NOSOTROS

THE HISPANIC PEOPLE OF OREGON

ESSAYS AND RECOLLECTIONS

NOSOTROS

THE HISPANIC PEOPLE OF OREGON

ESSAYS AND RECOLLECTIONS

Edited by
Erasmo Gamboa and Carolyn M. Buan

Designed by Jeanne E. Galick

Published by the
Oregon Council for the Humanities
Portland, Oregon

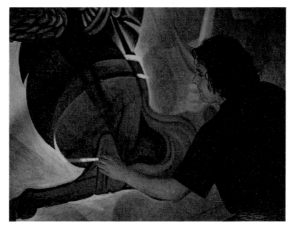

PREFACE

In 1992 the Oregon Council for the Humanities published *The First Oregonians*, a collection of illustrated essays on the state's native people, past and present. It was the first in a series of illustrated books to be published by the Council on the peoples of Oregon, and its success with the general public, students, and agencies that work with Indian clients was striking. The book sold out within two months and has been reprinted twice. That success confirmed our decision to create a series of publications and has led to this second volume, which focuses on the state's largest ethnic minority, the Hispanic people of Oregon. Both projects reflect the Humanities Council's commitment to increasing the public's understanding of Oregon's diverse ethnic character.

Our goal in this book has been to produce a visually engaging, historically accurate, and reasonably comprehensive picture of the Hispanic people of Oregon. The project originated in the scholarly work of Erasmo Gamboa, associate professor of history in the Department of Ethnic Studies at the University of Washington. Dr. Gamboa, whose family has a long history in Oregon, worked with the Council to help us gather oral histories from Hispanic residents all over the state and to identify writers for this book on the basis of a "call for essays." His expert knowledge, insights, and writing have been indispensible.

Carolyn M. Buan, his co-editor, has guided the editing process from the earliest contacts with writers through the many stages of revision and production that such a project inevitably entails. The book's consistency of tone and perspective and its readable treatment of a large, complex subject are due to her fine professional hand.

Jeanne E. Galick, the book's designer, has produced a volume of great beauty and visual meaning. Her work included the careful design that is evident on every page, the oversight of all production details, and the extensive photo research and coordination of new photography that make this such a unique publication.

Nosotros is aimed not only at the general public but at teachers and students. We are gratified to know that Merced Flores of the Oregon Department of Education and Luis Machorro of the Portland Public Schools consider it an important adjunct to the existing curriculum's focus on regional history and multicultural understanding.

Richard Lewis,
Executive Director
Oregon Council for the Humanities

ACKNOWLEDGMENTS

A project as complex as this is not possible without the help and cooperation of many people. During the early stages of the book's development, we sought advice from George Cabello (Portland State University), Susan Cabello (Pacific University), Luis Machorro and Tim Gillespie (Portland Public Schools), Efrain Diaz-Horna (a board member of the Oregon Council for the Humanities), Mary Jean Katz and Merced Flores (Oregon Department of Education), and George Rede (*The Oregonian*).

In addition to serving on the advisory group, Luis Machorro offered his help and advice at many stages in the book's development. Thanks, also, to Frank Martinez, Alan Apodaca, José Jaime, and José Romero for providing valuable information and photographs about the civil rights movement of the 1960s and 70s and to Francisca García and Gumesindo Gamboa, Jr. for providing information on the earliest Hispanic communities in Oregon during the years after World War II. Susan and George Cabello, José Jaime, and Patricia Rivadeneira provided some of the Spanish translations in the book, and Patricia Rivadeneira and Paula Mendez translated and transcribed some of the oral history interviews from Spanish. Meg Larson generously donated her time and talent to proof sections of the book.

Oral history interviews were expertly conducted by Frances Alvarado, Maria Rius, Eva Castellanoz, George and Susan Cabello, and Noël Wiggins. We thank them for their involvement. We also thank our essayists for their fine contributions and for their patience during the long production process.

Photographs, both historical and modern, are a big part of *Nosotros*, so we have been fortunate to work with some excellent photographers and archivists. Francisco J. Rangel is not only a fine artist whose photographs appear throughout this book, but a man whose interest and contacts in the Hispanic community have been of immeasurable help. He has given generously of his time and talent. Jan Boles, another fine photographer, put his contacts and research skills to use for us in eastern Oregon; Gerry Lewin, a photographer with the Salem *Statesman-Journal*, provided strong archival images; Michal Thompson, a photographer with the *Hillsboro Argus,* was most helpful in opening his files to us; gifted art director Natalie Brown and the Southern Oregon Historical Society were extremely generous, letting us have unlimited access to their photo files and providing photographs free of charge; Eliza Buck and Nancy Nusz of the Oregon Folk Arts Program gave us many photos of folk celebrations and artists; Priscilla Carrasco photographed some of our subjects on assignment and provided a moving photograph of a hungry child that was used often to promote the United Farmworkers Union's cause; and Barry Peril and Tom Robinson shared outstanding photographs from their personal files. In addition, Larry Landis at the Oregon State University Archives, Mikki Tint at the Oregon Historical Society, Sherrain Glenn at the Schminck Memorial Museum, Linda Dodds at the Cowboy Museum, Phil Wikelund at The Great Northwest Bookstore, and Peggy Sitz at the Harney County Library provided a great deal of help in finding historical photos. We also thank the individuals who agreed to be photographed for this project and to tell us about their lives and work.

Printing such a colorful, beautiful book would not have been possible without the generosity of the folks at Premier Press—especially owner Arnold Wheeler and staff members Lauren Van Bishler, Pam Mullins, Nancy Brock, Pat McIntyre, and Karen Hurtle. For help in publicizing the book to the Hispanic community, we thank Juan Prats, owner of *El Hispanic News*; Maria Elena Campisteguy-Hawkins; and the Oregon Council for Hispanic Advancement. We are also grateful to Gale Castillo and Hispanics in Unity for financial support and the time their board took to discuss the book's purpose and content with us.

Without the financial support of several other individuals and organizations, we could not have afforded to produce our book. Generous contributions were given by:

The Collins Foundation	Hispanics in Unity
The Rose Tucker Charitable Trust	Custom Roasting, Inc., Armando Miranda, President
The Holzman Foundation	Richard Herrera and Family
The Oregon Department of Education	Adelante Sí Hispanic Organization of Lane County
Carlos Rivera and Lisa Andrus-Rivera	Oregon Council for Hispanic Advancement

A major gift from First Interstate Bank has made it possible for us to distribute *Nosotros* to Oregon high schools.

TABLE OF CONTENTS

INTRODUCCION

La gente hispana de Oregon constituye una comunidad compleja y en crecimiento que todos los habitantes de Oregon deben comprender mejor. Esta comunidad bilingue y multicultural, con raíces en muchos países, ahora forma parte de la historia de Oregon extendiéndose desde las primeras expediciones de los exploradores españoles hasta la actualidad.

La primera parte del relato comienza en el siglo 16, que es cuando los exploradores españoles navegaron por nuestra costa en expediciones scientíficas y de dominio territorial. El relato se reanuda a mediados del siglo 19, cuando vaqueros mexicanos introducen una cultura vaquera al "Desierto Alto de Oregon" y arrieros mexicanos llevan provisiones vitales a los poblados aislados y a los remotos puestos del ejército.

La segunda parte comienza en los años 30 y 40 cuando los campesinos migratorios y los braceros se convierten en trabajadores indispensables para la industria agrícola de Oregon. Este capítulo acaba cuando trabajadores migrantes empiezan a establecerse en el estado.

La tercera parte tiene que ver con la lucha que se llevó a cabo durante los años 60 y 70 para conseguir que los mexicano americanos pudieran vivir con más dignidad. El resultado de esta lucha fue que se iniciaron nuevos programas sociales, oportunidades en el campo educativo, y nuevas leyes.

Hoy en día, como vamos a ver en el último capítulo, emigrados de América Central, América del Sur, Puerto Rico, y Cuba se han unido a los primeros pobladores que fueron los mexicano americanos. No estando limitados a sólo trabajar en el campo, los hispanos estan creando nuevas empresas, practicando en una gama de profesiones, y creando una entidad artística emocionante. Sin embargo, todavía mantienen su cultura tradicional mediante su arte folklórico, festivales, y ritos religiosos.

Para poder relatar parte de esta importante historia (porque no podemos decir que la hemos relatado toda), hemos contado con la ayuda de escritores que la han estudiado y de individuos que la han vivido. Que sus experiencias y recapacitaciones nos ayuden a comprender mejor al grupo mas grande de minoría étnica de Oregon.

Nota Sobre Nombres, Acentos y Guiones: *En este libro hemos reproducido los nombres tal como nos los han dado o en la forma como generalmente aparencen. Hay variación en el uso del acento debido a factores como periodos históricos, contextos geográficos, o americanismos. La expresión "Mexican American" lleva guión cuando es usada como adjetivo.*

INTRODUCTION

The Hispanic people of Oregon comprise a large, complex, and ongoing community that all Oregonians should better understand. Bilingual and multicultural, with roots in many other countries, theirs is now an Oregon story, extending from the earliest period of exploration and discovery to the present day.

Part one of the story begins in the sixteenth century, when Spanish explorers first sailed along our coast on expeditions of scientific discovery and territorial imperative. The tale is taken up again in the mid-nineteenth century, as Mexican *vaqueros* introduced a new cowboy culture to the Oregon High Desert and Mexican mule packers brought vital supplies to isolated settlements and army outposts.

Part two begins in the 1930s and 40s as the migrant laborer and the *bracero* became key workers in the state's agriculture industry. That chapter ends when the migrants began to settle in the state.

Part three concerns the struggle that took place in the 1960s and 70s to ensure that Mexican Americans could live their lives in dignity. That struggle resulted in new social programs, educational opportunities, and laws.

Today, as the final chapter unfolds, the original Mexican-American settlers have been joined by emigrés from Central and South America, Puerto Rico, and Cuba. No longer confined to agricultural jobs, Hispanics are starting new businesses, entering a wide range of professions, and creating an exciting body of art. Yet they still maintain their traditional culture through folk arts, festivals, and religious observances.

To tell parts of this important story (for we by no means claim to have told it all), we have relied on writers who have studied it and individuals who have lived it. May their insights help us better understand Oregon's largest ethnic minority.

A Note About Names, Accent Marks, and Hyphenation: *We have reproduced proper names in this book in the way they were supplied to us or in the way that they normally appear. Our use of accent marks varies in different parts of the book, depending upon such factors as the historical period, geographic context, or Americanization of the subject at hand. "Mexican American" is hyphenated when used as an adjective.*

INTRODUCING OURSELVES

Oregon is a land of immigrants, whose
largest ethnic minority comes from Mexico; the Spanish-speaking countries
of Central America, South America, and the Caribbean; and Spain.
This population is vibrant and complex, drawn to the state
from many countries and many walks of life.
This complexity makes the question of "what to call ourselves"
difficult to answer. Latino, Chicano, Mexican American,
South American, and Hispanic (the term used most often in this book)—
the possibilities abound. Not surprisingly, the answers
are as varied as the individuals who give them.

PERMITANNOS PRESENTARNOS

Oregon es un territorio de inmigrantes, cuyo grupo más grande
de minoría étnica proviene de México; los países hispano parlantes
de América Central, América del Sur, y el Caribe; y España.
Esta población, vibrante y compleja, que atrae este Estado
proviene de muchos países y diversos ámbitos sociales y laborales.
Esta complejidad hace la pregunta "cómo llamarnos"
difícil de contestar. Latino, chicano, mexicano americano,
sudamericano, e hispano (el término mas usado en este libro)—
las posibilidades son innumerables. Por lo tanto,
no debe sorprendernos que las respuestas
sean tan diversas como las personas que las ofrecen.

WHAT'S IN A NAME?
THE QUESTION OF WHAT TO CALL OURSELVES

BY CARLOS BLANCO

*The word Nosotros (We or Us) in the title of this book includes
Mexicans, Mexican Americans, Central and South Americans, Puerto Ricans,
Cubans, Spaniards, and their descendants who live in the United States.
But what should a group as diverse as this be called?*

The term Hispanic is used extensively throughout the book, but the terms Latino and Chicano appear, too. The editors have not chosen any single term—precisely because the question of what we call ourselves is currently under debate in a number of circles in this country.

A few years ago, the term "Chicano" was in vogue. This term has its roots in the Chicano civil rights movement of the 1960s. It was adopted by many Mexican-Americans who thought "Chicano" better described their unique experience and reality in the United States. According to some, the term originally had a mildly pejorative significance in Mexico. Today it is less popular.

The term "Latin American" was originally coined by the French in the 1800s. They wanted to increase their influence by appealing to the language kinship they thought existed between France and a region where two major Romance languages (Portuguese and Spanish) were spoken.

The term "Hispanic" was first officially used by the U.S. government to classify individuals for purposes of the 1970 census. The term includes people of Mexican, Puerto Rican, Cuban, Central American, South American, and other Spanish culture or origin.

According to Uncle Sam, national origin or culture—but not race—defines one as a Hispanic. This may be just as well because when it comes to Hispanics, defining who belongs to what race can be a prickly, inexact matter.

To grasp this issue, one has to understand that Latin America was colonized in much the same manner as the United States. When the English were settling the thirteen colonies, albeit at the expense of Native Americans, the Spanish were doing much the same thing in regions to the west and south and both were exploiting Africans.

Later, many immigrants from all over the world arrived, both to the English-speaking north and the Spanish-speaking south. Thus, the American continents—English and Spanish speaking—are constituted of nations composed of other nations. However, a major difference is that in the Spanish colonies, Caucasians, blacks, and Native Americans intermarried more freely than in the English colonies.

Within the Spanish colonies, though, differences in the population's makeup existed and continue to exist today. Due to strong indigenous influences in Mexico and Central America, the region's culture tends to celebrate its aboriginal heritage. However, countries located in the cone of South America, which have experienced major migrations from Europe, have a more European orientation. And African influence is most evident in the music and customs of the Caribbean nations.

When these racially mixed Hispanics migrate to the United States, our national obsession with labels and classifications creates great confusion. The question of what they call themselves—posed to a sample of Hispanics in a 1990 poll—elicited several answers. Among other things, the poll revealed that Mexicans, Puerto Ricans, and Cubans strongly identify with their own national-origin groups and want to be called "Mexicans," "Puerto Ricans," and "Cubans." The poll also revealed that members of these groups do not identify themselves as one community, see themselves as being similar culturally and politically, or have much contact with individuals from the other groups.

Ramiro and Teresa Silva of Gold Hill (center) and their children Victor, Karin, Edgar, Ramiro, and Ricardo.

The data also suggest that:

> ...while there may be a foundation for the creation of a "pan-ethnic" identity that includes Mexicans, Puerto Ricans, and Cubans, such a move will require respect for national-origin distinctiveness. It also depends on a recognition that what U.S. Hispanics have in common is more a function of their place in American society than of an alleged Latin American or Hispanic cultural heritage.
>
> —Rodolfo O. De la Garza, *Latino Voices*

The fact remains, however, that Hispanics can be of any race. In the 1990 census, most Hispanics chose "white" when answering the race question. However, of those who checked "other race," 98 percent also claimed Hispanic origin on the ethnicity question.

In 1992, the year of the 500th anniversary of Columbus's fateful voyage, furious debates ensued about what the event signified to Hispanic self-identity, and fissures around this topic were immediately evident in the Hispanic community. To those who are proud to consider Columbus Day a cultural birthday, the event signified the start of the process that made Hispanic culture what it is today. In the opinion of other Hispanics, however, that same process ruined the potential for an indigenous culture and instead imposed on the region an alien Spanish one. Thus, among some individuals, the term "Latino" is gaining favor over "Hispanic" because it implies that Latin America has a distinctive indigenous culture rather than being just a stepchild of Spain.

The Spanish *conquistadores*, consumed by greed, brought carnage and untold misery to the peoples they conquered. But modern Mexico and Peru would never have existed as they are now if they had missed the defining Hispanic element in their cultures. Hispanics who denounce the celebration of Columbus Day as an invasion rightly do so, but they cannot deny that they also carry in their veins the heritage of Spain. The common denominator in all Latin American cultures is their bond in the blood, traditions, and language inherited from Spain.

WHAT SOME CHOOSE TO CALL THEMSELVES

"I perceive myself as Afro-Cuban-American. I find I am obligated all the time to identify myself as Hispanic. I don't mind it. I think the labels and terms are not very important anyhow. I think I accept the political terminology which for now is Hispanic, that's fine; but if I'm called Latino, I'm fine. If I'm called Cuban, I'm comfortable with that, but my preferred term is Afro-Cuban-American because that one reflects everything about me. My children are great—they think they are Cubans. Both grew up in Portland."

—*Armando Laguardia (Cuba)*

"I am of Puerto Rican descent, so of course I prefer to be recognized as Puerto Rican, but I was born in New York, so I am a New York Rican. When I have to complete an application, I choose Hispanic. It has a broader sense than the other and you can include Spain. I can also accept Latin American because I am a Latin American."

—*José Solano (Puerto Rico)*

"Hispanic. I don't really have a preference."

—*Maria Picon (Venezuela)*

"Hispanic. I think this term covers the majority of the Latin Americans."

—*Laura Bergman (Ecuador)*

"South American because it is more explicit and I like the difference between South, Central, and North America."

—*Maria Luisa Baragli de Bevington (Argentina)*

"I love Latino because it covers all the Spanish-speaking people."

—*Carlos Camus (Chile)*

"I identify with South American. My ancestors were partly Jewish and partly Italian, French, Belgian, and Russian. Now they are proposing the term 'Indo-American' and I like it. My oldest child was born in Berkeley and the youngest in Palo Alto. The middle one was born in Argentina. They mostly identify themselves with Central America."

—*Nelly Link (Argentina)*

"When I have to fill out forms, I say I am Hispanic because that is the way we have been categorized within the five different groups. Within that category I would say, because I am a native-born Mexican, that I am a Hispanic of Mexican descent. My children are U.S. citizens, but if I have to say what they are, I would say they are Mexicans—from Oregon. I know that at one time you used to hear the word Chicano as a coined term to imply some political involve-

ment, and I think it was good. I think it brought people together with a political ideal to fight for. I would have called myself a Chicano, but now I just call myself a Hispanic of Mexican descent."

—*José Jaime (Mexico)*

"I'm obviously a Mexican American. I was born in Medford."

—*Roberto Gonzalez (United States)*

"I have no preference. I can call myself Latin American or Latino, Hispanic or Mexican. I'm from Mexico and that's within Latin America. Hispanic refers to anyone who speaks the language. And if I choose Mexican, it's because I'm a citizen of Mexico."

—*Armando Estrada (Mexico)*

"The first time I heard the term Hispanic was when I came to the States and had to fill out forms. I just fill them out differently each time—Indian, Black, Hispanic—who do I identify with? I am all of them.

The words 'Hispanic' or 'Latin American' omit the heart of South America—the Indian—the part that has nothing to do with being Latin. These labels may be easier but they reinforce barriers between groups of people."

—*Luciano Praño (Peru)*

"I prefer South American."

—*Roger Iparraguirre (Peru)*

"People assume you're Mexican if you're Hispanic. I found myself saying I'm Puerto Rican but I'm American. I was born here. Now I say I'm Hispanic or Latino and leave it at that."

—*Antonio "Tony" Sonera (United States)*

"Always our family considered ourselves as Mexican. We have never identified with the label 'Chicano.' Chicano to us is something undesirable...the word refers to one of little worth."

—*Celia D. Mariscal (United States)*

"I'm Chicano. *Cien por ciento Chicano. No soy Mexican Americano, no soy Mexicano, no soy Peruano. Cien por ciento Chicano.* I consider the term Chicano to be politically charged, to let people know we've researched our history, our roots, our culture, our traditions. The term has meaning, history, pride, and purpose. It lets people know who I am and where I'm coming from, rather than accepting someone else's label of Mexican-hyphen-American, Latino, or Hispanic."

—*José Romero (United States)*

OREGON

UNITED STATES

Atlantic Ocean

Gulf of
Mexico

MEXICO

CUBA

PUERTO RICO

BELIZE

HONDURAS

GUATEMALA

EL SALVADOR

NICARAGUA

COSTA RICA

PANAMA

Caribbean

VENEZUELA

GUYANA

SURINAME

FRENCH GUIANA

COLOMBIA

ECUADOR

Pacific Ocean

PERU

BRAZIL

BOLIVIA

PARAGUAY

CHILE

URUGUAY

ARGENTINA

ORIGINS OF HISPANIC POPULATIONS IN SELECTED STATES, 1990

	Total Hispanic Population	Mexican	Puerto Rican	Cuban	Other
U. S.	22,354,059	13,495,938	2,727,754	1,043,932	5,086,435
California	7,687,938	6,118,996	126,417	71,977	1,370,548
Idaho	52,927	43,213	665	164	8,885
Montana	12,174	8,362	437	124	3,251
Nevada	124,419	85,287	4,272	5,988	28,872
OREGON	112,707	85,632	2,764	1,333	22,978
Washington	214,570	155,864	9,345	2,281	47,080

Chart 1. The designation "Other" refers to the countries in Central and South America and to Spain.

2

HISPANICS IN OREGON:
A DEMOGRAPHIC PROFILE

BY RICHARD W. SLATTA

Oregon, like the rest of the United States, is a land of immigrants.
Between 1950 and 1990, Oregon's population rose 87 percent—
and our Spanish-speaking population became
Oregon's largest ethnic minority.

A STATE OF IMMIGRANTS

Since the end of World War II, 25 million people have immigrated to the United States. According to the 1990 census, 26 percent arrived from Mexico and Central America (four out of five from Mexico). Another 25 percent came from Asia, 22 percent from Europe, 9 percent from the Caribbean, 5 percent from South America, 4 percent from Canada, and 2 percent from Africa. From 1950 to 1990, the U.S. population increased 64 percent, as Oregon's population rose 87 percent—from 1.5 million to 2.8 million.

During that forty-year period, Mexicans, Mexican-Americans, and other Hispanics joined the rush to the Pacific Northwest. Migrants arrived each spring to harvest strawberries, peaches, prunes, walnuts, apples, and other crops. Over time, an increasing number of workers left the migrant stream and settled in the state. Other Spanish-speakers from Spain, Cuba, the Caribbean, and Central and South America joined the Mexican pioneers. By 1980 the Spanish-speaking population had become Oregon's largest ethnic minority.

In 1990 Hispanics comprised 112,707 of Oregon's 2,842,321 people, about 4 percent of the total. Approximately 45 percent of the nation's Hispanics live in the West, with some 34.4 percent in California. (Slightly more than 20 percent of westerners are Hispanic.) Hispanics comprise 25.8 percent of people in California, 5.3 percent in Idaho, 1.5 percent in Montana, 10.4 percent in Nevada, 4.0 percent in Oregon, and 4.4 percent in Washington.

THE NATIONAL SCENE

During the 1980s the nation's Hispanic population increased from about 15 million (6.4 percent of the total) to 22 million (9 percent), growing at a much faster rate than the general population. Political violence in Central America and

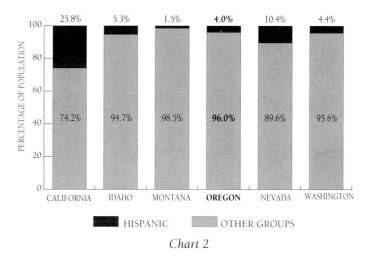

1990 HISPANIC POPULATION PERCENTAGES
IN WESTERN STATES

Chart 2

massive economic problems throughout Latin America drove many people to flee their countries (*see chart 3*).

During the 1980s some income and educational indicators improved for Hispanics. In 1990 Hispanics held about 5 percent of total aggregate household income, or about $173 billion. Compared with 1982, a higher proportion of Hispanic households had incomes of $50,000 (up from 10.6 percent to 13.4 percent). By the year 2000 an estimated 800,000 Hispanic-owned businesses will generate $49 billion in revenues.

While some Hispanics have enjoyed economic gains, poverty remains correlated with minority ethnic status. Despite the glitzy veneer of 80s prosperity, poverty deepened across the nation. By 1989, 13 percent of Americans lived in poverty. With 12.4 percent of Oregon's citizens living in poverty, the state ranked squarely in the middle of the states at number 25.

POPULATION GROWTH
IN THE UNITED STATES, 1980 to 1990

	1980	1990	% OF CHANGE
U.S. Population	226,545,805	248,709,873	9.8%
Total Hispanic	14,608,673	22,354,059	53.0%
Mexican	8,740,439	13,495,938	54.4%
Puerto Rican	2,013,945	2,727,754	35.4%
Cuban	803,226	1,043,932	30.0%
Other	3,051,063	5,086,435	66.7%

Chart 3

Children suffer the most from this state of affairs. Some 38.4 percent of Hispanic children lived in poverty in 1990, compared with 18.3 percent of non-Hispanic children. Children under eighteen years of age comprised nearly half of all Hispanics living in poverty. These unfortunate Hispanic youngsters represented 11.6 percent of all children in the country but accounted for 21.5 percent of all children in poverty.

Data for 1991 showed worsening conditions. Latinos were three times more likely to live below the poverty line than non-Hispanic whites. The median annual income of Hispanic men fell short of their non-Hispanic white counterparts ($19,769 versus $31,046).

Gender differences persist in the Hispanic community, more so than in the general population. There was a significant difference in labor-force participation between Hispanic men and women. The rate for Hispanic males in March 1991 was higher (78 percent) than that of non-Hispanic males (74 percent). In contrast, the rate for Hispanic women was lower than that for non-Hispanics (51 percent versus 57 percent). Hispanic women suffer higher unemployment rates and lower median incomes than their non-Hispanic white counterparts.

HISPANIC DIVERSITY

The Hispanic community is diverse and vibrant. In terms of national origin, the distribution of Oregon's Hispanics deviates somewhat from that of the nation at large. People of Mexican origin make up a substantially larger proportion of the state's Hispanic community (76 percent versus 60 percent in the nation as a whole).

Immigrants from Cuba and Puerto Rico have clustered on the eastern seaboard, rather than in the West. Oregon has 0.6 percent of all persons of Mexican origin in the United States, but only one-tenth of a percent of the Cuban and Puerto Rican populations. The state's Hispanics outnumber African Americans by more than two to one.

These figures for national origin, however, do not mean that most of Oregon's Hispanics are foreign born. On the contrary, most Oregonians, Hispanic or not, are American born. Only 5.7 percent of Oregonians were born in a foreign country. About 31 percent of Hispanics were foreign born, the great majority in Mexico.

GEOGRAPHICAL DISTRIBUTION

The majority of Oregon's Hispanic population is clustered in eight counties: Clackamas, Jackson, Lane, Malheur, Multnomah, Marion, Umatilla, and Washington. The map below includes those Oregon counties with a 1980 population of

Hispanic populations tended to cluster along agricultural corridors like the Willamette Valley in western Oregon, where jobs were plentiful.

The shaded counties are those that had a Hispanic population of 2,500 or more in 1990. Since then, Hispanic populations have increased in all counties of Oregon with the strongest growth occurring in Yamhill, Washington, and Clackamas counties.

GROWTH OF THE HISPANIC POPULATION IN SELECTED OREGON COUNTIES, 1970 TO 1990

COUNTY	1970	1980	1990	1990 TOTAL POPULATION
Clackamas	2,084	3,624	7,129	278,850
Jackson	1,571	3,954	5,949	146,389
Lane	2,662	5,581	6,852	282,912
Malheur	2,546	3,801	5,155	26,038
Multnomah	8,356	11,239	18,390	507,890
Marion	4,215	9,702	18,225	228,483
Umatilla	746	2,682	5,307	59,249
Washington	2,457	6,419	14,401	311,554

Chart 4

2,500 or more Hispanics. In some of these counties, population figures nearly doubled or did double every decade between 1970 and 1990 (*see chart above*).

URBANIZATION

Unlike the rural Spanish-speaking population of the 1950s, today's Hispanic community is predominantly urban. Not surprisingly, Oregon's largest city also includes a large concentration of Hispanics. In 1990 Portland had 13,874, and more than 9,100 people lived in homes where Spanish was spoken. In Salem 4,873 persons reported Spanish being spoken in the home. Hispanics have also located in many small towns in the Willamette Valley. Chart 5 highlights a few towns with proportionately large Hispanic minorities.

HISPANIC POPULATIONS IN SELECTED OREGON TOWNS, 1980 & 1990

TOWN	1980	%	1990	%
Independence	688	17%	1,070	24%
Nyssa	1,150	40%	1,262	48%
Ontario	1,195	14%	2,019	21%
Woodburn	2,035	18%	4,211	31%

Chart 5

EDUCATIONAL CHALLENGE AND PROMISE

The educational system remains a sore point with the Hispanic community. The high school dropout rate for that group in the Portland Public Schools doubled from 1982 to 1992. In fact, during the 1992-93 school year, the rate jumped an alarming 5 percent, as more than one out of five Hispanic students (20.7 percent) dropped out. This was the highest rate for any ethnic group; during the same period just under 6 percent of Asian, 8.2 percent of white, 9.5 percent of African-American, and 16.7 percent of American Indian high school students dropped out.

Portland's dropout problems came at a time when Hispanic graduation rates were rising nationally. (The proportion of the nation's Hispanics aged 25 and over completing high school rose from 46 percent in 1982 to 51 percent in 1991.) Once again, Portland's Hispanic community leaders have called for bilingual education and greater cultural sensitivity in the schools—although such pleas have gone mostly unanswered for several decades.

Nationally, three-quarters of adult Americans had graduated from high school in 1990. Twenty percent had a bachelor's degree or higher. Oregon exceeded the national level of high school graduates with 81.5 percent and closely matched the national level for college graduates. These impressive overall figures made the plight of Hispanics in the public school system all the more disturbing.

Poverty hampers the efforts of many Americans to obtain an education. Many of them, especially Hispanics, must work at low-paying jobs just to survive. Children must drop out to contribute to the family income. Completing one's education remains a luxury beyond reach.

THE FUTURE

Despite the problems that plague Oregon's Hispanics, they have contributed to a delightfully varied mosaic of cultures and ethnicities in the state. Today, Oregonians enjoy Mexican Cinco de Mayo fiestas as well as Scandinavian festivals, German Oktoberfests, and other ethnic celebrations.

As subsequent chapters attest, the state's fastest growing ethnic minority is also beginning to make important contributions in cultural, business, and political arenas. As it does, its accomplishments will become more visible and better appreciated.

3

A PERSONAL SEARCH FOR OREGON'S HISPANIC HISTORY

BY ERASMO GAMBOA

When I was growing up in the years following World War II,
my family lived in Independence, then "The Hop Capital of the World."
Oregon was not our permanent home.
It was one of several stops in an annual migration route
through Washington, California, and Oregon.

In Independence we lived at the Golden Gate Hop Ranch, considered the largest such ranch in the world. Years later, we worked at the McLaughlin Hop Ranch, also located outside Independence.

These hop farms were immense complexes, where we lived in long barracks-like, rough wood dwellings that could literally house hundreds. At the Golden Gate Ranch, Anglo migrant families worked alongside Mexican Americans and Native Americans.

Both of these hop ranches were microcosms of change in Oregon during those post-war years, when gasoline, tires, and automobile parts were no longer rationed and migrants traveled the nation's highways in search of work as they had during the Depression.

Mexican-American families like ours traveled to Independence from Texas, Colorado, Wyoming, New Mexico, Washington, and California. We arrived as if on cue to begin picking string beans or harvesting hops, and when work on the last hop field was completed in September, we left as quietly and systematically as we had arrived.

Years later, my interest in the history of Hispanic communities in Oregon and the Pacific Northwest forced me to develop a context for that phenomenon. I tried to understand the significance, if any, of that World War II generation of Mexican-American families that came to Independence and other

Oregon communities. Were they the first Hispanics in the state? If not, did the circumstances of their arrival differ from those of previous Hispanic Oregonians? Finally, what did the World War II generation of Spanish-speaking men, women, and children have in common with present-day Hispanics?

THE YEARS BEFORE WORLD WAR II

Hundreds of years before my family came to Independence, other Hispanics had preceded them to Oregon. Beginning in 1542, and lasting through the 1800s, Hispanic maritime expeditions explored, mapped, and laid claim to much of the Pacific Northwest coast, including Oregon. Later, under the terms of the Transcontinental Treaty of 1819, the United States purchased title from Spain/Mexico to the Northwest region. It now became the Oregon Country. For the remainder of the century, Hispanics traveled continuously to Oregon from Mexico. (It is well to recall that until 1848, the northern border of Mexico was just a few miles south of present-day Ashland.)

At the time, the border was little more than an imaginary line separating the United States from "Mexican" California. It did not constitute a barrier—political, legal, or otherwise—that would keep Hispanics or their cultural and economic influences from crossing into Oregon. Well before the Civil War,

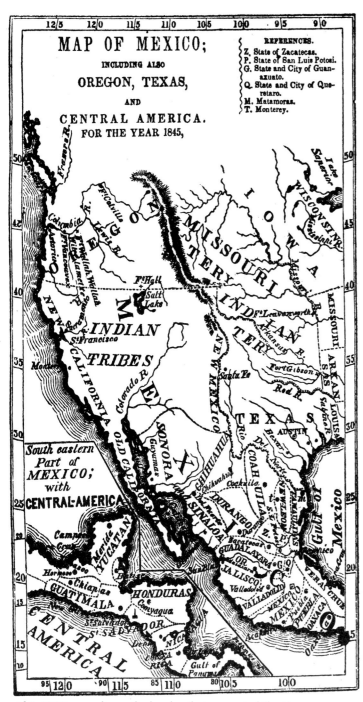

MAP OF MEXICO;

INCLUDING ALSO

OREGON, TEXAS,

AND

CENTRAL AMERICA.

FOR THE YEAR 1845,

REFERENCES.

Z. State of Zacatecas.
P. State of San Luis Potosi.
G. State and City of Guanaxuato.
Q. State and City of Queretaro.
M. Matamoras.
T. Monterey.

This 1845 map shows the border that separated the Oregon Country from Mexico. It lay just south of present-day Ashland.

sion on the Willamette, established in the 1830s. Until mid-century and the minting of "Beaver" coins, Mexican silver pesos made up most of the currency circulating in Oregon. Ships out of San Francisco unloaded "Mexican produce and goods" in Portland. Today, place names like Chaparral Creek, Umatilla, Cape Perpetua, and Spanish Gulch serve as powerful reflections of that early Hispanic presence in the state.

Early in the 1900s an influx of Hispanics, led by immigrants from Mexico, began to enter the state. Some were self-exiles from revolutionary Mexico. Others came from the Southwest, attracted by job opportunities in Oregon. Since the census was limited to foreign-born Hispanics, no one knows, or will ever know, how many came to the state during the first two decades of this century.

Oregon's proximity to California encouraged Hispanics to come to the state—now linked by a growing system of railroads and highways. More than any other factor, however, burgeoning farm production pulled Hispanic migrant workers. In the years after World War I, Hispanic families from New Mexico and Colorado lived in Nyssa and worked on farms in that area of the state.

The Great Depression and a lack of jobs slowed, but did not entirely halt, the flow of Hispanics coming to Oregon. Even as unemployment soared and relief lines grew, Anglos avoided hard "stoop" labor farm jobs. Of necessity, Oregon farmers recruited substantial numbers of Hispanic laborers—enough that Congress singled out the state as one of the principal users of interstate migratory laborers. Many came from California's Imperial Valley to Hood River and the Willamette Valley. At the same time the Oregon Short Line, Oregon Railroad and Navigation Company, and Union Pacific Railroad hired increasing numbers of Hispanics to maintain their tracks.

WORLD WAR II AND THE POST-WAR YEARS

World War II brought full employment and quickly ended the Depression. When the nation mobilized all available resources in order to win the war, a critical shortage of workers developed. This was particularly hard on Oregon's farms. Now workers had more reasons to avoid farms in favor of more attractive jobs. During the war, many of them, Hispanics included, came from throughout the nation to take jobs in the state. The most sophisticated recruitment program, however, involved Mexico. Between 1942 and 1947 the federal government recruited an estimated 15,136 Mexican men to the state to alleviate the farm-labor shortage (*see Chapter 6 on the Bracero Program*). This contract labor force made all the difference in the food-for-victory campaign in the state.

With the war's end in 1945, Oregon gradually phased out the use of Mexican contract labor. However, since farms remained stable after the war, out-of-state workers were just as necessary. To fill the gap, state and federal agencies helped farm employers secure many Mexican-American migrant families. In the years following the war, these families came to the state

Hispanics came to mine gold, to organize and operate the mule pack system of transportation, to settle, and to live the lives of ordinary adventurers. Once in Oregon, Hispanics served in the early volunteer state militia during the "Indian wars," had a hand in developing the livestock economy of the eastern range lands, and were part of the general process of development.

When Hispanics themselves were not present, their influence and products were very evident. "Castellan" roses, brought from Mexico, adorned the grounds of the first Methodist mis-

An early "Spanish" restaurant in Portland, photographed ca. 1915.

in increasing numbers—it was a turning point in the history of Oregon's Hispanics.

Some of those who came had been in Oregon before the war. One who hoped to come was Claro Soliz. In one of his last letters from Europe, he wrote of hoping to survive the Battle of the Bulge, adding, "If I come back, I will build my house in Oregon. That is beautiful country. Everywhere you look around, it looks like you are in Heaven with the angels and the saints." Claro did not survive the war to see the beauty of Oregon again, but many others did move to the state in the post-war era.

Across the nation and in Oregon, Hispanics found new opportunities after the war. Although still relegated largely to the hard, low-wage jobs on farms and railroads, some were able to find work as farm-equipment operators, crew leaders, and supervisors. And because many non-Hispanic agricultural workers did not return to their jobs after the war, it was now possible for Mexican Americans to drive tractors, combines, and trucks and work in warehouse and food processing. For Hispanics in Oregon, a new epoch was under way.

This type of opportunity was the magnet that attracted my father to Independence two years after the war ended. In Edinburg, Texas he learned from his relatives, Rafael Reyes and Felix Barrientes, that with careful planning between jobs in Oregon, Washington, and California, year-round employment for the entire family was possible. He was not alone—the Luna, Alvarez, Gonzales, Coronado, Morales, Navejar, Castilleja, Carrillo, Garcia, Delgadillo, Armijo, and Partida families, also of Edinburg, traveled to Independence, too.

Oregon was particularly attractive due to its lush vegetation and—because we were heavy consumers—to the absence of a sales tax. Moreover, we were *needed*, and in comparison to residents of Texas and other states, Oregonians treated us surprisingly well.

Although seasonal life at Independence was far from ideal, jobs were plentiful. Nearby at Buena Vista, young and old, men and women entered the fields several times to strip the rows clean of mature beans. Hispanics called this *la pisca del ejote*. By the time the harvest ended, hop fields elsewhere in the valley beckoned.

Families picked hops by hand according to a hierarchical order of jobs. The lowest and worst paid was the picker. Workers who lowered the wires, weighed the hops, or supervised the crew were higher in the pecking order. The latter positions, which were once reserved for Anglos, now opened for Hispanics.

A Mexican Independence Day celebration begins in a 1940s labor camp as the Mexican flag is raised (far right).

Hop picking during the early 1940s. (Left) Willamette Valley braceros (men brought to Oregon as contract laborers) weigh hops. (Right) Braceros on the Horst Ranch in Polk County gather empty baskets in preparation for the day's harvest.

When mechanization occurred, a division of labor by gender took place. Women, and sometimes children, went on the belt lines removing leaves and doing other "light jobs" that required more dexterity, while males took the "harder" positions. No females worked in the more specialized areas of the kiln where the hops were "cooked" or dried. Naturally, a differentiated wage system for women and men also developed.

CAMP LIFE

Away from the workplace, Hispanics quickly adapted to the dynamics of camp life. The Golden Gate hop ranch, located south of Independence, had facilities for an estimated 1,500 adults. A camp manager described the housing as little more than "rough shelter."

The Gamboa family at the Golden Gate Ranch. Matriarch Paula Gamboa Coronado stands second from left, back row. Her daughter Francisca Garcia (far left) and Francisca's husband Irineo (far right) settled in Woodburn (see Francisca's story on page 148).

Long wood buildings, divided into separate cabins by unfinished lumber, defined the periphery of the camp complex. An electric bulb, a small wood-burning stove, a table with wooden benches, and two bunks or metal folding cots with straw mattresses furnished each cabin. Water was available at spigots located outside the rows of cabins. The sanitation setup consisted of outdoor privies and garbage cans. Small mountains of log trimmings located throughout the camp were available for our cookstoves.

Tall firs, asphalt roads, a camp store, a community center, and the roughly constructed cabins gave the facility a rustic, recreational-camp appearance, but camp life was far from relaxing. When Hispanics arrived after the war, it was already in bad condition. Lack of material for improvements during the war had resulted in deterioration, and the shift from hand harvesting to mechanization had cut down on the number of workers, leaving many cabins unoccupied and in disrepair. Although the Oregon Council of Churches tried to enforce minimal health regulations on private property, living conditions were substandard and unhealthy.

The camp population itself was also changing ethnically and racially. At one point, poor white seasonal families, many from Oklahoma and other Midwestern states and from Oregon, had lived in the camp along with Native Americans. By the end of the 1940s, the camp residents were almost exclusively Hispanic.

When Mexican-American families began to arrive, the camp became an arena of contention among the different groups. In reality, segregation along racial lines existed. Hispanics, being new, and Native Americans received the worst housing in the least desirable sections of the camp. The camp administrators, a deputized marshal, a jailer, the store operator, and a housing manager were all Anglos. Camp life was nevertheless an arena of social interaction among the diverse residents, and ethnic

After a long day in the fields, workers might gather to sing and play guitars. Otherwise, leisure-time activities were few.

and racial lines sometimes became blurred. This was especially true among the younger population and at social or cultural events. Hispanic families, for example, organized entertaining dances outdoors on weekends. Sometimes musicians like guitarist Francisco Rodriguez and his brother accordion player Ramon Rodriguez at the Golden Gate were available in the camp. Otherwise, couples danced to music from a phonograph and records pooled for the occasion. Since these were very public and fun-filled gatherings where the music was easy to dance to, young adults mixed despite racial and cultural differences. I still recall Louis Doney, the Golden Gate's camp marshal and a former logger from Coos Bay who enjoyed dancing in spiked logging boots sporting his holstered gun and his badge.

In addition to the dances and other events, the end of the hop harvest meant Oktoberfest. This celebration provided the final opportunity for the workers to get together before leaving the camp. Growers provided free food, drink, and entertainment in celebration of the harvest's end, but Hispanic workers, who were unfamiliar with the idea, called it *el fin de la corrida* (the end of the harvest) and looked forward to it as a unique annual occasion.

Acculturation was evident in other ways. Although not a common practice, Hispanics socialized with and even married non-Hispanics. On Sundays, Baptists and other evangelical dominations visited the camp and vied for the residents' attention with prayer and offers of free coffee and doughnuts. Although there were few converts among the predominately Catholic population it was not uncommon to hear children singing hymns like "This Little Light of Mine" in English. Mexican food became another avenue of cultural exchange. The versatile tortilla, corn or flour, was immediately popular among Anglos because it could be eaten hot or cold, alone or with a variety of fillings.

As the farms around Independence drew more Hispanic families, the town felt their cultural and economic influence. (At the peak of the harvest the hop-ranch population was larger than that of the local community.)

The place where Hispanic families bought their food supplies was a small grocery store located on Main Street, whose owner tried to cater to our needs by carrying canned tortillas, tamales, and other food items from Texas. My father thought that the canned tortillas and tamales tasted terrible and told the store owner so. When the storekeeper asked for suggestions, my father produced a wrapper from El Ranchito Tortillas from Zillah, Washington—at the time the only commercial tortilleria in the Pacific Northwest. The store contacted El Ranchito and after that a full line of Mexican food items was available to the Mexican-American workers in Independence.

The purchasing power and economic effect of the Hispanics in the post-war years was important. In the same way that Washingtonians cross the Columbia River to avoid a sales tax, Hispanics were quick to recognize the advantage of making major purchases while in Oregon. Even if families did not buy new vehicles locally, they licensed out-of-state cars and trucks in Oregon because it was less costly than in Washington or California, and Oregon plates were renewable in months other than January. As poor as they were, Hispanics also bought nonessential consumer items. Now that the war was over and

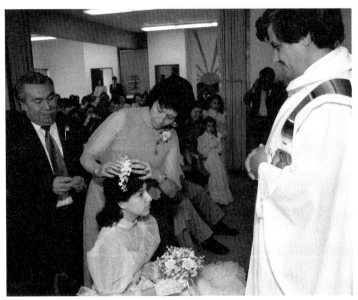

radios, washers, refrigerators, musical instruments, and other "luxuries" were available, Hispanics wanted them. These items were sometimes necessary and more affordable in Oregon, but also they represented material evidence of the advantages of working in the state. My father, for example, came to Oregon in a used truck obtained in Mississippi, but at Independence he bought a brand new Chevrolet truck. Although the family was heavily in debt for years because of this purchase, friends in Texas and California who had not made the trip north envied our more reliable means of transportation.

Even in the 1940s businesses recognized the value of the Hispanic market and used various ploys to get us to buy. The Palace Tavern in Independence welcomed Hispanics from the beginning. It sometimes took advantage of the fact that the workers had few places to spend their leisure time by selling liquor to those who were well beyond the point of intoxication. A local brewery took a different approach by bringing free cases of "Brew 77" beer to camp.

Nevertheless, public establishments sometimes rebuffed Hispanics and their hard-earned dollars. Some stores and taverns refused to serve them because they caused "trouble," spoke Spanish, or "discouraged" other customers. These were rationalizations for simple and odious discrimination.

Clearly, Independence does not tell the whole story of Hispanics for the rest of Oregon in the 1940s. The same process of social and economic adaptation between Hispanics and non-Hispanics took place in other parts of the state. One year after the war ended, ground was broken for new farm-labor camps at Yamhill, The Dalles, Hillsboro, Klamath Falls, Wasco, and other areas. Two years later the federal government put up thirty-six temporary and eight permanent camps for sale to private groups to use as housing for migratory labor. Hispanics were becoming commonplace throughout Oregon.

FROM MIGRANTS TO PERMANENT COMMUNITIES

The annual pursuit of seasonal farm jobs led eventually to the development of permanent Hispanic communities. Throughout the state the pattern was similar. One or two families would decide to stay rather than migrate elsewhere, and the next year others would do the same. Generally, it began with those families that had visited the state for several years. Once families made the decision to remain, they experienced considerable isolation from the cultural surroundings of their hometown and separation from lifelong friends. However, traditional cultural practices that brought Hispanics together—

Top. After coming back to Oregon for several years, many families chose to stay permanently and some were able to buy houses. Middle. As conditions improved, a family might enjoy a Sunday outing at the state capitol grounds. Bottom. Traditional celebrations like the quinceañera that marks a girl's fifteenth birthday gave the Hispanic community its own identity.

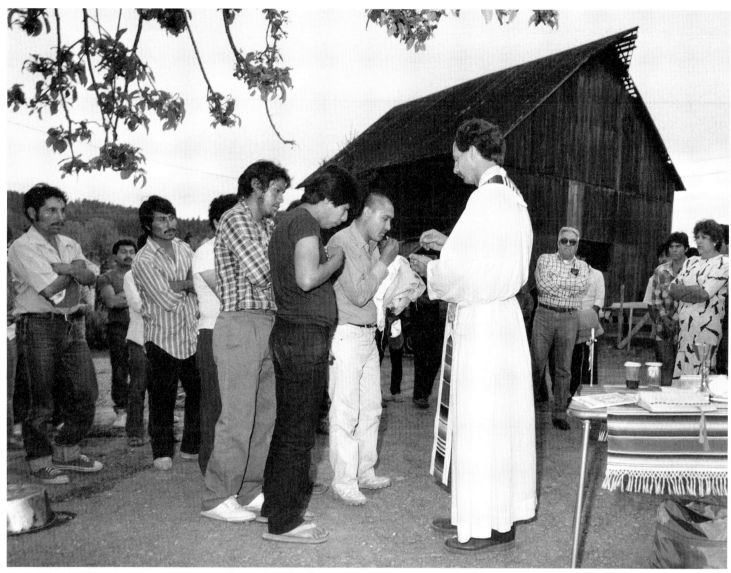

The Catholic Church has been a major unifying force for the Hispanic community and has worked to improve both the practical and spiritual sides of workers' lives. Besides providing Spanish-language services in parishes, priests conduct services at migrant camps.

baptism and marriage celebrations, weddings, dances, and other fiestas—helped to soothe the feeling of alienation.

The social matrix of these communities was complex. While changes intruded into the traditional lifestyle, some social customs and relationships remained constant—for example, addressing someone of higher status required *usted* rather than *tu* or the term *Don* or *Doña*. In this new resident community, wealth did not define social status entirely. Folk healers and individuals able to provide spiritual guidance were important, as were the elderly, those who could speak English, and those who had been in Oregon a long time.

Other important cultural characteristics gave identity to the community. Cooperation in making food for Christmas *tamaleras* (gatherings where tamales are made), *quinceañeras* (young women's fifteenth birthday celebrations), and other events united several families. Both women and men who pos-

sessed the expertise to prepare traditional food for large numbers of people were important, particularly when they could also organize the efforts and contributions of many others. Culture, therefore, mitigated change.

This should not suggest that Hispanics remained culturally static. Oregon provided a welcome escape from constant dislocation, and many took advantage of the opportunity. As former migrants, they understood the value of education and did what they could to enroll their children in school. Adults also attended evening English classes when available. Some purchased homes and when they did, it was because they took non-farm employment. As they established themselves, visits to their home states became more infrequent, and years later they stopped visiting entirely. In time, the post-war generation's successful adaptation persuaded other Hispanics to consider making Oregon their home. In the space of a decade after the

Haydee Gutierrez (center), director of the school of Oregon Ballet Theatre, started dancing at an early age in Cuba and trained with prominent Cuban dancers. She came to Oregon in 1993.

Miltie Vega-Lloyd, originally from Puerto Rico, is now human resources and facilities manager at KPTV-12 in Portland. She is also active in Hispanic community affairs.

first enclaves developed, the outlines of established Hispanic communities were discernible across the state, and steps were taken to meet their cultural needs. Hispanics approached local theaters to schedule Mexican films for the Spanish-speaking community and in response, theaters scheduled these films Wednesday or Sunday evenings. In the process, owners did a brisk business on otherwise "slow nights." Some families at-

Part of the new wave of immigrants in the 1980s, the Felixes fled their native Guatemala because of political upheaval. Here they pose in front of the home they bought in Salem.

tempted to establish restaurants or other businesses that catered to the growing Hispanic community.

The Catholic church was also quick to recognize the growing number of Hispanics in attendance and began to bring in Spanish-speaking missionaries during the summer months to conduct Spanish mass during the hours when English mass was not being held. The Catholic ministry also gave Hispanics an uncommon opportunity to use local community facilities for religious celebrations. This opened the door to nonreligious events because sympathetic priests sometimes initiated the first social and cultural community gatherings on parish property. This was important because Hispanics did not have their own meeting places and other "public" or fraternal halls were not always available to them. In this way, the church helped them maintain and reinforce their culture in the state.

THE DECADE OF THE SIXTIES

The 1960s were a watershed decade for Oregon's Hispanics. By then, community organization had intensified considerably. In 1965 former migrants obtained a federal grant from the Office of Economic Opportunity to establish the Valley Migrant League. Located in Woodburn, this organization served seven counties in the Willamette Valley with adult education, job development, and day-care services. That same year, Treasure Valley Community College in Ontario organized a similar migrant program. Besides offering adult education, the college's Migrant Center developed citizenship courses, a credit union, and a housing program. Two years later, Oregon State University Extension Service began a Spanish-language newsletter for homemakers. By 1969 the visibility of Oregon's Hispanics was no longer in question. That year, Governor Tom McCall established Oregon's Advisory Committee on Chicano Affairs to begin to bring Hispanic issues before state government.

In 1966 Club Latino Americano and the Hispanic community at Woodburn organized their first annual Mexican Fiesta. Next the Oregon Council of Churches, especially the Portland Catholic Archdiocese, aided in purchasing the land for Centro Chicano Cultural at Woodburn—the state's first Hispanic cultural center. A migrant health clinic followed in the same community. In 1970 the University of Oregon enrolled about eighty young Hispanics, the first sizable class of its kind in the university's history. All of this, and a push for better conditions for farm workers, were reflections of the growing visibility and political influence of Hispanics.

THE LAST TWENTY-FIVE YEARS

Since the 1970s a variety of nationalities and ethnic groups have expanded the fixed boundary of Oregon's Hispanic community developed by Mexican Americans. The history of the arrival of these "new" Hispanic groups to Oregon is complex.

Congress passed the Immigration Act of 1965 to establish a more equitable 20,000-per-country access to emigrants from all nations. The new law also provided a system of preferences, by which Hispanic citizens and resident aliens in Oregon could petition to bring their families and immediate relatives without regard to per-country limits. In addition, Congress expanded the admission of refugees and individuals granted asylum.

Even as U.S. immigration policy enhanced admissions, civil war, oppression, poverty, inflation, and closed opportunity in the Caribbean and Central and South America motivated an increasing number of Latin Americans to emigrate. The decision to emigrate stemmed from these worsening conditions and also from an increased awareness about opportunities in the United States.

Once individuals made the decision to leave their homelands, they took several routes to the state. Some came as legal immigrants. Others came as tourists or students and then married U.S. citizens or chose to remain as permanent residents. Some Salvadorans, Guatemalans, and other Central Americans

As Oregon's Hispanic population grows, it is finding new sources of work. The family of Rafael and Olvido Rodriguez (left) and their son-in-law Daniel Robles (right) found steady employment in Newport-area fish processing plants. Before coming to Oregon, Rafael was a graphic designer in Mexico, working two jobs to make ends meet. Here, his family has a chance for a better life.

The family of longtime resident Dr. Joseph Gallegos came to Portland in the 1940s when his father heard there was work in the shipyards. A key figure in developing Colegio Cesar Chavez in Mt. Angel (described in Chapter 7), Gallegos is now director of Social Work and Gerontology Programs at the University of Portland.

work arenas—not surprising, considering the gulf that exists between, say, a Mixtec immigrant of rural origin who snuck across the border at night and a former South American landowner who arrived by jet.

On the other hand, moving to a different country is never easy, even under the best of circumstances. Refugees, migrants, and immigrants alike feel the same stress of separation from loved ones and of resettlement in Oregon—the same nostalgia for the past that love of Oregon, the birth of a second generation, and a search for commonalities with other Hispanic Oregonians will gradually replace.

Today, this rich and varied population continues to change the face of Oregon communities. In urban areas, Hispanics are active in the judicial system, politics, education, business, and the arts and humanities. Rural Hispanics are not different, except that in smaller towns with sizable Hispanic populations, true Mexican-American zones have emerged.

As each wave of Hispanic newcomers arrives, it replays the conscious balancing between the "old" and "new" culture that occurred in the post-war years. In Oregon the post World War II generation paved the way for later generations of Hispanic migrants and immigrants. Now, Hispanics find broad avenues of equality in social, educational, and economic opportunity.

A STATE COMPOSED OF IMMIGRANTS

When I am asked to define the Spanish-speaking community in Oregon, my immediate response is that Hispanics are not different from other residents of the state. We are the descendants of immigrants or are immigrants ourselves. The same is true for all Oregonians except Native Americans.

Said another way, Oregon does not belong to one people. The Hispanic culture and the cultures of other peoples are intertwined and intermingled. At Independence, you can still find the Guadalupe Alvarez and Ramon Coronado families, who settled there after the war. There you will also find Ovid Long, the son of Dr. Long, an Independence veterinarian who employed my father in the forties. The storefront where my father introduced "El Ranchito" tortillas still exists, although it is now an antique shop. Hispanics and non-Hispanics have, for the most part, existed side by side and often within each other's families and communities.

Over the past few decades a substantial growth of the number of Hispanics residing in the state has altered the configuration of Oregon society. These changes affect all Oregonians in several ways. Lack of familiarity with Hispanics may hinder the larger community's ability to accept and respect them as equal participants, while Hispanics themselves may be hindered in the quest for equality by a limited understanding of their own complex history. Above all, barriers that work against an open and fluid society challenge everyone to look beyond their own families and communities.

initially entered the country illegally but were later eligible to legalize their status under the amnesty provision of the 1986 Immigration Reform and Control Act. The Puerto Rican and Cuban American community eventually came to Oregon under still different circumstances. Citizens since 1917, Puerto Ricans are not immigrants and have an unrestricted right to migrate anywhere in the U.S. Most Cuban Americans entered the country under the 1966 Cuban Refugee Act and subsequent refugee admissions policies.

Oregon was not the primary destination of most non-Mexican Hispanics. Instead, the majority of newcomers from the Caribbean and from Central and South America "migrated" to the Pacific Northwest during the 1970s after residing elsewhere in the nation.

Central and South American immigration has reconfigured Oregon's Hispanic community forever. Mexican Americans no longer speak for all Hispanics. Moreover, there are formidable differences in the experiences and interests of the various groups. Often they find themselves in very different social and

EARLY EXPLORATIONS AND HISTORY

*Nearly four centuries ago, Spanish explorers sailed along the Pacific coast
and recorded detailed observations about the land and its inhabitants.
In the 1800s Mexican vaqueros helped establish the vast cattle ranches
of the Oregon High Desert and skilled Mexican mule packers
brought supplies to soldiers and settlers.
During World War II, when the state's farmers were desperate for help,
imported Mexican workers harvested the crops and aided the war effort.
When the war ended, Mexican Americans replaced these braceros and
laid the foundation for the present-day Hispanic community.*

LAS PRIMERAS EXPLORACIONES Y LA HISTORIA

*Hace casi cuatro siglos, exploradores españoles navegaron por la costa del Pacífico
y registraron en forma detallada sus observaciones sobre el territorio y sus habitantes.
En el siglo 19 vaqueros mexicanos ayudaron a establecer los amplios ranchos
de ganado del "Desierto Alto de Oregon" y arrieros mexicanos llevaban
las provisiones a los soldados y pobladores.
Durante la Segunda Guerra Mundial, los agricultores del estado necesitaban
ayuda desesperadamente e importaron braceros mexicanos para ayudar
con la cosecha y con los menesteres de la guerra. Cuando acabó la guerra,
estos braceros fueron reemplazados por mexicano americanos
y se fundó así la base de la comunidad hispana actual.*

SPANISH EXPLORERS IN THE OREGON COUNTRY

BY HERBERT K. BEALS

He was called Soto, and he claimed to be the son of a Spanish sailor who had survived a shipwreck near the mouth of the Columbia River. This elderly, blind individual was encountered near Beacon Rock in the Columbia Gorge on May 8, 1811 by Gabriel Franchère, a member of John Jacob Astor's fur trading enterprise. Franchère had witnessed living evidence of an early and little-known Hispanic presence in the Oregon Country.

At the Nehalem Sand Spit, thirty miles south of the Columbia's mouth, large quantities of beeswax on the beach, as well as nearby rocks with mysterious carvings, have long been suspected of having an Iberian connection. Farther south, midway between Yachats and Florence, there is a rocky promontory called Heceta Head that honors Bruno de Hezeta (his spelling), commander of a Spanish expedition that explored Oregon's coast in 1775. And on the coast's southernmost section, two capes—Blanco and Sebastian—bear the oldest European place names in Oregon, both of Spanish origin.

Looking north to Washington state, Hispanic place names are plentiful in the Strait of Juan de Fuca, the San Juan Islands, and the waters around them. At Neah Bay, once called *Núñez Gaona*, its Hispanic name failed to survive, but bricks used there in constructing an outpost settlement offer their own testimony to a Spanish role in the region's early history.

What impelled Spain's involvement in a land so remote from her Iberian homeland? Anyone seeking an answer to that question must return—figuratively at least—to when the voyages of Christopher Columbus were still fresh in the minds of their participants. Discovering that lands westward across the Atlantic could be reached from Europe by any competent, properly equipped seafarer was a mixed blessing for Spain. Fearing

Overleaf. Schooners Sutil *and* Mexicana *in the Strait of Juan de Fuca, 1792. Above. Artist José Cardero's depiction of Spanish fortifications under construction at Neah Bay, Washington.*

Portuguese encroachment in the lands Columbus had found, the Spanish sovereigns sought, with papal assistance, an agreement with Lisbon to establish a demarcation line to prevent their respective claims and colonizings from dragging each other into disputes or outright warfare.

With the urging of Pope Alexander VI, the two Iberian powers entered into a treaty on June 7, 1494, signed and sealed in a Castilian town named Tordesillas. They agreed to a north-south line located 370 leagues—1,110 nautical or 1,277 statute miles—west of the Atlantic Ocean's Cape Verde Islands. Spanish claims would be confined west of this line to territories not already ruled by a Christian prince, as of Christmas Day, 1492; Portuguese claims were reserved to such areas east of it.

It seemed a simple and effective solution. But means to fix the line's exact location in those days ranged from rudimentary to nonexistent. Moreover, the Tordesillas Treaty had been drawn up when Europeans knew little about the true configuration of the lands Columbus had found. Consequently, some surprises were in store for the treaty's signatories as geographic knowledge expanded and the line's location could be more accurately determined. Not the least of these was the discovery that a sizable part of Brazil was on the Portuguese side—the reason its inhabitants today speak the Portuguese language. More importantly, by the stroke of a pen, Spain was unknowingly assigned most of the Pacific Ocean and all lands it touched along its eastern periphery.

The Pacific's existence was unknown to Europeans until 1513, when Vasco Núñez de Balboa, standing atop a Panamanian mountain, saw its shimmering oceanic expanse. He called it the *Mar del Sur* or South Sea because it stretched southward from his vantage point. Seven years later it acquired a different, more permanent—if slightly inappropriate—name, *Mar Pacífico*, when Ferdinand Magellan crossed it without encountering a single storm. He also located an archipelago in the western Pacific, today's Philippines, which became the keystone of Spanish commerce between East Asia and Hispanic America for two and one-half centuries.

From 1565 to 1815, ships variously called *naos de China*, China ships or Manila galleons, annually crossed the Pacific between Acapulco, Mexico, and Spain's Philippine entrepôt at Manila. Their westbound cargoes, which consisted mostly of silver from the mines of Mexico, Peru, or Bolivia, were used to purchase a variety of East Asian goods. Laden with Chinese silks, fine porcelain wares, exotic jewelry, and less exalted items such as beeswax (for candles), needles, nails, or gunpowder, the galleons returned to Acapulco by crossing the North Pacific. They were sometimes perilous and always arduous voyages, which often brought them in sight of northern California's Cape Mendocino or possibly even Cape Blanco on the southern Oregon coast.

A number of these ships never reached Acapulco, and it is likely that one or more may have been blown off course in bad

Model of the Santiago, one of the Spanish ships used in exploring the Pacific Coast.

EARLY SPANISH DESCRIPTION OF THE OREGON COAST

First Recorded European Sighting of Yaquina Head on the Oregon Coast, From the 1774 Diary of Juan Pérez.

Día 13 al Domº 14 de Agosto de 1774

Proseguimos costeando con Trinquete y Gavia y el Velacho sobre un rizo en buelta del SSE. Viento N. fresco y mucha Mar del O.: los tiempos claros por lo que al ponerse el Sol se hallaba la Costa ahumada en tal conformidad que no se pudo divisar de ella, solo lo que se hallava frente del Barco, la que demoraba al LNE. distancia de 7. a 8 leguas. Anochecieron los orizontes claros y hermosos y en dicha conformidad amanecieron, y al aclararse el dia me demoraba la que se percevía [sic] demás al S. de la costa SE. distancia de 18 leguas. Y la de más N. al N. la misma distancia poco más o menos, corre dicha costa al NNO-SSE.: de la más cerca de la costa 4 Leguas al LNE. A las 7 1/2 cargamos la Cevadera. A las 9 1/2 se cazó el Puño de la mayor de estribor se largo el rizo del Velacho y Velas menudas: A las 11 se bolvieron aferrar. A las 12 observé en la Latitud de 44 gs. 35 ms. N.* me demoraba la S. de la costa al SE 1/4 S. y la del NO. NO1/4 N. distancia de 5 a 6 Leguas de la más cerca por el LNE desde la altura susodicha corre la costa NNO-SSE. tierra alta y doblada como la distancia de 12 legs. y muy Poblada de Arboleda hasta las cumbres de los cerros, y luego corre por el mismo rumbo de más mediana altura y empieza de una punta tajada al Mar y gruesa y tiene una Barranca de color entre blanca y amarilla mui conocida.**

13th to Sunday 14 August 1774

We proceeded on along the coast with the foresail, and the main and fore topsails under one reefing, turning to a course SSE. The wind was N. fresh; a heavy swell out of the W.; the weather clear. At sunset, the coast was found to be so hazy that we were able to see only that part directly in front of the ship, which bore ENE. a distance of 7 to 8 leagues. At nightfall the horizons were clear and beautiful; they were the same at dawn. As daylight came on, the S. extreme of the coast was perceived to bear SE. a distance of 18 leagues; the N. extreme bore N. the same distance, a little more or less. The said coast runs NNW-SSE.; nearest to the coast 4 leagues, ENE. At 7:30 we loosened the spritsail. At 9:30 the starboard corner of the sail was hauled aft. The reefings in the fore topsail and minor sails were loosened. At 11 they were furled again. At 12 I observed the latitude at 44° 35' N.* The S. extreme of the coast bore SE 1/4S., and that on the NW. [bore] NW1/4N; nearest distance 5 to 6 leagues, ENE. From the aforesaid latitude the coast runs NNW-SSE. The land is high and mountainous for a distance of about 12 leagues and very heavily forested up to the mountain summits. It then runs in the same direction at a more moderate height, beginning with a point that slopes steeply into the sea. It is massive and has a very prominent cliff that is between white and yellow in color.**

*Within two nautical miles of the mouth of Yaquina Bay.

** This point is almost certainly Yaquina Head (lat. 44° 41' N.), about three nautical miles north of Yaquina Bay's mouth, near Newport, Oregon.

AMONG THE EARLY EXPLORERS WERE...

ALEJANDRO MALASPINA (1754-1809)—Born Mulazzo, Parma, Italy; died Milan, Italy, age 55; commander of frigate *Astrea* on voyage of circumnavigation,1786-1788; commander of Pacific exploring voyage, with corvettes *Descubierta* and *Atrevida*, 1789-1794; imprisoned 1795 at La Coruña because of involvement in court intrigue; released after eight years through Napoleon's intercession.

ESTEBAN JOSÉ MARTÍNEZ (1742-1798)—Born Sevilla, Spain; died Loreto, Baja California, age 56; pilot aboard *Santiago*, 1774; commander of expedition to Alaska, 1788; major figure in Nootka Controversy, 1789-1792.

CAYETANO VALDES (1767-1835)—Born Sevilla, Spain; died Madrid, age 68; commanded schooner *Sutil* as part of Malaspina expedition; participant in Battle of Trafalgar, 1805, in command of 80-gun ship *Neptuno*; wounded but survived to reach rank of admiral.

JUAN FRANCISCO DE LA BODEGA Y QUADRA (1744-1794)—Born Lima, Peru; died Mexico City, age 50; captain of schooner *Sonora*, 1775; captain of frigate *Favorita*, 1779; major figure in Nootka Controversy; commander of the "boundary expedition" (*expedición de límites*), 1792.

DIONISIO ALCALA GALIANO (1762-1805)—Born Cabra, Córdoba Prov., Spain; died Trafalgar, age 43; commanded schooner *Mexicana* as part of Malaspina expedition, 1792; participant in Battle of Trafalgar, 1805, in command of 74-gun ship *Bahama*; killed in action and buried at sea.

JOSÉ CARDERO (1766-ca.1811)—Born Ecija, Córdoba Prov., Spain; died Cádiz (?), about age 45; artist with Malaspina expedition.

BRUNO DE HEZETA Y DUDAGOITIA (ca. 1744-1807)—Born Bilboa, Basque Country, Spain; died Málaga about age 63; captain of frigate *Santiago* and expedition commander, 1775; captain of Manila galleon *San Felipe*, 1784; participant in naval engagements of Napoleonic Wars; retired as vice admiral; recalled to command naval base at Málaga at time of death.

JUAN PÉREZ (1725?-1775)—Born Balearic island of Majorca, possibly at Palma; died off Monterey, California, about age 50; pilot aboard Manila galleons; participant in Spanish colonization of present-day California; captain of frigate *Santiago*, 1774; first pilot and second-in-command of *Santiago*, 1775; died and buried at sea, reportedly of typhus.

---

weather and been cast ashore on the northwest coast of America. This could offer an explanation as to how Soto's shipwrecked father and the Nehalem beeswax reached Oregon's shores.

If losses to natural hazards were not excessive, the Spanish crown had no particular incentive to explore and map the coasts above Cape Mendocino. And as long as Spanish dominion in the Pacific went unchallenged, the Manila galleons sailed securely without fear of foreign corsairs. That security was first shaken in 1578 when English mariner Francis Drake entered the Pacific to raid and plunder the largely undefended Spanish ports and shipping on the western seaboards of South and Central America. Although Drake captured several Spanish vessels, he failed to take a Manila galleon—a distinction that would instead fall first to his countryman Thomas Cavendish, who captured the *Santa Ana* off Baja California in 1587.

These events compelled a Spanish response. Among other things, a search was begun for harbors north of Baja California that could be used by Manila galleons in distress. There are claims that a certain pilot, Juan de Fuca, undertook the first such attempt in 1592, sailing from Mexico, and supposedly discovered a strait linking the North Pacific and Atlantic oceans. Although his name is immortalized in the Strait of Juan de Fuca, his voyage remains unauthenticated. In 1595 a better documented voyage left Manila on a mission that tried mixing exploration with a commercial venture. The ship *San Agustín*, under Sebastián Rodrigues Cermeño, was wrecked trying to conduct a coastal survey. News of the tragedy reached Mexico with survivors who escaped in an open boat.

A Spanish expedition sent north from Mexico in 1542 to explore the California coast, led by Juan Rodríguez Cabrillo and Bartolomé Ferrelo, may have gone beyond the 42nd parallel (the present-day California-Oregon border). But the first such expedition to see and name landmarks on the southern Oregon coast was that of Sebastián Vizcaíno in 1602-03. The names of capes Blanco and Sebastian are traceable to this expedition, which surveyed and mapped harbors along the entire California coast—omitting only San Francisco Bay. No participant in the expedition, however, is known to have gone ashore in present-day Oregon.

When Vizcaíno returned from his voyage, he urged the viceroy of New Spain, Gaspar de Zúñiga, to authorize another expedition to plant a settlement at Monterey Bay. Zúñiga was supportive, but he was nearing the end of his term in office. His replacement, Juan de Mendoza, did not share his predecessor's enthusiasm, believing the expense too great for the benefits promised. The pall Mendoza's rejection of Vizcaíno's proposal cast over exploration on the California and northwest coasts was so pervasive that it would be nearly a century and a half before Spanish exploring vessels would ply those waters again.

What eventually brought Spain to end its long neglect of America's northwest coasts was news that in 1741 two mariners, Vitus Bering and Aleksei Chirikov, serving the Russian crown, had successfully reached Alaska by sailing eastward from Kamchatka. They were followed by other Russian venturers in the Aleutian Islands who were seeking to make their fortunes in furs while advancing Russian claims to Alaska. These events alarmed Madrid, and in 1768 a special crown's representative, José de Gálvez, was dispatched to New Spain with orders to initiate settlements at San Diego and Monterey. They would be useful in countering the Russians and supporting subsequent exploring voyages to formalize Spanish claims in the North Pacific issuing from the Treaty of Tordesillas.

The first three exploring voyages sent north were organized under the auspices of Antonio María de Bucareli, who became viceroy of New Spain in 1771. Using ships built at a naval base founded by Gálvez at San Blas on Mexico's west coast, these voyages were governed by similar instructions. They were to sail north to the 60th parallel (the latitude of Prince William Sound, Alaska), where they were to go ashore and take formal possession in the name of the Spanish king, Carlos III. They were to return south, exploring the coast, landing, and taking possession wherever possible until they reached Monterey. They were to search for Russian settlements but avoid contact with them. Native peoples were to be treated with kindness, and the use of force against them was strictly enjoined except in cases of self-defense.

The members of Malaspina's expedition gathered valuable scientific information about the flora, fauna, and climate of the Northwest Coast. Unfortunately, much of the knowledge they collected was suppressed.

Juan Pérez, a former Manila galleon pilot, led the first expedition in 1774. Employing a lone frigate named *Santiago*, he made the first European reconnaissance of the Oregon Country's coastline and the first direct contacts with its indigenous population. Pérez visited Langara Island, northernmost of the Queen Charlottes, and Nootka Sound on Vancouver Island and sighted Washington state's Mount Olympus. He had friendly exchanges with the Haida people at Langara Island and the Nootka Sound natives. The luster of his career as an explorer, however, suffered because Pérez neither made landings nor took possession, and only reached latitude 54°40' N., over five degrees short of the viceroy's goal. A second expedition was needed.

It embarked from San Blas in March 1775, commanded by an officer of Spain's *Armada Real* named Bruno de Hezeta. Pérez served as pilot aboard the flagship *Santiago*. A small escort vessel, the schooner *Sonora*, was commanded by another *Armada* officer named Juan Francisco de la Bodega y Quadra. This expedition achieved considerable success, making several landings and taking possession at northern California's Trinidad Head, at Point Grenville on Washington state's coast, and at Bucareli Bay and Krusov Island in southeastern Alaska. The expedition experienced tragedy on July 14, 1775, when a seven-member landing party from the *Sonora* was attacked and killed by natives near the Quinault River. The two ships later became separated in high seas, following which Bodega y Quadra reached Alaskan waters just short of the 59th parallel before adverse weather and scurvy forced him back. Meanwhile, aboard the *Santiago*, Hezeta sighted and mapped the mouth of the Columbia River on August 17, 1775, a discovery of no little importance. He failed to enter the river because so many of his crewmen were ill.

A third expedition, which sailed in 1779, was deemed necessary by Viceroy Bucareli. Under the leadership of Ignacio Arteaga, senior officer at San Blas, and Bodega y Quadra, it consisted of two frigates, the *Princesa* and *Favorita*. Determined to gain high latitudes, they sailed directly to southeastern Alaska, bypassing the Oregon Country. After surveying Bucareli Bay, they reached the 60th parallel as originally specified in Bucareli's instructions, where they explored and mapped Prince William Sound and the Kenai Peninsula. They encountered neither Russian individuals nor settlements. After the expedition returned to Mexico, it would be nearly a decade before

José Cardero's depiction of an encounter at Loughborough Inlet, British Columbia.

Nootka Chief Tlupanamabu's portrait was one of several made by Tomás de Suria.

other exploring ships would put to sea from San Blas for northwest America.

A new round of Spanish exploration commenced in 1788. Initially a response to the growing presence of British fur trading vessels, it also came to include the pursuit of knowledge apart from purely geopolitical considerations. The Age of Enlightenment sweeping Europe in the eighteenth century had produced a boundless appetite for greater knowledge of the natural world. The Spanish king, Carlos III, one of Europe's monarchs who keenly supported the Enlightenment, had a vast colonial empire ripe for scientific investigation. With His Majesty's encouragement, Hispanic exploration in the Americas aspired to the scientific ideals of the Enlightenment. Unfortunately, Carlos III died in 1788, just as Spain's Pacific explorations resumed.

Over thirty voyages by vessels flying the red-and-yellow banner of Bourbon Spain plied Northwest waters between 1788 and 1795. It proved a futile effort to stem the tide of foreign encroachment, but its scientific achievements—though little publicized—would be of more enduring value.

Esteban José Martínez, pilot and second-in-command under Pérez in 1774, would be a key figure in Spanish efforts to stave off Russian and British threats. Martínez, accompanied by Gonzalo López de Haro, located Russian settlements on Alaska's Kodiak and Unalaska islands in 1788. Encounters there with representatives of the Shelikhov-Golikov Company (later the Russian American Company) were guardedly cordial.

But in July 1789, when Martínez confronted British fur traders at Nootka Sound, serious trouble ensued. Seeking to persuade them to vacate the Sound, which he considered Spanish territory, Martínez ordered James Colnett arrested, his ships seized, and their personnel sent off as prisoners to San Blas. This incident ignited the Nootka Controversy, bringing Spain and Britain to the brink of war. The outbreak of the French Revolution, however, seems to have prevented armed conflict over the issue.

In 1790 Martínez returned to Nootka to establish a fortified outpost overlooking *Cala de los Amigos* (Friendly Cove). Garrisoned by Catalonian volunteers, it became a base of operation for Spanish vessels charting the coasts of Vancouver Island and the Strait of Juan de Fuca. Most surviving Hispanic place names in these areas are traceable to this period and the tireless mapping efforts of little-known Spanish navigators such as Manuel Quimper, Francisco de Eliza, Salvador Fidalgo, Jacinto Caamaño, Cayetano Valdés and Dionisio Alcalá Galiano, to name only a few. In 1792 Fidalgo initiated a settlement on the south side of the entrance to the Strait of Juan de Fuca, which he called *Núñez Gaona*, today's Neah Bay. Part of a strategic withdrawal from Nootka, it would prove short lived. Yet it enjoys the distinction of being the earliest attempt at European settlement in what is now Washington state.

Spanish explorations in the Pacific culminated in a voyage led by Alejandro Malaspina, an Italian-born officer of the *Armada Real*, and his Spanish co-commander, José de Bustamante y Guerra, in 1789-94. Its two splendidly equipped ships, the corvettes *Descubierta* and *Atrevida*, embarked from the Spanish seaport of Cádiz. In the Enlightenment spirit, the expedition was as much concerned with scientific as geopolitical objectives. It proved remarkably successful in gathering botanical, zoological, ethnological, meteorological, and other data along the Pacific seaboards of the Americas, from Cape Horn to Alaska's Prince William Sound. In an unhappy twist of fate, the reform-minded Malaspina later became entangled in Madrid's court intrigues, resulting in his imprisonment and depriving him and his colleagues of public recognition for their accomplishments. Equally unfortunate, the expedition's records and scientific data were suppressed and scattered.

An Indian dance recorded at the Spanish outpost on Friendly Cove, Nootka Sound, established in 1790 by Esteban José Martínez.

BODEGA Y QUADRA, BIOGRAPHICAL SKETCH & JOURNAL EXCERPT

Born in Lima, Peru, May 22, 1744, Juan Francisco de la Bodega y Quadra Mollinedo was descended from noble ancestors deeply rooted in northern Spain's Basque country. His birth in the Americas classified him as a *creole*, placing him at some disadvantage in Castilian society. Nevertheless, in 1762 he entered the *Academia de Guardia Marina* (Spain's Naval Academy) at Cádiz. In over twenty years of naval service, he rose to the rank of *Capitán de Navío* (Captain). During most of his naval career he was involved in exploration and international diplomacy on the Northwest Coast of America. On the occasion of Bodega y Quadra's untimely death, March 26, 1794, at Mexico City, British explorer George Vancouver paid tribute to his erstwhile rival with these words:

Having endeavoured, on a former occasion to point out the degree of admiration and respect with which the conduct of Senr. Quadra towards our little community had impressed us during his life, I cannot refrain, now that he is no more, from rendering that justice to his memory to which it is so amply entitled, by stating, that the unexpected melancholy event of his decease operated on the minds of us all, in a way more easily to be imagined than described; and whilst it excited our most grateful acknowledgments, it produced the deepest regret for the loss of a character so amiable, and so truly ornamental to civil society. (W. Kaye Lamb, ed., *The Voyage of George Vancouver, 1791-1795, IV, 1396-97*; The Hakluyt Society: London, 1984.)

During Bodega's exploring voyage to the Northwest Coast in 1775, in command of the 38-foot schooner *[goleta] Sonora*, he and his long-suffering crew struggled against many adversities to sail their miniscule vessel into Alaskan waters, where scurvy and foul weather nearly overwhelmed them. Writing early in September 1775, he describes their plight:

Hallándome con la gente picada de este contagioso mal, sin tener con qué medicinarlos y expuestos a extenderse a todos...conocí que era imposible por más que me esforzase el subir a más altura... y así me resolví a regresarme, aprovechando los vientos que me fuesen favorables, y conformarme con reconocer la costa cuando me fuese posible.

Desde el día primero de septiembre anduvieron los vientos escasos y variables hasta el día 6, que afirmaron por el sueste con tanta fuerza que, a las doce de la noche, no se podían aguantar las mayores con los rizos tomados y me puse a la capa con proa al sursudueste, pero cada momento iba aumentando la mar y el viento, de suerte que a las dos de mañana no se podía resistir; no obstante, se hacía el último esfuerso para mantener la capa a causa de la corta distancia que estaba la tierra. Estando en estas reflexiones, rompió tan fuerte mar en toda la embarcación que, arrancadando batayolas, candeleros, grampones y bordas de la todilla,* se llevó

al agua cuanto había sobre cubierta, creyéndonos al impulso de la mar enteramente zozobrados, pues en el espacio de cuatro minutos no se vio sino una mar espumosa en todo el barco,...se principiaron a oír quejidos y lamentos, pues las batayolas habían estrellado al contramaestre contra un ancla, dejándolo sin movimiento. También fueron maltratados algunos marineros, aunque no de cuidado, pero quedaron inútiles para ayudar a maniobrar, de modo que, en tan crítica hora, me vi con sólo dos marineros, el piloto, el guardián y un criado mío; y, conociendo que el manteneros sin zozobrat era imposible, dispuse dar la popa al viento siguiendo el rumbo del norueste, obligado a perder la poca distancia que estaba de la costa y sin otro esperanza de librar que la de que cesase la tempestad antes que diésemos con la costa.

Finding myself with men smitten by this contagious evil, without having anything with which to medicate them, and it is at the point of spreading to everyone...I knew it was impossible for me to exert any more effort to go up to a higher latitude....And so, I resolved to turn back, availing myself of the winds that were favorable to me, resigning myself to examining the coast as much as possible.

After the 1st day of September, the winds abated and were variable until the 6th, when they blew steadily from the southeast with so much force that at midnight the mainsail with two reefings taken in was unable to endure it, and I lay to with the bow to the south southwest. But the sea was increasing by the minute, and the wind in such a manner that at two in the morning I was unable to resist, despite making the utmost effort to remain lying to, on account of the short distance I was from the land. Being in these circumstances, a wave crashed over the entire vessel so powerfully it tore off rails, stanchions, clamps and boards of the round house. It carried away into the water everything topside. We believed ourselves about to founder at the wave's impact, because in the space of four minutes nothing was seen but sea foam throughout the ship....moans and wails began to be heard, because the rails had dashed the boat-swain against an anchor, leaving him motionless. Some of the sailors were also badly shaken up, although not dangerously so. But it left them useless for helping to work the ship, so that in such a critical hour I saw myself with only two sailors, the pilot, the watch and my servant. Knowing that it would be impossible for us to remain without foundering, I gave the order to head the stern into the wind, continuing from a northwesterly direction, obliged to lose the little distance that I was from the coast; and with no other hope of deliverance except that the storm might abate before we met with the coast.

*The term *todilla* (round house in English) refers to the curved roof above the covered quarters at the ship's stern. It was essentially the *Sonora's* quarterdeck or (in Spanish) *alcazar.*

Portrait of Chief Tetaku's wife by José Cardero. Tetaku was a notable Indian leader on the Strait of Juan de Fuca.

With the recent bicentennial celebrations of Robert Gray and George Vancouver, it seems only fair that the contributions of Spanish mariners be recognized as well. The Hispanic presence here was not only early and of considerable duration, but peopled by individuals who displayed courage, intelligence, and diligence, to say nothing of all the usual human foibles.

From the perspective of diplomatic history, the United States owes a particular though seldom acknowledged debt to the achievements of Spanish explorers in the Oregon Country. When the American and Spanish governments reached agreement on the Transcontinental Treaty of 1819, that treaty provided among other things for the United States to assume all Spanish claims north of the 42nd parallel. The slogan "Fifty-four Forty or Fight" rested on no American exploit, but on the voyage of Juan Pérez in 1774. Claims based on Robert Gray's entry into the Columbia River in 1792 were bolstered by Bruno de Hezeta's sighting of the same river seventeen years earlier.

And in one final and improbable case, the United States secured ownership of the San Juan Islands (north of Puget Sound) in an arbitration decision made in 1871 by the German emperor, Kaiser Wilhelm I, who based his decision on maps prepared in 1790-91 by such mariners as Narváez, Quimper, Eliza, and López de Haro.

THE PÉREZ-CAÑIZARES MAP OF THE NORTHWEST COAST OF AMERICA

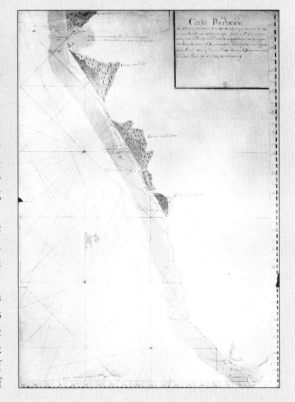

In 1989 two researchers from the Library of Congress, James Flatness and John Hebert, uncovered an unusual map in the U. S. National Archives in Washington, D.C. It was among some fifty-seven other Spanish-language maps and documents dating from the late 18th and early 19th centuries, all of which were in the National Archives' Army and Old Navy Records section. This particular map was undated, but an inscription on it states that it was drawn by a certain Josef de Cañizares at the request of Juan Pérez and that it depicts discoveries made during the latter's voyage to explore the Northwest Coast of America in 1774. Pérez's official report at the conclusion of his expedition states that he intended to have such a map prepared and submitted to Viceroy Bucareli in Mexico City. But no such map has hitherto been located in Spanish or Mexican archives.

Josef de Cañizares was a young naval officer who was skilled in hydrographic surveying, and he was someone with whom Pérez was well acquainted. Thus, although Cañizares was not a participant in the voyage, he would have been a likely choice to prepare the map Pérez had promised the viceroy. Cañizares later gained a certain amount of modest fame by conducting the first detailed hydrographic mapping of San Francisco Bay.

Assuming the map's authenticity—and there is no particular reason to doubt it—how did it come to be in the U. S. National Archives? The most probable explanation seems to be that after it was submitted to Viceroy Bucareli it was misplaced and remained lost among other papers accumulating in the viceregal residence at Chapultepec, southwest of Mexico City. In the course of the war between Mexico and the United States (1846-48), Chapultepec, which by then the Mexican government had converted into the Colegio Militar, was assaulted by U. S. Army forces in September 1847. At that time, the Pérez-Cañizares map must have been captured along with various other maps and documents and later brought to Washington D.C.

Whatever the case was, it represents the earliest European charting of the North American coast from Monterey, California, northward to the Alaskan panhandle, based on something more than imagination or fantasy.

5

VAQUEROS
ON THE HIGH DESERT
RANGELAND

BY BOB BOYD

*In the summer of 1869, a young California cattleman named John Devine
arrived at recently abandoned Fort C. F. Smith on Willow Creek
in the High Desert of southeastern Oregon.
With him were a herd of trail-worn cattle, a dozen California vaqueros,
and the outfit's cook and chuckwagon.*

There, amidst a landscape of sagebrush and rimrock bordered by the Trout Creek Range and Steens Mountain, Devine founded the Whitehorse Ranch, the region's first ranching empire. At the same time, his Hispanic *vaqueros*, who had trailed the herd north from the Sacramento Valley, introduced traditions in the High Desert that had originated in Spanish California a century before and continue to be used today, over a century and a half later.

THE CALIFORNIA VAQUERO CULTURE

Vaqueros had entered California in 1769, when Gaspar De Portola, governor of Baja California, and Franciscan missionary Fr. Junípero Serra first established a Spanish presence there. Between 1769 and 1848, when Mexico lost California to the United States, these horsemen developed a unique culture on the mission lands and large *ranchos*. To assure enough workers to manage their tremendous herds of

In the Oregon High Desert, buckaroos on a cattle drive carry on traditions introduced by Hispanic vaqueros *in the mid-1800s.*

horses and cattle, the Franciscans would select their most reliable Indian converts, or neophytes, to learn the skills and work of the *vaquero*. Meanwhile, the *hacendados*, with their tremendous *ranchos* given as land grants by the Spanish or Mexican government, looked to their large families for skilled horsemen. Their sons literally grew up in the saddle and were skilled at an early age.

Sea traders calling at California ports to barter manufactured goods for hides and tallow often commented on the California horsemen. Whether roping a steer, leaning from the saddle to snatch a buried rooster by the neck at a *fiesta*, or working as a team to capture a fierce California grizzly bear, the *vaqueros* loved to demonstrate the responsiveness of their well-trained horses.

It was the California method of training horses, the equipment and style of horsemanship developed in the days of the missions and *ranchos*, which John Devine's *vaqueros* introduced to the Oregon High Desert (*see sidebar on page 33*).

The men who had mastered these skills looked on their life's work as more than just a job. It was a calling in which they took great pride, and that pride was reflected in their finely tooled California stock saddles, beautifully engraved silver bits and spurs, and carefully crafted rawhide equipment.

NORTH TO OREGON

With Mexico's independence from Spain in 1821, the subsequent loss of official support for the California missions, and the American invasion in 1848, the golden age of the missions

1831, near the San Francisco Mission. Skilled horsemanship and finery characterized the early California vaqueros.

and *ranchos* came to an end. However, *vaqueros* continued their work under the new flag, perhaps for *hacendados* who had managed to retain a fragment of their former holdings or for an Anglo-American gold rush entrepreneur turned cattleman.

By the 1870s, however, stockraising and mining were no longer the economic backbone of the state. Agriculture was king in the great inland valleys along the San Joaquin and Sacramento rivers, and the California legislature passed a law imposing heavy penalties against stockmen whose cattle strayed onto agricultural land. The "herd law" signaled a migration of California cattle and *vaqueros* beyond the Sierras to Nevada and Oregon.

By that time, John Devine had already headed north, but he was soon joined in Oregon by Pete French. French was employed by a doctor named Hugh Glenn, who had come West at the time of the gold rush but found his fortune in supplying beef to the miners. In the summer of 1872, he decided to focus his California operations on wheat ranching and searched out new rangeland for his cattle herds. To lead the trail drive to Oregon, he chose French, a foreman at his Jacinto Ranch who spoke Spanish and was popular with the outfit's *vaqueros*.

The young 23-year-old trail boss found what he was seeking as he gazed from a rimrock overlook and saw before him the vast natural meadows along the Blitzen River at the western edge of the Steens Mountain. The temporary camp along the Blitzen was to expand into a ranching empire of almost 70,000 acres, running over 45,000 head of cattle.

THE EARLY OREGON VAQUEROS

Many of the *vaqueros* who rode for French at the P Ranch in the early days had made the initial drive north. Vincente and Juan Ortega, Francisco "Chico" Chararateguey, and Juan and Jesus Charris brought their California customs to Harney County and taught their ways to the young Anglo-Americans

At John Devine's Whitehorse Ranch, the vaquero *tradition was strong. Devine brought the first* vaqueros *to Oregon.*

The work was never hurried. While a *vaquero* might devote much of his time to training the horses assigned to him, big outfits might also employ a skilled *amansador*, or tamer. A colt would first be accustomed to a braided rawhide nose band held in place by a light leather bridle. Together, nose band and bridle were called *jáquima*, today's hackamore. Tied at the base of the *jáquima* was a twisted horsehair rope, or a *mecate*, which served as reins. The colt's nose was sensitive to the pressure applied by the nose band, or *bozal*. A smart colt soon learned that the discomfort of the *bozal* could be avoided by reacting to the feel of the rough horsehair reins moving on his neck before the *bozal* was tugged. Gradually, softer *bozals* and finer *mecates* were employed as the colt grew more and more responsive to neck reining.

At this point, the *vaquero* or *amansador* might for the first time place a bit in the horse's mouth. No reins were attached and the animal simply grew accustomed to the feel of it. Eventually, braided rawhide reins were attached to the bit with woven buttons along their length to allow the colt to feel the movement of the reins. For a time, the rider might employ both the *jáquima* and the bit, using two pair of reins before switching control to the bit and reins entirely. To those unfamiliar with their techniques, some of the bits of the *vaqueros* might appear quite harsh and uncomfortable, especially the spade bits. However, a skilled *vaquero* with a well-trained horse needed only to rely on the feel of the reins to signal his wishes to the animal—he never jerked roughly or in any way hurt the horse's mouth.

A *vaquero's* primary tool for working cattle was a hand-braided rawhide *reata*. Woven from strands of carefully cut rawhide strings, some *reatas* were up to 100 feet long. With a sharp eye and a good arm, a skilled *vaquero* could rope a fast-moving steer up to 70 feet away. As the loop sailed over the cow's horns, the rider took a couple of turns around the horn of his saddle, a move known as *dar la vuelta*. To ease the shock to the animal of pulling the *reata* tight, the *reata* was left to slide a moment before being tied off.

These illustrations by Maynard Dixon were done for Harper's Magazine *after he and fellow artist Ed Borein took a horseback trip to Harney County in 1901. Dixon reflects the image of the* vaqueros *who worked for the big cattle ranches in Southeastern Oregon at the turn of the century. Both young men later became two of the most prominent western artists of their day.*

Some vaqueros' wages would end up on the gaming tables, at the bar, and in the back rooms of the local saloon.

John Devine and his crew outside his race horse stable at the Whitehorse Ranch.

who signed on with French. Prim "Tebo" Ortega was French's range boss, and at a salary of $100 a month was the highest paid of the P Ranch crew. "Tebo," due to his station, had the privilege of maintaining a small herd of his own, from which he periodically sold cattle at the stockyards in Winnemucca, Nevada. Apparently much of the proceeds ended up on the gaming tables of that Nevada cow town, but upon his return to the ranch, the old *vaquero* always insisted that "he made them work for it." In later years, Joaquin "Chino" Berdugo served as the ranch's range boss.

At the Whitehorse Ranch, the California *vaquero* heritage was equally strong. Devine himself favored a stiff-brimmed, low-crowned black hat, short tailored jacket, and tight trousers once fashionable on the *ranchos*. He enjoyed raising race

Life on the range centered around the chuckwagon. It fed the outfit on trail drives and carried the men's bedrolls. Next to the wagon, on the right, is Frank Lorenzana, one of the area's last vaqueros.

horses, which he rode with the finest of tooled and silver-mounted saddles and bridles.

At the Whitehorse and Alvord ranches, day-to-day range activities were in the hands of an experienced *vaquero*. For twenty-five years, under Devine's ownership and later when Miller and Lux Company owned the outfit, Juan Redon served as foreman.

Evelyn Gilcrest, whose father managed the ranches for Miller and Lux at the turn of the century, later reminisced about those days:

> In addition to the ranch foreman, there was a vaquero foreman who was directly responsible for the cowhand's assignment. For the Alvord, Mann Lake and Juniper this was Juan Redon, a Mexican whose knowledge of the cattle business was of great assistance. He lived with his Irish wife Maggie at Wildhorse where he had a little ranch of his own. With his clean colorful shirts and levis, bright neckerchiefs, expensive sombreros and beautifully tooled and polished boots, he made a very dapper appearance.

Also on the east side of the Steens lived Amanda Mirandi. At one time a *vaquero* in the Harney Valley, Mirandi later established a ranch near Wildhorse, known today as Andrews. When relatives came up from California, the Mirandis would celebrate the occasion in traditional fashion with a big barbecue and a *fiesta*.

ON THE RANGE AND AT THE RANCH

Vaquero life on the ranches of the High Desert followed an annual cycle. In the springtime, outfits hired on extra hands for a busy season of roundups, moving cattle to summer rangeland, and trail drives. In the days before fences, all the ranches in a region would join together to gather their scattered cattle. A crew of *vaqueros* and a chuckwagon from each ranch would join neighboring ranches in rounding up and separating their cattle. The year's new calves would be branded, then each outfit would drive its herd to summer range. As the snow melted in the high country the cattle were moved up into the Steens, Pueblo, Warner, Trout Creek, and Owyhee mountain ranges to graze on the season's fresh grasses. Life for the *vaqueros* during this time was spent in the open, or in the rough shelter of a cow-camp shack or dugout.

At the close of summer, the herds would be moved back to the desert. At that time, a beef roundup might be held to select the cattle that were to be driven to market and sold. Winnemucca, Nevada, with its stockyards and loading chutes for the Central Pacific Railroad, was the most common destination of the trail drives from eastern Oregon. Other herds might head north to The Dalles or Umatilla Landing, where special cattle boats of the Oregon Steam Navigation Company would carry them down the Columbia to Portland.

On both roundups and trail drives a *vaquero's* home was his bedroll; a large, heavy, canvas tarp which carried his blankets and quilts and also protected him from the weather when he slept out in the open. This bedroll also served as his "suitcase," carrying spare clothes, equipment, and personal belongings.

The *vaquero's* bedrolls were carried in the chuck wagon, or for large outfits, in a separate bed-wagon. In fact, life on the range was centered around the chuck wagon, which carried staples like beans, rice, flour, and spices in sacks and barrels.

Joaquin "Chino" Berdugo (left) and Prim Ortega worked as foremen at the P Ranch.

Bolted to the rear was a compartmented storage box for dutch ovens, pots, skillets, and other essentials for providing a meal in the open and on the move. Often, the chuck wagon was the domain of a Chinese cook—men like "Charley On Long" and "China Gow" at the P Ranch, and "Payne" of the ZX. These men were noted for ruling the chuckwagon or ranch kitchen with efficiency and a fierce, possessive pride. Woe to the *vaqueros* who fell a-foul of them!

As winter approached, only the ranch's permanent crew of *vaqueros* was kept on, while seasonal hands were laid off and left to fend for themselves. Winter work consisted of watching over the herds as they grazed the lower elevations of the desert and helping the cattle weather that difficult time by breaking ice on frozen waterholes, feeding them stored hay when natural forage was covered with snow, and dragging mired-down cows out of muddy wetlands. As spring approached, wild horses rounded up on the desert were driven to the ranch and "broken" in preparation for the work ahead in the next season's roundups, trail drives, and ranch work. Some outfits had

It was the old-time California vaqueros of southeastern Oregon like Amanda Mirandi (far left) who passed on their horsemanship and cattle-working skills to a new generation of Anglo-American buckaroos.

LUIS ORTEGA & THE ART OF RAWHIDE BRAIDING

The traditions of the California *vaquero* have endured for three centuries because generations of horsemen have believed in the value of their skills and the importance of passing them on. Perhaps no one has played a more significant role in preserving the *vaquero* culture than Luis Ortega, a fifth generation Californian who worked in Oregon in his youth. A descendent of Sergeant José Francisco Ortega of the Portola Expedition of 1769, Ortega and his forebears continued as horsemen on the California landscape well into the twentieth century.

As a boy growing up on the Spade S Ranch, near present-day Lompoc on the central California coast, Luis Ortega was fortunate to have as a friend and mentor, Fernando Librada, a 110-year-old Tulare Indian who had been a *vaquero* in the days of the Missions and great *ranchos*. Librada taught Ortega the art of braiding rawhide, a craft essential to *vaquero* life. Skilled rawhide braiders produced *reatas*, *bozals*, reins, and other key pieces of a *vaquero's* outfit. Luis Ortega developed his skill over the years, pursuing it in his spare time while working as a *vaquero* in the early years of this century. Like other adventurous young men he occasionally sought out new experiences and country, on several occasions working the roundups on the Oregon desert at outfits like the MC and ZX. There on the High Desert, a half century after the first *vaqueros* came into the country, Ortega noted a prevalence of hackamores, light-

Young Luis Ortega poses with his horse Fish at the Spade S Ranch about 1912.

Luis Ortega and his wife Rose with an exhibition of his rawhide work at the National Cowboy Hall of Fame. Ortega's reatas, *bridles, and other pieces are collector's items.*

handed riders with spade-bit horses, and ropers still favoring rawhide *reatas*.

A chance meeting with western artist Ed Borein, who praised Luis for his rawhide work, encouraged the young craftsman to pursue his braiding on a full-time basis. When he gave up the life of a buckaroo, Ortega promised himself that he would "get so high up on the rawhide game that nobody would ever catch up," and he did. For over fifty years Luis and his wife Rose were familiar figures at livestock shows and rodeos, where Ortega's prized work was purchased by horsemen and collectors. On other occasions they toured the sagebrush country of Nevada and Oregon, where his *reatas*, bridles, quirts, and other rawhide work were equally appreciated and sought after.

Ortega's efforts to preserve his California heritage went beyond his rawhide work. He wrote two books on the subject, *The California Stockhorse* and *The California Hackamore Horse*, as well as numerous articles for *Quarter Horse Journal* and *Western Horseman*. He was honored with exhibits of his work at the National Cowboy Hall of Fame and in 1986 was awarded a National Heritage Fellowship by the National Endowment for the Arts in recognition of his accomplishments. Luis Ortega died April 6, 1995.

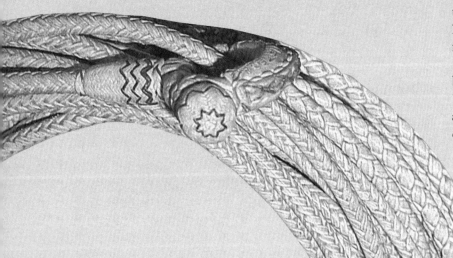

specially built barns for training horses in the winter, like the "round barn" at the P Ranch.

A *vaquero's* winter home was a bunkhouse fashioned from timber, stacked stone, or sod and furnished with wooden bunks or iron bedsteads and a substantial stove.

When the men were not at work, they played cards, repaired their saddles and gear, and passed the long evenings with good conversation. For those who could read, most bunk houses had out-of-date issues of *Harper's Magazine*, or the *Police Gazette*, or perhaps newspapers from Sacramento, Chico, or Red Bluff that told what was happening at home. And—a bunkhouse favorite—there were catalogs filled with the latest *vaquero* gear by G.S. Garcia of Elko, Nevada or the Visalia Stock Saddle Company of San Francisco, or silverwork by Mike Morales and Raphael Gutierrez.

VAQUEROS WHO MADE THEIR MARK

In this era of the big open-range ranches, before fences and homesteaders changed the landscape, *vaqueros* like Juan Redon, "Tebo" Ortega, and "Chino" Berdugo spent their lives in the saddle working for one outfit. Other Hispanic riders remembered by old timers or captured on aging photographs include "Chappo" at Riley and Hardin's Double O Ranch west of Harney Lake, "Ankle" Bustamento at the Home Creek Ranch in Catlow Valley, and Augustine Gilbert at the Roaring Springs Ranch. Later, at the turn of the century, Placedor Bravo was a well-known horse trainer and trader in Harney and Grant counties. And in the 1920s Frank Lorenzana, a second-generation *vaquero* who grew up in the Harney Valley, was a top hand on the Miller and Lux ranches in Oregon and northern Nevada.

Other young men with the skills to find a job with any outfit often worked their way through the region. It was a way to see the country, make new friends, and ride fresh horses. Unless recorded in a ranch ledger or one of the few photographs taken during this period, however, these itinerant *vaqueros* disappeared quietly from our memories.

After a long day's work, many a vaquero *would pore over catalogs that pictured the latest riding gear. This "full flower stamped" saddle is from an early catalog published by L. D. Stone Company, San Francisco. The spur is advertised as "silver inlaid, nicely engraved" by M. Morales of Portland, Oregon.*

VAQUEROS BECOME BUCKAROOS

The year 1900 not only ushered in a new century, it marked a turning point on the rangeland of the High Desert. Homesteads were now scattered across the landscape, a landscape traced with fence lines and marked by farmers' fields. Most of the old *vaqueros* were fading from the scene. Some, like Juan Redon, returned to California to live out their remaining years. A few stayed on at the ranches but no longer took part in the more rigorous work with the cattle. "Tebo" and

Chino Berdugo holds Lawrence South, son of the P Ranch manager.

"Chino" continued at the P Ranch in a life of retirement. They were respected for their role in the early settlement of the country and counted among the pioneers of Harney County.

Esther South, whose father managed the P Ranch after Pete French was shot in a land dispute, remembers the old *vaqueros* as they were in their later years. She remembers that "Chino" and "Tebo" took it upon themselves to help keep an eye on her and the other South children. One time, Esther remembers, she slipped away to ride her horse through the Blitzen River, only to find a worried and angry Tebo waiting on the other side to give her a spanking and send her back to the ranch house.

Those aging *vaqueros* who remained in the High Desert must have felt a great deal of pride and satisfaction, knowing that the skills and customs they brought north from California

In 1985 in Hood River, three former vaqueros from Zacatecas and Jalisco, Mexico, formed a charro association to keep alive the fancy riding and roping traditions of their youth and to provide entertainment for the local Hispanic community. An aspiring charro must subscribe to a code of ethics and demonstrate proficiency in breaking horses and roping and riding horses and bulls. The Dos Coronas Charro Association, the only one in Oregon, has a close working relationship with The Dalles Rodeo Association.

were still valued on the ranches of the region. The young Anglo-Americans who took up their work anglicized *vaquero* into buckaroo. A *la jaquima* became hackamore, *chaparreras* evolved into chaps, and *mecate* become McCarty. But except for altering some of the old California terms, most buckaroos continued to follow the old ways as horse trainers, reinsmen, and ropers. Today, a wide selection of traditional rawhide gear, silver-mounted bits and spurs, and California rigged saddles continue to be produced and used on the Oregon ranges.

A visitor to the Whitehorse Ranch will find the original stone and wooden barn, topped by a weathervane in the form of a white horse, dating from the era of John Devine a century ago. A close look at the equipment hanging in the tack room, and the riders at work among the cattle, make it readily apparent that the transition from *vaquero* to buckaroo has survived remarkably well. At the MC, the ZX, the Alvord, the Roaring Springs, and most other historic outfits, the visitor can see that the Spanish California legacy which began in 1769 continues in the sagebrush ocean of the Oregon High Desert.

MEXICAN MULE PACKERS AND THE ROGUE RIVER WAR

During the period of Oregon's provisional and territorial governments, volunteer militias often served in times of crisis. One such time was 1855 and 1856, when the Rogue River War raged in southern Oregon. While the volunteer militia in that war—the Second Regiment Oregon Mounted Volunteers—has received considerable attention from historians, the packers who supplied the troops with food and other necessities have scarcely been mentioned.

In the mid-1800s, transportation of supplies to troops in Oregon was a vital and tricky business. For the most part there were no roads, just muddy or snowy trails over the mountains. Therefore, wagons could not be used and mule packtrains were required. Because of the rugged conditions, Mexican mules—bred for use in packtrains—were preferred over other pack animals. At the time, the animals had to be brought in from Mexico or California, and keen competition among miners, settlers, and private packtrain owners drove prices up quickly.

Although Oregon had a sprinkling of Anglo mule packers who had learned their skills in California or Mexico, Mexican packers were dominant in the trade. Mexicans had

been mule packing throughout the Southwest and Mexico as well as California for centuries, and when the mining population moved north, the Mexicans came too. In 1851 Mexican packers were the first to move supplies of every kind from distribution points in northern California to settlements as far north as the Illinois Valley in Oregon. As a result of their early presence along southern Oregon trails, they were also among the first casualties of the Rogue River Wars.

The first Mexican packers were hired on December 1, 1855; the last served through May 31, 1856. The men worked an average of eighty days at a substantial wage of $6 per day—the same wage paid to Anglo packers.

The Mexicans who served with the Second Regiment Oregon Mounted Volunteers did so shortly after the Mexican-American War, when anti-Mexican feeling ran high. Yet these men demonstrated that the prevailing stereotypes of Mexicans as irresponsible, lethargic, and docile were just that—stereotypes. The men proved their value during the Rogue River War and played a significant part in the frontier and military history of the state.

—Erasmo Gamboa

6

THE BRACERO PROGRAM

BY ERASMO GAMBOA

*More than any other period, the World War II years
pulled Mexican Hispanics to Oregon and the rest
of the Pacific Northwest in unprecedented numbers.
They came for one reason—to fill the critical labor shortages
that threatened agricultural production.*

In Oregon, labor was desperately needed everywhere, but especially on the state's farms, which were expected to produce unprecedented amounts for national consumption and for distribution abroad. Yet among non-Hispanics, farm jobs went begging because they paid badly and involved poor working conditions.

To avoid losing the crops, employers and state officials tapped all potential sources of labor, including school children, housewives, business employees, and state prisoners. Even so, labor shortages continued to threaten farm production. One year into the war, Oregon farmers turned to Mexico for help.

THE BINATIONAL WARTIME LABOR AGREEMENT

In August 1942 Mexico and the United States signed a binational wartime labor agreement—Public Law-45—and the federal government began to contract with Mexican men (*braceros*) for temporary employment in the United States. The agreement guaranteed, among other things, that the men would be paid a minimum wage; receive health care, adequate housing, and board; and not be subject to social discrimination.

In Oregon the Emergency Farm Labor Supply, or Bracero Program, as it was popularly called, was administered by the state college at Corvallis and by federal labor officials. In the next five years approximately 15,136 *braceros* contracted for farm employment in Oregon. The number alone was impressive, but more important was its labor potential. Once in the state, the men were reorganized into a highly regimented and effective labor force.

HOUSING THE WORKERS

The *braceros* were housed together, sometimes in mobile tent camps or in permanent farm labor camps that dotted the farming areas from Ontario to Salem and Hood River to Medford.

As a rule, six workers lived together in a 16-by-16 foot tent that was furnished with folding cots, one blanket per person, and heating stoves when available. Although each individual was entitled to bring seventy-seven pounds of personal effects from Mexico, in reality most arrived with little more than a change of clothes. With time, the workers scavenged for discarded crates or boxes and placed them inside the tents for storage and seating. These makeshift creations—along with

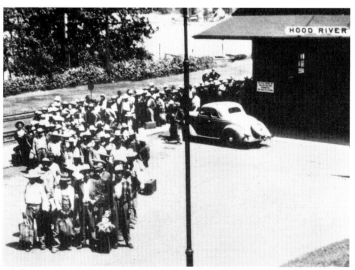

Under a wartime labor agreement, braceros *from Mexico arrive at Hood River. There, each was assigned to work for a farmer in the area.*

Top. Largely through the efforts of braceros, *Oregon produced an estimated 3,200 tons of cucumbers in 1945. Middle. Outside the cook tent, a group of men waits to pick up lunches before heading to the orchards. Often food spoiled because it wasn't refrigerated, and the men became violently ill. Bottom. Checking the mail wall at O'Dell Labor Camp, Hood River. Some* braceros, *away from their villages for the first time, became homesick or feigned illness so they would be sent back to Mexico.*

pictures of loved ones, tokens of remembrance, or knick-knacks purchased locally—completed the interior. The men were on call each day, including Sundays, and could be transferred at a moment's notice to meet labor shortages elsewhere.

During the summer, the men were often driven from the tents by 100-degree temperatures, and in fall and winter the fabric structures offered little protection from the inclement Northwest weather—leading to the specter of hypothermia. Stoves, if provided, were ineffective because the loose sides of the tent allowed most of the heat to escape. Moreover, the frequent lack of kerosene, coal, or dry wood meant that the stoves were often useless. When the stoves did work, the *braceros* sometimes faced a more serious threat—from fires in the highly flammable tents.

LEISURE-TIME ACTIVITIES

Leisure-time activities, a key to everyone's physical and social well-being, were just as precious to the *braceros*—yet the men had little to do during their off hours. In most camps, Mexican movies—projected outdoors on tent walls—were a bright spot in an otherwise dull routine. When films were not available, the men found other ways to pass the time. On Sundays, they sometimes requested Catholic priests to offer mass in camp. They also frequently pooled their resources to buy radios or jukeboxes (which they stocked with Spanish records). Some passed idle hours with handicraft work.

Beyond these limited leisure activities, the social highlight of the year at most camps was the celebration of Mexican Independence with festivities that were largely improvised but still provided a welcome break from the daily routine. Another much-celebrated occasion was Cinco de Mayo, the anniversary of the defeat of the French in Mexico.

At Medford in 1944 more than a thousand—including U.S. Senator Rufus Holman (a member of the Senate Appropriations Committee), the mayor of Medford, members of the chamber of commerce, students from local high school Spanish classes, many farmers with their wives and families, and several local barmaids—attended the celebration. The local radio stations broadcast the day's festivities, while Mexican music from a jukebox and musicians from the camp gave the day some authenticity. Three pigs were butchered for the noon meal and visitors dined on two thousand tortillas, fifty gallons of ice cream, and a thousand soft drinks. As a symbol of friendship, the workers raised the flags of both countries in a special ceremony as bugles called the crowd to attention. In the evening, the camp hosted a dance, complete with orchestra, where women from the community and the growers' wives and daughters danced with the Mexican workers.

PROBLEMS AND HARDSHIPS

Although the *braceros* were praised for their labor, the wartime farm-labor program was not without problems. In addition to living in tent camps under spartan conditions with few organized social activities, they suffered many accidents, not only because of their unfamiliarity with farm machinery but because farmers had little regard for their safety. As a rule, *braceros* received low wages, and when they organized strikes to win increases, they encountered quick and sometimes violent resistance from growers and local officials. Overall, the men endured much racial discrimination from employers and local communities alike.

The *braceros* also complained loudly about the poor quality of food served in the camps. The meals lacked variety and appeal because the kitchen facilities there were often makeshift and deficient by most standards. Contributing to discontent over meals was wartime rationing, which meant that desirable quantities and varieties of food were not always available. The Agricultural Workers Health Association, a government-sponsored cooperative that provided health care to farm workers in the Northwest, supported the *braceros*' complaints. In 1945 it reported that the poor, iron-deficient food was the main cause of nutritional anemia among the men. This disclosure prompted the Mexican embassy to take action that led to improvement in the quality of food served to the men.

Food services were inadequate in other ways. Sometimes sandwiches were prepared too early in the day and were taken to the fields unrefrigerated, leading to spoilage. Workers were not provided with containers for coffee or milk, so they used anything they could find without much thought to sanitation. This practice undoubtedly contributed to an unusually high incidence of food poisoning. During a nine-month period in 1946, there were five outbreaks, but the most serious outbreak had occurred three years earlier on a hop ranch near Grants Pass,

During the pea harvest at Athena, men feed the crop into machines that stripped the peas from the vines in preparation for canning.

where 500 of 511 men fell sick and 300 required hospitalization. Life was also difficult for the *braceros* because for most, the sojourn to the United States was their first separation from their immediate and extended families, which are extremely important in Mexican culture. Thus, they arrived ill-prepared to cope with the strain of hostile and unfamiliar circumstances and the tensions and emotions surrounding the war effort. Not surprisingly, many men became distraught and feigned illness or wrote to their families asking to be recalled—before their seasonal contracts ended—for reasons of illness or death at home. Federal farm labor officials from Portland expressed concern that many *braceros* in the North-

In a Umatilla County labor camp in 1943, trucks from several farms wait for the braceros *to learn their assignments for the day.*

In addition to working in the fields, braceros *were also assigned to work in food-processing plants.*

west would use any means to return early. They "definitely want to be sent home now," observed one official in what became a common complaint. "If there is a way to hasten their departure, they will find it...either by refusing to work or violation of the [wage] ceiling." In 1945 the Chief of Operations at Portland reported that 10 percent of all *braceros* contracted to the Pacific Northwest were either missing or had been granted an early repatriation.

The men also faced widespread anti-Mexican sentiment. The camp manager at Medford reported that a Mexican national was attacked in public "without provocation" and severely injured by five young men. After the assault, the battered man was arrested on a charge of being intoxicated. During his arraignment the judge acknowledged that "those who made the attack should have been arrested instead." As it turned out, the *bracero* had been staggering and presumed drunk "due to the beating received and not due to alcoholism as claimed." Such instances were not everyday occurrences, but they did reveal a pattern of racial animosity toward the Mexican workers.

Oregon employers soon tired of having workers complain about poor wages, harsh living conditions, hard work,

and racial discrimination. They tired of *braceros* refusing to work or walking away from the labor camps and their employers in protest.

THE END OF THE PROGRAM

When the war ended, the Bracero Program was gradually phased out, and migratory Mexican-American workers began to replace those who had earlier been imported. In Oregon and throughout the Pacific Northwest, the *bracero* labor force had been a decisive factor in the state's ability to sustain critical agricultural production, and the Mexican men therefore had played a significant role in winning the war.

At one point, Governor Earl Snell recognized their contribution in a letter to the Mexican government, in which he expressed the sincere appreciation of all Oregonians for the men's work.

Governor Snell was not alone in expressing his gratitude. Many farmers understood that Mexican labor was essential to Oregon agriculture. One farmer from Columbia County summarized it best: these "Mexican boys," he said, were "God-sent."

BECOMING ASSIMILATED

*The national civil rights movement of the 1960s and 1970s
had its Mexican-American counterpart in Oregon.
Here, the war against poverty and mistreatment of farm workers resulted
in a mix of social and educational programs, laws, and policies that over the years
have improved conditions and provided opportunities for Hispanics in the state.
Today, members of the Hispanic population continue to build on the foundation laid
by the civil rights movement and to strengthen the state's agricultural industry.
They also own a growing number of businesses and hold positions
in government, industry, medicine, law, and education.*

NUESTRA INTEGRACION

*El movimiento nacional de derechos civiles de los años 60 y 70
tuvo su equivalente para los mexicano americanos en Oregon.
La lucha contra la pobreza y contra el maltrato de los migrantes trajo como resultado
un surtido de programas sociales y educativos, así como leyes y normas que,
con el pasar de los años, han ido mejorando el nivel de vida de los hispanos de este estado
ofreciéndoles también oportunidades. Hoy en día, miembros de la comunidad hispana
siguen desarrollando los fundamentos dados por el movimiento de derechos civiles
y fortalecen la industria agrícola del estado. También son dueños de un gran número
de negocios y ocupan posiciones en el gobierno, en la industria,
en la medicina, en jurisprudencia, y educación.*

Symbols of the fight for equality—Cesar Chavez and the United Farm Workers Union flag

EL MOVIMIENTO: OREGON'S MEXICAN-AMERICAN CIVIL RIGHTS MOVEMENT

BY ERASMO GAMBOA

The Mexican-American civil rights movement of the 1960s and 1970s—
more popularly called the "Chicano Movement" or "El Movimiento" Chicano—
was one of the most important periods of Oregon's Hispanic history.
During those decades the pursuit of political, social, and economic rights,
which were long denied to seasonal workers and migrants in Oregon,
was significant because it provided the foundation for much that has affected
the civic culture of Hispanics in subsequent decades.

As noted elsewhere in this book, Hispanics had started to settle permanently in Oregon in the years following the end of World War II. In Independence, Woodburn, Ontario, and Nyssa, families gathered to create formal and informal benevolent or cultural organizations and celebrations. These efforts brought a certain amount of cultural and spiritual satisfaction, but in many Oregon towns, Mexican Americans experienced de facto segregation and did not feel accepted after 15 or 20 years of permanent residency.

Social alienation can be subjective. Political powerlessness, pressing educational and health problems, and poverty-level income, on the other hand, were objective problems whose solutions seemed beyond the ability and resources of Oregon Hispanics before the 1960s.

THE NATIONAL CIVIL RIGHTS MOVEMENT

The beginnings of Oregon's Mexican-American civil rights movement were rooted in the political and economic context of the nation in the 1960s. At the time, the national civil rights movement was beginning to be effective in its challenges to racial and discriminatory practices in American society. While that movement was primarily focused on African Americans, it also drew wide attention to the longstanding discrimination against Mexican Americans in states like Texas and California.

As it had with the civil rights movement, the federal government—under President Kennedy's "New Frontier" and President Johnson's "Great Society" programs—began to respond to increased demands by Mexican Americans for complete and equal citizenship. Under the Johnson administration, the Office of Economic Opportunity (OEO) provided federal funds to organizations intent on addressing social and economic problems of the poor at the "grass roots" level. When Congress passed the Civil Rights Act of 1964, a new era of nontraditional, sometimes confrontational, politics and heightened social and cultural consciousness was underway.

THE CHICANO MOVEMENT

In many parts of the nation, Mexican-American social progressives, farm workers, college and university students, and political activists used cultural pride and the issue of general deprivation to organize the Chicano Movement. Loosely defined in terms of its goals and membership, the Chicano Movement appealed to most Mexican Americans regardless of gender, class, age, political affiliation, or state of residence. Oregon's Mexican-American civil rights movement was part of this broad, complex national movement taking place in Chicano communities throughout the Southwest, Midwest, Washington, and Idaho.

THE SITUATION IN OREGON

Although part of the larger national social movement, Oregon's Mexican-American civil rights movement was also

Mexican priest Father Ernesto Bravo (right) came to Oregon under the sponsorship of the Catholic Church to serve the needs of Mexican Americans in the Willamette Valley.

particularly suited to the state. In the 1940s and 1950s a Mexican-American migratory and resident seasonal labor force was becoming more and more commonplace in the Willamette and Treasure valleys, and this labor force was comprised of families that were among the poorest in the state. Therefore, it was not coincidental that President Truman's Commission on Migratory Labor chose "Library Hall" at Tenth and Yamhill in Portland as the site for its only hearing on migratory labor in the Pacific Northwest in October 1950. For three days, the commission listened to recommendations to improve the availability of farm labor to state farmers, but because the majority of speakers were farmers or their representatives the commission heard very little testimony about ways to improve the working and living conditions of the migrants themselves.

Eight years after the hearing, the farm labor supply had stabilized but conditions for the workers had not improved appreciably. Don S. Wilner, state senator from Multnomah County, remarked that "discriminations have contributed in making migrant workers the poorest members of our society." Their average income, he continued, is between "one and two thousand dollars per year."

THE CHURCHES' ROLE

The Oregon State Council of Churches was one of the first organizations to begin to address the migrants' needs. In the

years following World War II, the Council provided social services to migrant camp residents at Independence, McMinnville, and other locations. In fact, the Council of Churches provided testimony before the Commission on Migratory Labor urging inspection of health conditions at Oregon farm labor camps.

As more and more Catholic migrant families began to be employed on Oregon farms, the Catholic Church's involvement deepened. In 1955 the Portland Archdiocese established a Migrant Ministry to provide the migrants with spiritual assistance. However, although some priests took steps to welcome Spanish-speaking parishioners, most Mexican-American families felt alienated in the English-speaking parishes. Later, the Migrant Ministry took a bold step and sponsored Father Ernesto Bravo, a Mexican priest from Zamora, Michoacán, to provide culturally relevant masses, sacraments, and spiritual retreats to Mexican Americans in the Willamette Valley. In this way, Catholic parishes like St. Luke's in Woodburn started to emerge as the hub of the growing Mexican-American community.

Behind the scenes, the Catholic Church also began to assist Mexican Americans to organize politically. This action was critical because it eventually led to the beginning of a sweeping political consciousness among Mexican Americans throughout Oregon.

BIRTH OF THE VALLEY MIGRANT LEAGUE

A turning point occurred in 1964 when the Migrant Ministry changed its name to Oregon Friends of Migrants. That same year it organized a coalition of progressive clergy, legislators, farm-labor employers, and Mexican-American residents to apply to OEO for a demonstration grant to fund adult basic education, vocational training, summer school, and day care and health services for migrant workers. This affiliation of citizens, state legislators, and clergy, known as the Valley Migrant League (VML), was located in Woodburn.

With an initial grant of $700,000, the VML quickly developed into a community-based organization with many times its original budget and a service area of seven counties in the Willamette Valley. The importance of the VML as a catalyst for Oregon's Chicano movement as well as an entity that addressed the agricultural workers' needs cannot be emphasized too strongly.

It was the concern of the Valley Migrant League with civil rights and the support of funding agencies like OEO that swept in a period of high-pitched political activism and ethnic pride among Mexican Americans which was unprecedented in Oregon. One former VML employee recalled, "Mexicanos used to hang their heads" before their employers, teachers, police, and government officials. When the VML developed, there was "no more humility before Anglos."

The Valley Migrant League, a federally funded community-based organization, became politically charged and felt the pressure of various local and national interest groups like the United Farm Workers Union, with its boycott of California table grapes and lettuce. The result was a groundswell of determination among Mexican Americans to create fundamental social change in the Willamette Valley.

GROWING PAINS

In seeking change, VML experienced its own growing pains. In 1965 its board of directors was comprised of growers, legislators, clergy, migrants, and local citizens. As VML programs grew to encompass low-income migrant housing, VISTA, summer school programs, and a migrant health project, the incompatibility of the group's overall goals and the interests of its individual board members became apparent. The most obvious split was between farm owners and the migrants themselves, but rifts between growers and church and community activists also occurred.

Beginning in 1970 Chicano farm workers flexed their new-found political muscle and took total control of the Valley Migrant League. They did this by amending the bylaws to raise board membership requirements from 51 to 100 percent migrant representation. Thereafter, growers, labor contractors, crew leaders, and others no longer had a say in the organization's administration.

However, VML was still hampered by federal regulations that prohibited it from assuming a direct political role. This meant that the organization had to maintain a distance from local politics and politically sensitive issues—something that was not always possible or politically expedient. When national interest groups like the United Farm Workers Union (UFW), with its Oregon boycott of California table grapes and lettuce, sought VML's support and pushed for farm-worker unioniza-

Abysmal camp conditions facing migrants in the 1960s spurred Chicano organizations into action.

Many Valley Migrant League programs focused on the immediate needs of seasonal farm-worker families. One program provided surplus food. Another collected and distributed bedding to families that arrived in the spring when the weather was still harsh.

tion and improved worker-employer relations on Oregon farms, the VML could not respond. And although concerned with the health of migrants, the VML was prevented from filing complaints concerning conditions in labor camps.

The VML's difficulties were not unique. In Eastern Oregon, Treasure Valley Community College (TVCC) had set up a similar program to serve farm workers in the Ontario area in 1965. Barely two years later, TVCC dismissed all the program's staff because of alleged political involvement with the farm workers' union. Although the employees were later reinstated, prob-

In an attempt to make a fundamental change in the migratory cycle of farmworkers, the VML started Farmworker Housing Project, a program that helped workers to build and buy their own homes.

lems persisted and in 1970 the TVCC Migrant Program moved to Caldwell, Idaho.

For the Valley Migrant League, however, the real issue was the degree to which it would be allowed to create fundamental social change in the Willamette Valley. From one side, the federal government constantly investigated and audited the organization to clear it of charges ranging from use of government funds to transport pickets in support of the UFW to communist affiliation. From another quarter, employees were physically accosted, received death threats, were held under close public scrutiny, and were otherwise hampered in their work. To keep the organization in compliance and its workers safe, the VML advised its staff not to become directly involved with the UFW during working hours.

These limitations led to unfounded criticisms from some individuals, who wanted autonomy for VML programs that would allow them to solve the "real" problems of the largely Mexican-American farm working community. As some people left the VML, they began to join Volunteers in Vanguard Action (VIVA), Volunteer Oregon Citizens for Agricultural Labor (VOCAL), United Farm Workers of Oregon, and Campesinos Forum. Although the VML supported farm-worker issues, these individuals urged more attention to unionization and farm-worker unionization and less to VLM's multi-service approach.

Coming from both sides, this pressure only worked to strengthen VML's commitment to Oregon farm workers. Often working behind the scenes, the organization did much to alter their lives in a meaningful way. Because of its concern with health conditions in farm-labor camps and the migratory cycle of Oregon farm workers, the VML developed a federally funded self-help housing project called Farmworker Housing that allowed farm workers to build and own their homes. This project was funded by the Federal Housing Authority and Farm Home

This haunting 1966 portrait by Priscilla Carrasco became a poster promoting the United Farm Workers Union and its grape boycott.

Left to right. Chicano leaders included Junior Perez, Valley Migrant League area director in Woodburn; Sonny Montes (left), a founder of Colegio Cesar Chavez who also worked for the VML in Hillsboro, and Lavar Gonzalez of AGUILA, a Portland agency that focused on urban problems; José Jaime, an early director of Centro Cultural in Cornelius; Frank Rivera, chairman of the Valley Migrant League board; Cande Veliz, staff member of the Salud de la Familia Medical Clinic in Woodburn, and Ramon Gonzales, a VML board chairman. Their leadership and determination helped pave the way for gradual improvements in the lives of Hispanics in Oregon.

Administration but remained under the VML board of directors. Through self-help housing, the Valley Migrant League—and later Farmworker Housing Project —addressed problems that had persisted for decades, problems related to education, health, and temporary residency.

NEW FIELDS OF ENDEAVOR, NEW LEADERS

By 1970 El Movimiento, or the Chicano Movement, was underway in Oregon and migrant worker issues were no longer the only concerns. Mexican Americans were interested in promoting cultural pride, having access to higher education, advocating affirmative action in non-agricultural employment, reforming the criminal justice system, and protesting the disproportionate number of Chicanos serving in Viet Nam.

VML executive director Frank Martinez (left) listens intently to a speaker at a Poor People's Conference in Salem while Brown Berets provide security.

Although the Valley Migrant League was initially developed to serve migrants exclusively, it became the heart and soul of the Chicano Movement in the state. Two key components of VML governance permitted this central role. First, the board of directors, unlike those of "migrant programs" in Washington and Idaho, was composed primarily of migrants or former migrants who were representative of the people and sympathetic to the Chicano Movement. The board members were dynamic community representatives. Guided by the experience and leadership of Chairman Frank Rivera, most board members were actively involved in the VML programs as well as in the local community.

The other element critical to the Valley Migrant League's new role was its executive director. Until 1969 no one had remained long enough in that job to develop a well-defined plan to sustain the organization beyond each annual funding cycle. That year, Frank Martinez, a former priest from New Mexico, became the first Mexican American to serve as executive director. The board's selection of him to head the VML was extremely fortunate. As an "outsider," Martinez did not fret about social and political boundaries imposed by local Mexican-American kinship ties and was not dependent on the local Anglo power structure. Therefore, he was free to take certain administrative steps and positions that other directors might not have considered.

The timing of the decision to hire Martinez was also superb. Across the state the call for "Chicano and Brown Power" and the symbolism of various facets of the movement were energizing many formerly quiet Mexican-American communities. At the time, Frank Martinez was the right person to begin to channel the rising tide of cultural identity and self-determination, for both the VML directors and the local communities.

Well trained as an administrator and a powerful orator, Martinez moved the VML toward being a more inclusive social agency. He began by bringing the community into the decision-making process. Where board meetings had usually lasted one or two hours, sessions now ran much longer—with some ending after midnight. Once the VML allowed people to express their concerns and needs, the organization strained to get things done. In retrospect, it made an extraordinary effort to fulfill most of the people's expectations.

EFFECTIVE STRATEGIES

One part of the VML strategy was to make effective use of the network of OEO administrators, Congressmen, leading Chicano spokesperson Cesar Chavez, church leaders, and politicians such as Al Ullman. When OEO officials did not travel to Oregon, VML administrators went to Washington, D. C. to secure funding. More impressive yet, the VML worked behind the scenes and got Senators George McGovern, Edmund Muskie, Ted Kennedy, Mark Hatfield and Birch Bayh to learn first hand about the meaning of poverty in the Willamette Valley. In 1972, for example, the VML arranged for then Democratic presidential candidate George McGovern to visit Centro Chicano Cultural at Gervais. Once there, McGovern realized he could not refuse a visit to a local farm labor camp. At the camp, he was sickened by the repulsive conditions of outdoor privies and overall camp conditions, and the VML had made its point about migrants in Oregon.

On another occasion the Oregon legislature was debating passage of Senate Bill 677 concerning collective bargaining rights for farm workers. This legislation, which had been supported by the VML and the United Farm Workers of Oregon, was changed to favor farm-labor employers. In addition to lobbying against the bill, the VML arranged for Cesar Chavez of the United Farm Workers of California to visit a daycare center and meet parents of children attending a VML school in Hubbard. From there, he went to the state capitol at Salem and gave a powerful and moving speech against passage of SB677. This type of political mobilization eventually defeated the bill.

Locally, the Valley Migrant League also pushed to hold local politicians accountable to the needs of Mexican Americans. In 1969 the VML was instrumental in getting Governor Tom McCall to create an Advisory Committee on Chicano Affairs. The 15-member statewide board included Frank Martinez and Rafael Pablo Ciddio y Abeyta, also of the VML. While the advisory committee had no real legislative power, it was an influential and symbolic voice that made the governor's office and legislature more conscientious about farm workers.

The importance of this kind of political activism went beyond mere tokenism. Oregon's Mexican-American community could present its issues before state government in a way that

Cesar Chavez's brother "warms up the crowd" in preparation for Cesar's appearance during a rally in Salem.

had not been possible earlier. Moreover, public pressure for stricter enforcement of laws and regulations concerning agricultural workers grew, especially in urban communities.

In 1969 individual political activists from the Valley Migrant League borrowed a page from the national civil rights movement and used a direct and unconventional political tactic: they helped organize a "Poor People's March" on Salem to protest farmers' refusals to allow community organizers on their property and to pressure Governor Tom McCall for better farm-labor housing and improved working conditions. The following September, Frank Martinez, as chairman of Oregon Poor People's Council, held a two-day conference at the Salem Fairgrounds to find ways of fighting poverty among whites, Chicanos, Native Americans, Gypsies, Russians, and African Americans in Oregon. These were striking political maneu-

vers—beyond the scope of anything the VML as a federally funded entity could ever have attempted.

DEVELOPMENT OF CULTURAL AND HEALTH PROGRAMS

The Valley Migrant League was active in other arenas as cultural preservation and appreciation began to take a community-wide form. In 1972 the VML approached the Social Action Council of the Portland Catholic Archdiocese for help in purchasing 75 acres in Gervais to establish the Centro Chicano Cultural. The concept of a cultural center involved organized Mexican arts, crafts, and dance classes funded by the Catholic Campaign for Human Development—all aimed at strengthening cultural pride. The center also helped promote better community relations between Mexican Americans

SELF-HELP PROJECTS BECOME PERMANENT INSTITUTIONS IN WASHINGTON COUNTY

In the mid-1970s Mexican Americans in Washington County initiated two important volunteer efforts to help migrants and residents alike. The first, Centro Cultural, was founded by a handful of Hispanic families who wanted to provide for the basic needs of poor workers and their families; to educate Hispanic children; and to make sure that the language, customs, and cultural traditions of Mexico would be preserved. In 1971 these families asked a Jesuit priest, Arnold Beezer, to help them establish Centro as a nonprofit organization and be its executive director. After he left, Leonel Lucero was hired.

When monies were no longer available to retain an executive director, the families recruited Fr. José Jaime, who was willing to work without pay for a time. Between 1978 and 1980 Fr. Jaime was able to secure grants with which the organization could run its programs, build a center, and—eventually—hire a new director. Meanwhile he also worked as program director for another agency: Washington County Community Action.

One of Centro's early projects was a job-training center for auto mechanics. Another was a cooperative venture with Tektronix to provide local Mexican Americans with training and experience in assembling electronics products. Centro's many programs and volunteer efforts have led to the establishment of such spinoffs as Ayuda (an alcohol treatment program in Hillsboro), the Oregon Human Development Corporation, and the Virginia Garcia Memorial Health Center in Cornelius.

Virginia Garcia was a six-year-old who lived with her family in a migrant camp in North Plains and became critically ill after stepping on a rusty nail. At the hospital, no one

The original home of Centro Cultural in Cornelius.

spoke Spanish and could not determine what was wrong with her. By the time she received help, she was near death. After she died, Centro Cultural began to contact various agencies, including Salud Medical Clinic in Woodburn and St. Vincent Hospital in Portland, to help establish a clinic that could serve migrants and other low-income clients. The Virginia Garcia Memorial Health Center opened in the summer of 1979 in Cornelius in the building that had been intended for use as a garage for Centro's auto mechanics training project.

Today, Centro Cultural is in its third decade in a handsome building (see page 78), erected in 1981 with block grant funds from the federal government. Over the years, volunteers have cooked and served untold numbers of free meals—often between 100 and 1,000 a day for migrant workers who arrive destitute before the harvest begins. Centro has also offered hundreds of English-as-a-Second-Language and Spanish-as-a-Second-Language classes and other educational and cultural programs. Virginia Garcia Memorial Health Center, in operation for over twenty years, has established a solid reputation for providing comprehensive, bilingual health care to Washington County's poorest families.

Much of the credit for this impressive record goes to a cadre of volunteers—both Hispanic and non-Hispanic—who keep programs going, even when funds run out.

High-profile visits to Oregon helped dramatize critical issues facing migrant workers in the 1970s. Senator George McGovern (center) was taken to a migrant camp where the primitive conditions and lack of sanitation literally sickened him.

Senator Edward Kennedy (second from left) met with (from left) Jim Montoya and Patrick Mellany, co-directors of the Center for Chicano and Indian Studies (CISCO), and David Aguilar, executive director of Centro Cultural in Woodburn.

and Anglos, on the one hand, and Mexican Americans and local police on the other. The Centro Chicano Cultural also hoped to establish a farming cooperative for Chicanos, although such a cooperative was never developed.

Several years before the cultural center was established, a number of organizations had been concerned with the health of seasonal farm workers, many of whom suffered acute problems associated with living conditions at labor camps. The Oregon Migrant Health Program, for example, offered migrants home visits, routine physicals, nurse treatment, and referrals to doctors eligible for federal reimbursement for migrant care. The program, which started in 1963, served 13 counties where 90 percent of the migrants resided in 1970.

When this program ended in 1971, the VML fought bitterly to obtain federal funds to organize the Salud de la Familia Clinic in Woodburn. Funded in 1972, the clinic used an old building renovated by the Centro Chicano Cultural as its first facility. Later it became known as the Woodburn Salud Medical Clinic and served all low-income families, Mexican American and Anglo alike. Staffed with bilingual and bicultural practitioners and administrators, the clinic visited labor camps and dispensed general health information and comprehensive healthcare services, especially to expectant mothers and infants. The clinic also instructed farm workers on the proper use and handling of potentially hazardous herbicides and insecticides.

In 1979 a group from Salud Medical Clinic separated and joined Centro Cultural and St. Vincent Hospital to form the Virginia Garcia Memorial Health Center. The separation stemmed from a concern over the loss of Chicano administrative control of the Salud Medical Clinic and limited eligibility for health care services. Virginia Garcia was a Mexican-American child who died after failing to receive proper health services due to her family's inability to speak English.

The Valley Migrant League also obtained funding to establish a Job Options Program and Minority Business Enterprises. Under the latter, the VML received an inital grant of $75,000 and a subsequent grant of $150,000 to provide business support services to Mexican-American entrepreneurs.

ACCESS TO HIGHER EDUCATION

As young migrants gained access to education, they too began to insist on greater rights for their people. Effective during the 1968-69 academic year, the Oregon Board of Higher Education adopted a "three percent" policy to admit students "who have not met the basic admission requirements." The number of admissions under this policy could not exceed three percent of the previous year's freshman class.

The three percent admissions policy was in effect at the University of Oregon, Oregon State University, Portland State College, Southern Oregon State College, Reed College, and Pacific University. Programs to help educate disadvantaged Mexican-American students were also developed at various colleges and universities, both public and private. As a result, the first generation of Mexican-American students was enrolled in higher education programs in Oregon. In sociology, history, and political science courses, many of these students became sensitive to the marginalization of the Mexican-American community in Oregon and across the nation. Often, the students became politically involved on campus in United Mexican American Students and Movimiento Estudiantil Chicano de Aztlan, as well as in community organizations. Willing to take risks on campus and at home, these students were impatient social agents of radical change. Among other things, they almost single-handedly kept an effective boycott against California table grapes and lettuce going in Portland, Salem, and other communities.

MEMORIES OF COLEGIO CESAR CHAVEZ

José Romero, now a special projects coordinator with the Portland Public Schools, was recruited to teach at Colegio Cesar Chavez in 1973 when he was a Ph.D. student at the University of Oregon. His reflections about his experiences at the colegio brings the excitement and disappointments of those years into high relief. The colegio closed its doors in 1983, five years after Romero had left.

In 71-72 Sonny Montes was hired by Mount Angel College (soon to become Colegio Cesar Chavez) as a student services specialist to work with the Hispanic youth. When the college's dream of educating Chicanos was about to evaporate and they wanted to close it down, Chicano staff and students went out in the school van to Oregon State, to the University of Oregon, to wherever they could find individuals who were involved in graduate studies and had at least a master's degree and some teaching experience. They offered us no promises, no money, just a lot of hard work. I decided to take a year off from my benefactor, the Ford Foundation, to get some hands-on experience. A year turned out to be five years and I never went back. Although I never acquired my doctorate, I feel I got twice the education. I've never regretted my decision.

I came on board in '73 as the director of Chicano studies. I taught the history of Latin America, a three-term sequence of Chicano Studies from pre-Columbian history to the present, and U.S. history. Later, I was involved in student advising, academic work, faculty recruitment, and the external degree program. After our president departed, Sonny Montes was named director of administrative affairs and I became director of academic affairs. The colegio's board approved this administrative model. On December 12, 1973 students renamed the

José Romero remembers his years as a teacher and administrator at Colegio Cesar Chavez as the best of his life.

When local residents were given the opportunity to donate to the colegio, some declined to participate.

college for Cesar Chavez, who was one of the most active and inspirational leaders of our time. When we took charge of the college, it was a mess—no accreditation, no financial aid, a mass exodus of the former faculty. When we got back on the right track, we were accredited again. We applied for federal grants and financial assistance for our students. We were able to acquire some private monies from the Fund for the Improvement of Post-Secondary Education and the National Institute of Education. We were able to work out an arrangement with the U. S. Department of Housing and Urban Development to pay them 25 percent of the debt owed rather than having to bear the full amount, which was in excess of $10.5 million.

On a good month, when things went well, we had 500 dollars left over after we paid for the oil and utilities and legal costs and supplies. We would divide the money and get $100 each for our salary. But there were months when there was nothing.

In the early 70s we were on the cutting edge of what was called the *colegio sin paredes* (college without walls), where people were able to earn college credit for prior experience gained outside the classroom. We often relied on our own people and communities to be mentors, facilitators, part of the assessment team that verified the competencies the students were acquiring.

We also were on the cutting edge when it came to "getting the word out." Without the help of Centro Cultural, without the help of other community members who would join us on marches and sit-ins, we would never have succeeded. It was a community effort. We would call Seattle and ask our support group there to do a sit-in at the Office of Housing and Urban Development and demand justice for Colegio Cesar Chavez, and they would do that. We would ask the Chicano Student Union at New Mexico State University to host one of our students who was going there to give a talk. A lot of people learned about what was going on in Mt. Angel. It became a national issue. Cesar Chavez came to the campus at least three times. He also assisted us in Washington D.C. when a settlement between the Colegio and HUD was drafted.

The tragedy is that when something is in its developing stages, there's a lot of activism, a lot of notoriety and rallies and marches. That's how you turn something small into something big. But after you succeed and it becomes what it was intended, a new set of elements comes in and that's what I call institutionalization. You replace the activists with academicians. You shift from the community involvement movement and try to focus more on education. The agreements are forged and the struggle subsides. Now it's time to stop the rhetoric and provide good education.

The mistake the college made in its later years was to try to catch up with the Lewis & Clarks and the Linfields, and to show them that we were as good if not better. In the process of doing that, they forgot about the community and the non-traditional students. And having alienated the Chicano community and having lost the momentum of the movement, they became isolated. They got their federal grants but they went nowhere. They stagnated. And the NW Association came back to see how they were doing, and even though the programs were good, the accreditation people said, "Higher ed is not based on how good your programs are or how well prepared your students are. It's how much money you are making. What's your financial base? What kind of endowment do you have? What kind of financial base do you have? We feel that that represents over half of what higher ed is all about. What we see here are too few students and too much dependency on federal funds, so we're going to put you on probation again until you begin to have more students and find other sources of revenue." By that time the colegio had lost its momentum and the politicos had left. The Board was not the same individuals.

The Colegio Cesar Chavez experience was a truly grassroots movement. During its ten-year history, it became the only independent accredited and degree-granting institution for Chicanos in the country.

Efforts by the federal Office of Housing and Urban Development to close the college and collect on its unpaid debt prompted supporters to rally on the campus.

One year after the college opened, Cesar Chavez visited the campus. His leadership and belief in the importance of education had inspired college founders to name their institution for him.

"Having left school in the seventh grade, I began to realize how important education was. I knew that I would never achieve any of my goals if I did not educate myself.

During my twenties, I studied to improve my writing and reading skills. At the same time, I learned as much as I could about economics, the history of the labor movement, and the organizing of workers.

It was pretty rough at first. I was changing and I had to take a lot of ridicule from some rough characters. . .

Education does not change things overnight. It makes change possible and irreversible. It cannot be stolen or taken away. It can be given away without losing any of it. It is something to hand down to your children and grandchildren like a family treasure. For me education is very important."

—Cesar Chavez,
Quotation and translation from a colegio publication

"Después de haber dejado la escuela en el grado séptimo, yo empecé a realizer de la importancia de la educación. Me di cuenta de que nunca podría llevar a cabo ninguna de mis aspiraciones sin educarme.

Cuando me encontré en mis veinte años, estudié para mejorar mi habilidad de escribir y de leer. Al mismo tiempo, aprendí lo más que pude sobre la economía, la historia del movimeinto labrador, y como organizar a trabajadores.

Al prinicipio, fue algo difícil. Yo estaba cambiando y tuve que aguantar mucha burla de algunos rufianos. . . .

La educación no cambia las cosas de un día a otro. Hace el cambio posible e irrevocable. No puede ser robada ni negada. Se puede usar y no se pierde nada. Es algo que se pasa a sus hijos y nietos como un tesoro familiar. Para mí, la educación es muy importante."

The Valley Migrant League also worked to enhance opportunities for Chicanos in Oregon colleges and universities. Through the VML's scholarship program, the first four former migrants received degrees from Linfield College. (One of the four —Ramon Gonzalez—succeeded Frank Rivera as VML board chairman.) Frank Martinez also lectured at Clackamas Community College, Portland State College, Lewis & Clark, the University of Oregon, and numerous high schools. Everywhere the message was the same—more opportunity for Mexican-American youth. Once, at Corvallis, a person threw a chair at Martinez after he confronted Oregon State University President Robert MacVicar with his own school's record. Out of approximately 15,000 students, 23 were of Mexican descent.

When the established educational systems did not respond, the VML took a different approach. It helped to establish the Chicano Indian Study Center of Oregon (CISCO) at the former Adair Air Force Base. This coalition to address the educational problems of Native Americans and Chicanos was one more example of VML's leadership and farsighted strategies for solving pressing social problems.

COLEGIO CESAR CHAVEZ

One of the most potentially far-reaching developments for Mexican Americans in higher education occurred in 1973. That year, Mount Angel College, a private teacher preparatory college affiliated with the Order of Benedictine Sisters at Mount Angel, faced declining enrollments, financial debts, loss of accreditation, and certain closure. Sonny Montes, director of ethnic affairs and minority recruiters, and Ernesto Lopez, dean of admissions, along with several others seized the opportunity to take over the failing college and founded Colegio Cesar Chavez—a college for Chicanos and other minorities. An independent four-year Chicano college was unprecedented anywhere in the nation and became a nucleus of the Chicano Movement in Oregon. By 1975 Colegio Cesar Chavez received candidacy status from the Northwest Association of Schools and Colleges. Two years later, the colegio granted degrees to twenty-two graduates—a class that exceeded the combined number of Chicanos graduating from the University of Oregon and Oregon State University.

Unfortunately, the gulf between assuming control of the college and running the campus successfully became painfully clear to those involved. From day one, Colegio Cesar Chavez faced its most pressing problem—an immense financial burden in the form of a debt of nearly $10 million to the Department of Housing and Urban Development (HUD). Later, the debt was reduced but when the college was unable to service it, HUD attempted to foreclose on the college property. The property was sold at public auction to an anonymous buyer and returned to the Order of Benedictine Sisters in 1986.

In addition to facing severe financial problems, the leadership of the college, including the Board of Trustees, the college administration, and the faculty, made critical errors. One was the frequent decision to change presidents. Another was the failure in 1981 to maintain any hope of receiving accreditation through the Northwest Association of Schools and Colleges. Nor did the college's name elicit critical support from the state's farming sectors. In 1983 Colegio Cesar Chavez closed its doors, ending a promising and disappointing chapter of Oregon's Chicano Movement.

THE DEMISE OF EL MOVIMIENTO

By the time the colegio closed, support for addressing the kinds of social problems raised by the various Mexican-American organizations in Oregon had faded at both the state and federal levels. Yet in many ways, the Mexican-American civil rights movement in Oregon outlasted its counterparts elsewhere in the nation. As early as 1968 President Nixon had cut the funding of OEO programs that had given the VML its start, and by 1973 OEO had ceased to exist or shifted to other departments such as the Department of Labor. Instead—under the concept of revenue sharing—much of the federal funding for social programs, except education and health, went directly to state government. State politicians, few of whom were Mexican American, now held the purse strings.

In a very real way, the limits of change were reached in Oregon and the nation, as the liberalism of the 1960s was swept away by a growing political conservatism and a shift in federal fiscal priorities. To combat this new political order, Oregon's Mexican-American community needed real political power that it did not have. The OEO program of the 1960s had only allowed that community to enjoy political recognition by the federal government. Yet at the time, its members could not have appreciated the need to develop the real power necessary to affect *local* politicians. As the rules for funding social programs changed, Mexican Americans were caught unprepared.

Anglos were also critical of the various programs that had been developed during the 1960s and 70s. They were cognizant of the implications of programs controlled by Mexican Americans and the challenges that these programs posed to the established order. Many local communities considered the programs to lie outside the status quo and seemed to resist them at every possible opportunity. The struggle to maintain them was carried on in the face of almost insurmountable odds.

Even within the Mexican-American community, questions were raised. Some objected to the term "Chicano" and the con-

LOOKING BACK

"These were politically charged times. On one occasion, lunch at an educational conference in Portland included non-union lettuce. A young Chicana flipped her salad on the table in protest, and immediately others did the same. Today, this may seem little more than childish behavior. At the time, it was a powerful symbol of the people's unity."

—*A former elementary school principal*

"At the time, migrants were Oregon's 'forgotten population.' The Valley Migrant League was the first program to impact migrants directly."

—*Alan Apodaca,*
former director of Washington Migrant Education

"Overall, the Valley Migrant League proved itself a versatile vehicle for Chicano self-betterment and an effective catalyst in the formation of other service groups."

—*Richard Slatta, historian*

"The goal was to make sure that the Valley Migrant League would leave 'something lasting' when federal anti-poverty money dried up and VML went out of existence."

—*Frank Martinez,*
former director of the Valley Migrant League

"I was an adjunct faculty at the Colegio Cesar Chavez. While there, I was impressed with the Board of Trustees....As a young man, I only had ideas. Persons like Frank Rivera, who was the president of his own company, were inspirational role models because they had already acted on their own ideas. *Si Se Puede* (It can be done) was one of the most popular slogans of the period. In the midst of hard times, *Si Se Puede* gave people immediate empowerment."

—*Francisco Garcia, Woodburn businessman*

"We were establishing a Chicano college in a community that had been hostile to Cesar Chavez and what the name and the movement meant, a community that viewed Spanish-speakers more as farm workers and not as college students, a community that liked to drive by at night and shoot bullet holes in our signs. But we made it, and we gave the community—not just the one in the Willamette Valley but throughout the state—something to rally about.

I recently made a trip to Mt. Angel and discovered that in a way it is still alive. The murals are still there and the campus is in good shape. The sisters have reopened it as a residence for farm workers. When I see that the buildings are being used and that there are farm workers living in the dorms, and that there are training programs going on and that there's shelter there, I feel it wasn't a lost cause."

—*José Romero, Portland Public Schools*

"Today, I'm trying to pass on some of the lessons a lot of us learned during our time at Colegio Cesar Chavez, so that the young people of today don't have to go through all the hassles we did. We need to prepare them so they are competent. Otherwise, they will fail."

—*Sonny Montes, Portland Public Schools*

"I think a lot of times people are idealistic in these types of organizations, thinking that what is important is the long-range goals. But once they get working, they put the long-range goals aside because the immediate needs are so imperative and demanding. I think they make an impact in the sense that they create awareness of the problems in existence and they make the ethnic group aware that it can do something about them....I can see areas in which—because of the Hispanic presence—a lot of programs have become really good programs."

—*José Jaime, former director of Centro Cultural*

frontational tactics the VML used, while others recognized VML's inability to address the causes of problems facing seasonal farm workers. Indeed, some referred to the VML as "el program" or "a program of bureaucrats" and saw it as being a part of new community politics that challenged their own interests. Despite everything that the organization had accomplished, some locals viewed the administrators who had come from the Southwest as "outsiders."

Some of the criticism was justified. Federal aid was usually provided for one year, leaving programs contingent on refunding. Many projects were underfunded. By their very nature, federal programs were so bound up in rules and restrictions they had little real power to make effective and lasting change and could be cancelled if they antagonized local governments.

By the 1980s both the Valley Migrant League and El Movimiento in Oregon had come and gone. Frank Martinez, whom Governor McCall had once referred to as the "governor of Chicanos," had resigned in 1973 and left Oregon. Shortly thereafter, a California-based corporation took over the VML and it became Oregon Rural Opportunities.

THE SIGNIFICANCE OF THE MOVEMENT

In retrospect, we must ask what the upsurge in Mexican-American activism accomplished. Most importantly, the combined efforts of many people made Oregon more cognizant of the social, political, and economic needs of its Mexican-American citizens. The struggles of that period also went far in establishing a modern presence for the Hispanic community. Chicanos, working with Anglo activists, guided the state toward enacting legislative and legal reform in many areas affecting the Spanish-speaking community.

The Valley Migrant League and its sister agencies were the catalysts for all subsequent Hispanic community organizations, some of which still exist today. They include Centro Cultural of Cornelius, Salud Medical Clinic, the Virginia Garcia Memorial Center, and El Aguila Federal Credit Union, but there are many more, too numerous to mention here.

It is also well to recall that the importance of the VML did not end with the close of the Mexican-American civil rights movement. The lives of that generation—and of Mexican-American men, women, and children in subsequent decades— were better off because of it.

Many individuals benefited personally during the Mexican-American civil rights movement. As they responded to the challenges of those years, they forged new careers and assumed important leadership positions in social and human services, education, government, and business. They became role models, and in so doing they paved the road of opportunity for future generations of Mexican Americans.

Hispanics of non-Mexican heritage also benefited immensely from the efforts of the Mexican-American civil rights movement. Because they arrived in the state later, they encountered an atmosphere that was more receptive to Spanish-speak-ers. Some obtained employment in Mexican-American community agencies or received direct social services from them. Also, non-Mexican Latinos did not fit under the terms Chicano or Mexican American but wanted to be included in the state's "minority" category. For this reason, the state's legislative conduit to the Spanish-speaking community, originally called the Advisory Committee on Chicano Affairs and later the Commission on Mexican American Affairs, is now called the Commission on Hispanic Affairs. Its purpose is to serve all Hispanics, regardless of nationality or history in Oregon.

Retrospection always urges caution. The Mexican-American civil rights movement did not change everything, and in some cases change was only temporary. When the President's Commission on Migratory Labor asked about Oregon in 1951, "...does a Mexican [Mexican American] or Negro [African American] worker have difficulty going to a restaurant, theater, school?" the response was yes. "That is [true] not only in farm areas, but we are having difficulty along that line right here in Portland."

As this book goes to press, Oregon has just escaped the effects of HB2933, which would have imposed the same sanctions on undocumented immigrants and their children as those contained in California's Proposition 187, which voters passed in 1994. The legislation would have withheld all social services from undocumented residents, but it would also have affected *legal* immigrants and U.S. citizens who *look* Mexican. Working with the Immigration and Naturalization Service, state officials would have been required to verify the legal status of adults and children who "appear" to be in the country illegally.

Although HB2933 died in committee, the general economic, social, and political climate today is making discrimination against Hispanics more noticeable in many communities in Oregon. In light of these manifestations of prejudice, one might be tempted to wonder if the Mexican-American civil rights movement changed anything at all.

No matter how much progress was made, awareness of such gains is sometimes overshadowed by present-day evidence of oppression or maltreatment. Still, it is clear that the status of Mexican Americans, as well as other Hispanics, improved from the early days of the VML. In the 1990s the changes that resulted from the social and political activism of that era are evident throughout Oregon. Discriminatory practices against Hispanics in Portland or Madras do not go unchallenged. In place of dead-end agricultural jobs that commonly lead to a migratory life style, Hispanics train and retrain to meet the demands of the state's diverse labor market.

The most important result of "El Movimiento" is seen in the people themselves. Thirty years ago, the Mexican-American civil rights generation battled anybody who stood in the way of achieving self-respect and full participation in the civic culture of the state. Today, Hispanics will contest anybody who tries to undo the gains of the 1960s and 70s. In their own way, Hispanics continue to keep the spirit of "El Movimiento" alive.

IMPROVING THE LOT OF MIGRANT FARM LABORERS: NATIONAL AND STATE LEGISLATIVE REFORMS OF THE 1980s

BY DANIEL P. SANTOS

In November 1986 President Ronald Reagan signed into law the Immigration Reform and Control Act (IRCA), the most comprehensive revision of the Immigration and Nationality Act since 1952. The law was intended to help stem the flow of undocumented aliens into the United States, while addressing the plight of those aliens who had long lived and worked within our borders yet were often detained by immigration officials intent on rounding up undocumented workers.

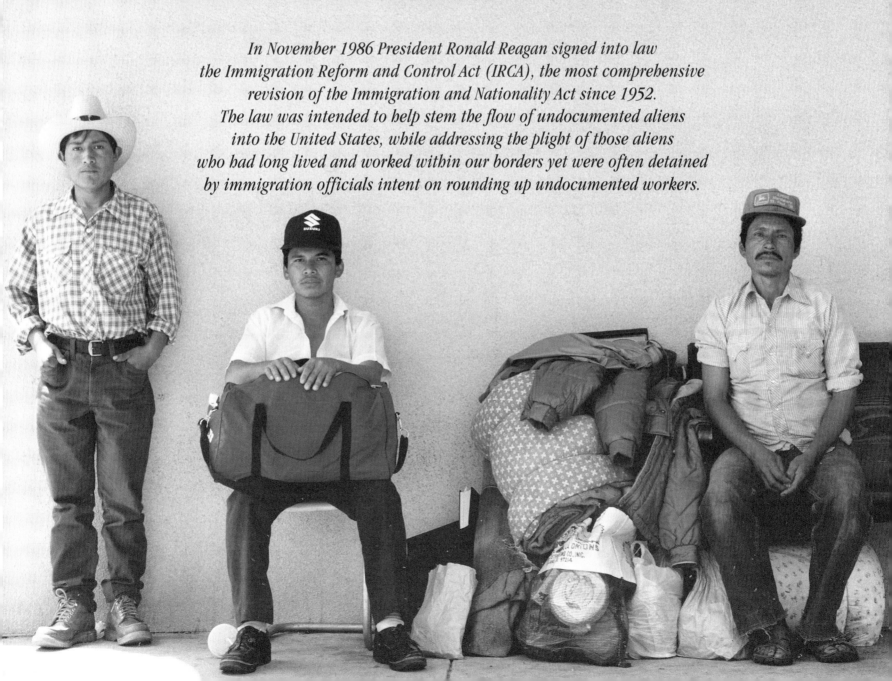

In seeking to strike a balance between control of the borders and protection of those citizens, Congress included several provisions in IRCA that allowed for the legalization of several million undocumented aliens in this country, additional protection against discrimination in employment practices, a guest worker provision, and appropriations for the delivery of certain social services to this newly legalized population.

The law was designed to eliminate the employment magnet that was drawing a mass of aliens across our borders. Recognizing that the border enforcement efforts were doomed to fail, the new law imposed an obligation on *employers* to hire only documented legal residents or risk sanctions. For its part, the industry was able to gain support for and passage of amendments that helped address its concerns about the availability of farm workers. Significant provisions of the 1986 law included legalization programs, employer sanctions, anti-discrimination provisions, State Legalization Impact Assistance Grants, and the National Commission on Agricultural Workers (*see sidebar on page 64*).

The 1986 legislation immediately created problems for undocumented laborers who were now expected to seek information from the Immigration and Naturalization Service (INS), their historical enemy. A great many of the aliens eligible to apply for amnesty or legalization communicated primarily in Spanish, and many who might qualify spent their fall and winter seasons in Mexico or other Central American countries. Further, it was difficult to distribute elementary information to potential applicants about a law that many "experts" had

Two labor contractors (left) talk with state officials in 1957. They had brought workers to Oregon when no jobs or housing were available, forcing state agencies to intervene to take care of the laborers. The 1980s legislation attempted to solve such problems.

problems deciphering. Finally, the $185 per-person filing fee made it hard for many aliens to file.

On May 1, 1987, just four days before the legalization program began, the INS adopted regulations for the legalization provisions and community and social service organizations were established as Qualified Designated Entities (QDEs) to assist aliens interested in applying for legalization. Meanwhile, Oregon's agriculture harvest was rapidly approaching.

THE LAW'S IMPACT
ON THE 1987 HARVEST SEASON

The confusion of the new immigration law resulted in a reduced and late-arriving alien work force. Aliens were unsure what immigration enforcement existed and uncertain about their eligibility for legalization. Even those who thought they were eligible were unsure where to apply—in their native country or here in the United States. Further, employers were unsure about immigration enforcement regarding "alien sweeps" and the new employer sanctions.

All these factors led to a shortage of pickers for Oregon's first major harvest of the season—strawberries—and the fear that there would be an insufficient work force to harvest other crops throughout the summer and fall. To supplement the INS's informational efforts, Oregon Governor Neil Goldschmidt issued a statement clarifying common misperceptions and inviting alien farm workers to the Northwest to work and seek legalization. The governor also pointed out that agricultural employers were not subject to sanctions during the 1987 harvest season. Despite this effort, an estimated eighteen to twenty million pounds of strawberries remained unpicked during that bumper crop year, as the percentage of undocumented aliens decreased.

As the harvest season progressed, more information was obtained by the workers and the growers, and the harvest resumed at a somewhat normal rate. However, there was an increased focus on the workers' plight. As the 1987 harvest came to a close, many strawberry growers concerned about having an adequate labor supply for the 1988 season reduced their strawberry acreage and planned greater reductions for 1989.

THE 1988 HARVEST SEASON

In 1988 workers began arriving in Oregon as early as February in response to a message spread by contractors, farm workers, families, and friends that workers would be needed. But confusion about the immigration law continued. Aliens who did not qualify for the amnesty legalization program still believed they had an opportunity to apply before the May 4, 1988 deadline and those eligible for Seasonal Agricultural Worker (SAW) programs believed that they, too, needed to apply prior to May 4, when in fact they had until November 30.

It also became widely known that the agricultural employer sanctions would not become effective until December 1, 1988. Therefore, unscrupulous labor contractors, or "coyotes," knew they could reap high profits from transporting illegal aliens into the country.

Besides the traditional means of attracting aliens, coyotes also took advantage of confused and unsuspecting aliens by claiming that they could qualify under the new legalization provisions. Coyotes even were able to recruit those few aliens who knew they might not qualify, by stressing that false documents abounded "up north." Often coyotes would double their profits by charging workers for transportation and documents.

From February 1988 on, the migrant workers continued to arrive, but few were able to find work and all had difficulty locating adequate housing and social services. By April a group of social service and worker advocate organizations in the northern Willamette Valley met to express their concerns about the growing number of migrants and their needs.

To complicate matters, the strawberry harvest began later than normal due to the cooler, wetter weather. Social service groups and some growers organized food and clothing drives, but the number of workers continued to grow. Meanwhile, the traditional domestic migrants from the Southwest had yet to arrive. As May rolled around, migrant workers exceeded the demand by thousands in the Willamette Valley alone.

A large labor pool, although advantageous to employers, strained farm laborers' working and living conditions. What normally, at best, was inadequate farm-worker housing became even more deplorable. Reports were received about workers and families living in chicken coops, barns, and garages; on river banks; and crammed into apartments or rented houses.

Due to the problems faced by migrant workers, farmers, and those providing social services, public awareness of and concern about the migrant issues reached an all-time high in the spring of 1988. As the harvest got under way, the availability of field work helped alleviate some problems but social service providers continued to experience a strain on their limited resources.

The Joint Legislative Committee on Labor held hearings on the migrant situation, looking at agricultural labor issues and farm-worker living conditions. Senator Larry Hill, as co-chair, and Adriana Cardenas, as the committee administrator, compiled information on the issues by visiting labor camps and work sites and interviewing farm workers and social service organizations.

The closing of the harvest activities did not result in the customary suspension of interest in migrant issues and social concerns. Compared to the previous year, wages were lower and jobs more difficult to find. Also, some aliens remained in debt to their coyotes. For these and other reasons, many migrants were stranded in Oregon without work and without resources to return home. In addition, the number of SAWs who had applied for temporary residency far exceeded the INS estimates. This resulted in long delays in processing applications. As these applicants waited for their interviews and physical

For the migrant population, housing was often substandard or nonexistent. Above, a mother and child occupy a squalid room in Washington County, 1990. Below. A car trunk serves as a bed, Cornelius, 1988.

exams, they too found themselves stranded in Oregon without many job opportunities.

A repeat of the farm-worker housing and social service dilemmas experienced during the spring was appearing again as fall set in. Again, community action groups, growers, and state agencies were frustrated in their attempts to meet the migrants' needs. This prolonged migrant crisis again increased awareness and concern among the general citizenry and the legislature.

Because many believed that the state had failed to provide a coordinated, comprehensive response, increased pressure was asserted on the governor to act. In November 1988 former Governor Bob Straub, Department of Human Resources Director Kevin Concannon, and Governor Neil Goldschmidt requested $500,000 from the Oregon Legislative Assembly Emergency Board to help address the needs of the migrant farm workers stranded in Oregon. Shortly thereafter, Governor

PROVISIONS OF THE IMMIGRATION REFORM AND CONTROL ACT OF 1986

Legalization Programs

1. Amnesty (Section 201)

The Amnesty provision allowed aliens who had resided illegally in the United States before January 1, 1982 to apply for legal resident status through a two-step process of temporary residency and eventual permanent residency. Eligible aliens had a one-year period in which to apply. In Oregon, approximately 3,000 aliens applied for amnesty.

2. Seasonal Agricultural Worker Program (Section 302)

The "SAW" provisions permitted certain agricultural workers to apply for temporary residency that would become permanent residency after two years. To qualify, aliens had to document that they had one of two specific employment histories. They could show that they had worked in a perishable commodity for at least ninety days, from May to May in 1984, 1985, and 1986 and had resided in the United States for six months during each twelve-month period, or they could document that they had worked for ninety days in agriculture between May 1, 1985 and May 1, 1986.

Eligible aliens had to apply for SAW status by November 30, 1988, and 23,817 in Oregon did so.

3. H-2A Guest Worker Program (Section 303)

This provision created a new category of temporary non-immigrant work visa that enhanced the existing H-2 provisions. The program has some requirements that created financial and procedural hurdles for the agricultural industry. Among the prerequisites were: certification of a shortage of domestic workers sixty days in advance of the harvest, provision of approved housing, transportation, guaranteed starting work days, and pay at the prevailing wage rate. (Industry representatives indicated that these requirements made the H-2A program unfeasible for most growers.)

4. Replenishment Agricultural Workers (Section 303)

The "RAW" Program was intended to help meet agricultural labor demands created by the potential departure of Seasonal Agricultural Workers from field work to other employment, based on annual assessments of shortages of Seasonal Agricultural Workers.

If admitted into the program, Replenishment Agricultural Workers would be required to work ninety days in agriculture for a three-year period in order to be eligible for permanent residency. If RAW applicants wished to become naturalized citizens, they must work ninety days per year in agriculture, for a total of five years. However, after working the ninety days in a given year, they could seek employment in any other occupation.

Employer Sanctions (Section 101)

On November 6, 1986, it became illegal to hire or recruit unauthorized aliens. A verification program was set up and employers were required to establish every potential employee's identity and eligibility or face fines of between $250 and $10,000 per unauthorized employee and further fines for not maintaining employment eligibility verification records.

Anti-Discrimination Provisions (Section 102)

Recognizing that some employers might deny employment opportunities to "foreign-looking or sounding" individuals to avoid sanctions, Congress prescribed new anti-discrimination provisions under IRCA. The provisions made it unlawful for any employer with four or more employees to discriminate against any authorized workers, citizens, or resident aliens. In order to enforce these new anti-discrimination provisions, the Office of Special Counsel for Immigration-Related Unfair Employment Practices was created within the United States Department of Justice.

State Legalization Impact Assistance Grants (Section 204)

As the states faced a potential increase of eligible clients for social service programs, Congress appropriated $1 billion per year for four years beginning in 1988 for public assistance, public health, and educational assistance. Educational programs were designed to assist legalizing aliens in completing permanent residency requirements.

National Commission on Agricultural Workers (Section 304)

Congress established the Commission on Agricultural Workers to monitor and analyze the impact of the new legalization on the agricultural industry. Among other things, the Commission was to determine whether certain regions needed special programs to meet their unique labor demands; whether the admission of additional foreign workers was appropriate; and whether the IRCA provisions were having an impact on the U.S. agricultural industry's competitiveness in the international market.

During an inspection in 1989, immigration agents check the identification cards of workers at a farm in Washington County.

At a 1991 meeting to discuss racial harassment, a farm worker describes his experiences during a recent INS raid in North Plains.

Goldschmidt issued an executive order establishing the Governor's Commission on Agricultural Labor and directed the commission to address the long-term issues of attracting a stable supply of skilled and legal workers and enhancing their working and living conditions.

The Legislative Emergency Board's approval of the request provided much-needed resources and served as a signal of the legislature's receptiveness to addressing agricultural labor issues.

1989 LEGISLATIVE REFORMS ON AGRICULTURAL LABOR ISSUES

Besides having a decade of reports concerning farm-worker issues, the Sixty-Fifth Oregon Legislative Assembly came to the Capitol having experienced two harvest seasons filled with agricultural labor problems. The two years of deplorable working and living conditions caused constituents to demand action. Furthermore, the agriculture industry was facing a potential inability to attract an adequate work force.

With the passage and implementation of the IRCA, employers no longer had a surplus of readily available cheap labor. Oregon now would be in competition for the available farm workers. More than job opportunities and wages were at issue: housing, child care, and medical and educational services would be needed to attract a stable and skilled work force.

The legislature had to address both issues. If reforms concentrated solely on enhancing working and living conditions or on incentives for the industry, the balance between their mutual needs would be jeopardized. The major package of farm-worker legislation was put together under the leadership of Senator Hill and the Coalition of Farmworker Advocates.

The package comprised Senate Bills 731, 732, 733, 734, and 735, which covered farm-labor contracting, labor-camp operation, camp access, tax credits for farm-worker housing, and clarification of farm-worker housing siting provisions. It was truly a comprehensive package.

Senate Bill 731. Senate Bill 731 expanded the farm-labor contracting provisions. These provisions responded to the actions of unscrupulous contractors and coyotes who abused farm workers. The responsibility of administering and enforcing the farm-labor contractor laws remained with the commissioner of the Bureau of Labor and Industries (BOLI).

The expanded provisions included the requirement that at the time of hire, before work starts, the contractor must execute a written agreement with the worker, outlining the working and living arrangements of the job offer. A provision was included in this section to require this written agreement be provided in the language used by the contractor to communicate with the workers. If a farm-labor contractor employed the workers, he or she must comply with the field sanitation laws.

A 1988 demonstration sponsored by the labor union PCUN called attention to unfair labor practices and poor living conditions—problems addressed in the 1989 farmworker bills.

Likewise, if the contractor owned or operated housing for the workers, he or she must assure that the facilities comply with laws relating to health, safety, and habitability.

The bill included language to avoid the type of situation that occurred in the spring of 1988, when contractors brought workers into the state well before the harvest season, by requiring contractors who recruit workers ahead of the harvest to provide lodging and food supplies at no charge until work begins. If the job does not begin within thirty days of the date agreed upon, the contractor must pay costs to either return the worker to the point of recruitment or to another work site the worker selects.

To enforce these provisions, anyone using an unlicensed contractor is subject to a civil penalty of up to $2,000—the monies to go to the Housing Development Account of the Housing Agency. This account has been a key resource in addressing the deficiencies in the quality and quantity of farm-worker housing. Finally, in order to assure that a contractor could pay any penalties and the costs for violations, the contractor's bond was increased from $5,000 to $10,000.

Senate Bill 731 had substantial support in both chambers, passing in its final form by votes in the Senate of twenty-two ayes, three nays, one excused, and four attending legislative business and in the House of fifty-seven ayes and three excused. The bill became effective with the governor's signature on May 23, 1989.

Senate Bill 732. Senate Bill 732 enhanced existing statutes on labor-camp enforcement activities. It required that every labor camp operator register his or her farm-worker housing with the Bureau of Labor and Industries. It stipulated that camp operators be licensed as farm-labor contractors, have an endorsement from BOLI, and maintain a bond of $15,000. This bond also would satisfy the farm-labor contractor's bonding requirements of Senate Bill 731.

The registration process outlined in the bill required that camps registered prior to January 1, 1989 undergo a pre-occupancy inspection. The camp operator could also request an inspection. If the camp failed to conform with the Accident Prevention Division's (APD) occupational health and safety rules, the Bureau would not register the camp until it was in compliance. To enhance enforcement, the bill mandated that BOLI and APD adopt an interagency agreement to conduct joint pre-occupancy visits of proposed farm-labor camps and exchange information about possible violations. APD would report health and safety violations related to housing, while BOLI reported on matters involving labor contractors, civil rights, and wage-and-hour issues.

Camp operators also had to comply with building codes and health and safety laws. The bill prohibited camp operators from discharging, evicting, or discriminating in any way against any person who filed a wage claim against them, instituted a proceeding under the bill's provisions, testified in such a proceeding, or consulted with anyone about his or her rights un-

der the act. The aggrieved party would bear the burden of proving such discrimination. This law did not prohibit camp operators from removing workers who have completed their employment or have been dismissed.

Now, camp operators would be responsible for making alternative housing arrangements if the camp were closed due to health and safety violations. If the APD closed the camp, the operator would be required to provide, free, above-standard lodging for seven days or until the camp was made habitable, whichever time was shorter. Such closures historically resulted in workers being cast out of bad housing into no housing, overcrowded housing, or housing arranged by social service organizations. Under the new law, community service groups would be better able to utilize their resources.

Because state agencies had to rely initially on their list of registered camps as a basis for conducting inspections, unregistered camps often avoided regulatory scrutiny. Also, because

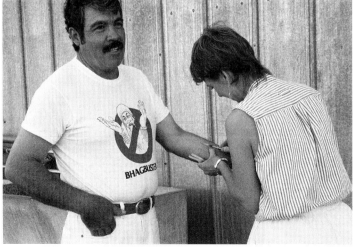

Many workers return to Bear Creek labor camp near Medford, drawn by such amenities as clean living conditions and health care. A stable, trained work force benefits the employer, too.

of staffing and resource limitations, the APD was sometimes unable to respond quickly to complaints about unregistered camps. If APD arrived after the camp had been vacated, a labor camp situation no longer existed and no sanctions could be imposed, regardless of how bad the conditions appeared. The previous rules also allowed a waiver of civil penalties for first-time offenders.

Senate Bill 732 addressed the problems of unregistered labor camps—in part by allowing any aggrieved party to bring suit for violation of the registration requirements and the other provisions under the act. This private right of action was meant to encourage camp operators to register their camps and to provide aggrieved parties an additional remedy beyond that provided by the APD. The automatic waiver of first-time violations was eliminated.

Senate Bill 733. Senate Bill 733 focused on increased access to labor camps. The right to enter farm-worker housing

Top. The Bear Creek complex includes a "rec" room where employees can enjoy a game of pool. Bottom. Nutritious meals are served cafeteria-style in the camp dining room.

areas was expanded beyond government officials, doctors, county health officials, and certified education providers to include religious organizations and any other providers of services for farm workers funded in whole or in part by state, federal, or local government.

For their part, authorized persons had to provide credentials identifying them as representatives of qualifying groups. However, they did not need to disclose the identity of the individual who had asked for a visit, although the employer could request such information and deny access until the invited person obtained an order in a judicial proceeding. Employers could also adopt reasonable rules on the use and occupancy of the housing, including the hours of access.

Senate Bill 733 also provided residents of labor camps with 24-hour access to a telephone. The employer also was required to provide a private or pay phone within two miles of the farm-worker housing to allow reasonable opportunities for private use. If these requirements represented an unreasonable hardship on the employer and the camp had an approved emergency medical plan, the employer could request a waiver of these telephone access provisions.

Senate Bill 733 enhanced the farm workers' ability to associate freely with religious, governmental, and social service organizations, as well as with invited guests—reversing their isolation from the larger community somewhat.

Senate Bill 734. Enforcement of housing standards was only part of the dilemma, so legislation also was passed to provide incentives to build and rehabilitate farm-worker housing. Senate Bill 734 was intended to increase the availability of farm-worker housing by providing Oregon tax credits to commercial lending institutions and to taxpayers who conducted such projects.

The Oregon income tax credit for the taxpayer would amount to 50 percent of the costs paid or incurred on a seasonal or year-round farm-worker housing project. The credit was to be taken in equal installments over five consecutive tax years, starting when the project was completed in years prior to January 1, 1996.

To qualify for the credit, the farm-worker housing construction or rehabilitation had to produce facilities that complied with health and safety laws as well as the provisions of Senate Bill 732. If, at some later date, the housing failed to "substantially" comply with construction standards or operation requirements, the taxpayer's credit would be disallowed and all prior tax relief forfeited. The Oregon Department of Revenue would then proceed to collect taxes not previously paid because of the tax credit.

For commercial lending institutions, the Oregon tax credit amounted to fifty percent of the interest income earned during the tax year on loans for the construction or rehabilitation of farm-worker housing located within the state. The lender's credit was intended to help make some financial resources available for farm-worker housing and to make such loans com-

NUEVO AMANECER:
Livable Spaces for Farmworkers

Candace Robertson, principal of Robertson Merryman Barnes Architects of Portland, says Farmworker Housing Development Corp. is "a client to die for." The nonprofit organization was established to help provide affordable housing to the estimated 2,500-plus Marion County farmworkers living under bridges and in their cars and is the developer of Woodburn's Neuvo Amanecer Apartments. The Farmworker Housing Development

Corp. has received grants or loans from thirteen organizations, and the hope is the Nuevo Amanecer will become a national model. "Their agendas are all positive," says Robertson. "And they've been continually involved in the design all the way. As architects, we can feel we're making a viable contribution to the fabric of the community."

In the $2.2 million Phase One of the project, the corporation built fifty units of housing, a laundry facility, and meeting rooms. Eventually, forty more units will be added, plus day care and community centers, for a total eleven-acre development. In the design, Robertson Merryman Barnes has veered far from what Merryman describes as the "stacked shoe boxes" of low-income housing. Such projects are driven by profit margins or, in the case of non-profits, by skittish banks fearful they might have to take over. Instead, the architects have created a cross between the rowhouse and the Mexican-style courtyard house—pairs of units, which share a common yard fenced by a low, step-down wall.

The courtyards offer a sense of private space, but still allow public interaction with the sidewalk. They are also a place for the kids to store their bicycles and for families to grow flowers, vegetables, and medicinal herbs. The apartments stand back against the development's boundary and have no back doors—the openings were eliminated for cost, safety, and to reinforce

the frontward focus on the common community.

Landscape design is integral to the project, according to Carol Mayer-Reed, a landscape architect and principal of the design firm

Mayer/Reed of Portland. Mayer/Reed was in direct consultation with Robertson Merryman Barnes in designing courtyards that incorporated "personal space" for each unit. For Carol Mayer-Reed, Nuevo Amanecer was an opportunity to "relax preconceived notions" about affordable housing projects and strengthen residents' "pride of ownership" and personal connection to the development. Within the larger development are three neighborhoods that surround a paved plaza and two

parks—one triangular, the other rectangular. Each neighborhood is further demarcated by the color of the predominant trees, and all are knit together with plenty of paths for the paseo, or evening promenade. Mayer/Reed developed the larger social areas as "extroverted spaces" to be used and enjoyed by the residents rather than "linear, leftover spaces."

The units themselves are cozy, ranging from 760 square feet for a two-bedroom apartment to only 1,200 square feet for four bedrooms. The firm, however, has taken great pains to make the apartments feel expansive. Rooms are lit by windows at both ends, and scissor-trussed roofs vault the ceilings. All the two-story units have balconies overlooking the first-floor space. Inside the front door is a "mud closet" to store dirty boots and clothes. The carpets are made out of recycled plastics collected in the Woodburn community.

"All the small details add up to an attitude of paying attention," says Robertson. "But what drove the idea of these apartments is that they are a community."

Reprinted, with permission, from the Fall 1994 issue of Oregon Heritage, *a publication of the Southern Oregon Historical Society, and with permission of* The Oregonian, *which published a longer version of the article on May 25, 1993.*

Farmworker housing doesn't have to be cramped and ugly. Nuevo Amanecer, a 90-unit housing development in Woodburn, features attractive, well-lighted apartments in a setting that promotes a sense of community.

petitive. However, to qualify, loans could not exceed an interest rate of 13.5 percent per annum.

Senate Bill 735. Cities and counties across the state reacted differently to farm-worker housing needs. Some counties recognized the importance of farm workers to their local economies and were willing to work on standards and guidelines that permitted the building of permanent farm-worker housing. Other localities were reluctant to permit permanent housing facilities among their communities. Senate Bill 735 served to summarize the value of farm workers and to declare state policy regarding the need for adequate accommodations for agricultural labor.

In that the agricultural workers in this state benefit the social and economic welfare of all the people in Oregon by their unceasing efforts to bring a bountiful crop to market, the Legislative Assembly declares that it is the policy of this state to insure adequate agricultural labor accommodations commensurate with the housing needs of Oregon's workers that meet decent health, safety, and welfare standards. To accomplish this objective in the interest of all the people in the state, it is necessary that: (1) Every state and local government agency that has powers, functions, or duties with respect to housing, land use, or enforcing health, safety, or welfare standards, under this or any other law, shall exercise its powers, functions, or duties consistently with the state policy declared by this 1989 Act and in such manner as will facilitate sustained progress in attaining the objectives established; (2) Every state and local government agency that finds farm worker activities within the scope of its jurisdiction must make every effort to alleviate unsanitary, unsafe, and overcrowded accommodations; (3) Special efforts should be directed toward mitigating hazards to families and children; and (4) All accommodations must provide for the rights of free association to seasonal farm workers in their places of accommodation.

Although Senate Bill 735 highlighted agricultural labor issues in Oregon, its emphasis was to clarify siting provisions for farm-worker housing. The bill identified housing for seasonal and year-round farm workers within urban settings as one of its concerns. Cities and counties also were prohibited from imposing standards, conditions, or procedures that would discourage or discriminate against farm-worker housing. The legislation clarified that construction of farm-worker housing was a permitted use in exclusive farm-use zones.

To provide a coordinated and consistent approach in building farm-worker housing, the bill designated the Building Codes Agency as the final authority on construction codes and rules. The Agency would interpret, execute, and enforce state and local building codes and issue building permits to rehabilitate existing farm-worker housing if, after the proposed rehabilitation, the facility would meet the APD health and safety standards.

A BALANCED APPROACH

Senate bills 731 through 735 represented a balanced approach to agricultural labor issues. The farm-labor contractor, camp access, and labor-camp operation provisions were progressive steps that helped alleviate workers' employment, health, and safety concerns. The tax credits and clarification of farm-worker housing siting provisions have served as incentives to improve Oregon's farm-worker housing.

ADDITIONAL FEDERAL LEGISLATION— THE 1990 IMMIGRATION ACT

This chapter is based on an earlier article by Mr. Santos. More recently, a new federal law, the 1990 Immigration Act, was passed. That law also aimed to control immigration. Whereas the 1986 Immigration and Reform Control Act was passed to control illegal immigration, the 1990 Immigration Act sought to reform *legal* immigration while addressing some of the problems created by the 1986 law.

One of those problems centered on reports of discrimination against job seekers who *looked* foreign—a result of employers' attempts to comply with the 1986 IRCA requirement that they verify the legal status of their workers or face sanctions. (Although employers should verify the legal status of *all* prospective employees, many singled out only non-Anglos.)

Among its other anti-discrimination provisions, the 1990 law called for stiff penalties for employers who made job applicants provide more or different documentation than that required by law.

Another part of the 1990 law gave the Immigration and Naturalization Service authority to bring civil actions against individuals who produced false documents and to levy fines of up to $5,000 for every document used or received. Before the law was passed, U.S. Attorneys had to bring criminal prosecutions, and few cases were prosecuted. The 1990 law increased the INS's workload in other ways—by expanding the agency's ability to deport criminal aliens and allowing its agents to carry firearms and make arrests for federal offenses that they witnessed. However, the Act did not substantially increase the agency's staffing and, thus, placed a new burden on its investigative branch.

The new law also eased the threat of deportation for the families of aliens who became legalized under the amnesty provision of the 1986 law and made it easier for family members of permanent residents from Mexico and certain other countries to obtain visas and thus reunite their families in the United States.—*The Editors*

SOCIAL POLICY AND THE OREGON HISPANIC COMMUNITY

BY ANTONIO SANCHEZ

The first introduction Hispanics may have had to social policy
in what is now called Oregon could very well have occurred
just after the coastal Indians encountered the first Hispanic explorers.

Although we have no historical documentation of what transpired among the Indians during this collision of destiny, we can surmise that their "social policy" was to deal with these new people as "intruders" and threats.

In many ways Hispanics in Oregon are still treated as "intruders." Recently, the Oregon Commission on Hispanic Affairs reported that, "Political rhetoric has often singled out the Hispanic community as a source of many societal ills. Oregon Latinos collectively have been portrayed as an immigrant, alien, and separatist population that overburdens our institutions and resources, while clinging to a culture and language that many view as a threat to American values and unity."

More often than not, social policy affecting Hispanics has been developed in response to misperceptions and fears that local and state policy makers hold concerning the demographic growth of the Hispanic population. Grass-roots Hispanic organizations and religious and civic groups have in turn served as the counterbalance, exerting public pressure on policy makers to recognize the impact and implications of their policies and trying to hold back the negative tide of public opinion.

Recently, however, Hispanics are responding by becoming *directly* involved in attempting to effect positive policy changes through galvanized social action at all levels of government and politics. Whereas Hispanic involvement was once *reactive*, it is now *proactive*. At no time since the early 1970s was direct Hispanic community activism in Oregon more pronounced

than during the months after passage of California's anti-immigration proposition 187 in November 1994. Fearing that similar legislation might spread to Oregon, organizations like the Oregon Chicano Concilio, the Commission on Hispanic Affairs, and the Metropolitan Human Rights Commission of Oregon, as well as members of the Hispanic media, increased their policy-related activities. In December 1994 the City of Eugene Human Rights Commission organized a community forum to discuss the anti-immigration issue. The meeting drew a vocal crowd of over 100. At another level, the chair of the Oregon Commission on Hispanic Affairs organized a group to deal directly with policy makers. In addition, student groups like Portland State University's Hispanic organizations established community meetings on campus. The focus of these activities was to stop proposed anti-immigration legislation that had been officially drafted but not yet formally introduced to the Oregon legislature.

Over the past fifteen years, both the numbers and composition of Oregon's Hispanic population have changed radically, and the development of social policy has mirrored this evolution. The population growth is a direct result of federal immigration policies, economic pressures in Mexico and California, and increased labor needs in the state's service-related industries such as restaurants, reforestation projects, farms, and dairies. We are finding that as the number of Hispanic seasonal migrant workers grows steadily, many of them are choosing to remain in the state. This phenomenon has magnified the already existing two-tiered stratification within the Hispanic population. At one level we have the highly mobile seasonal migrant farm-worker population consisting often of young, unmarried Mexican or Mexican-American males. At another level are the Hispanics who choose to remain in the state. In general terms, this segment of the Hispanic population tends to be married with children, Mexican or Mexican American, and generally more educated than their migrant counterparts. The recognition of this two-tiered stratification within the Hispanic population is of fundamental importance in understanding Hispanic social policy issues and the process undertaken by the community to address them.

Despite sharing many of the same basic social needs and policy concerns (adequate health care, education, employment, and fair treatment under the law), Hispanic migrant workers and more permanent residents have different needs and corresponding social policies. For migrants, the social policy debate most often focuses on access to affordable and safe migrant housing; access to affordable and appropriate basic health care, emergency health care, or dental care, often in rural areas; job safety issues (for example, controls on the use of pesticides and regulations concerning child labor); local and state criminal justice concerns; immigration services due process and other immigration issues; and bilingual education and other migrant educational challenges such as student placement, retention, and discipline. For Hispanics who reside in the state on a more permanent basis, these concerns remain important, but education, housing, and employment issues—as well as discrimination problems—are of special interest.

HEALTH CARE

Hispanics in Oregon tend to be in a poorer state of health than the general population. Their health is affected by income, education, age, gender, language, the ability to adapt to American society, and the ability to access care, have a family physician, and obtain health insurance.

This population is two to four times more likely than whites to have communicable diseases, including tuberculosis, and sexually transmitted diseases such as gonorrhea, chlamydia, and syphilis. Although Hispanic babies tend to be healthier than those born to white mothers or to mothers from other ethnic groups, mortality rates for their mothers is twice that of the white population. In addition, Hispanics have far greater rates of mortality for many preventable conditions, including cancer of the cervix, chronic liver disease, and diabetes. Compared to non-Hispanic whites in the United States, Hispanic Americans tend to under utilize preventive health-care services such as prenatal checkups, routine physical examinations, and dental and eye examinations. When Hispanics visit the doctor, their illnesses are often at a late and severe stage and for many, the access point most frequently used is the hospital emergency room. The result is poor care, little or no followup, and higher

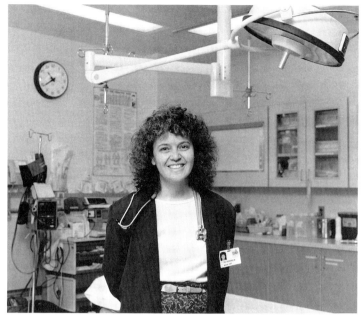

Dr. Tina Castañares is the Hood River County health officer, a staff doctor at the local hospital, and a part-time physician at Clinica del Cariño, which she helped found. Too few clinics like this exist to provide bilingual health care in farming communities.

costs for the patient, third-party payers, the hospital, and the government.

Access to affordable and appropriate care continues to top the list of health-care policy concerns among Hispanics in Oregon. Approximately four out of every ten Hispanics have no medical insurance, due in large part to high unemployment rates and to employment in industries that seldom provide health-care benefits. Although the 1994 Oregon Health Plan tried to expand coverage to most Oregonians, it failed to provide adequate access for seasonal farm workers, whose income may fluctuate and leave them unable to qualify for state-funded Medicaid services or to buy their own insurance.

Significant barriers to adequate and accessible health care are especially pronounced for Hispanics who only speak Spanish, for the unemployed or under employed, for the elderly, for those who live in rural areas of the state, and for those with mental health problems. The lack of Hispanic health professionals, especially physicians who understand the culture and language of their patients, is also a problem. Shortages of Hispanic physicians have been reported throughout the state and are especially acute in rural agricultural areas and during the harvest season.

In addition, government health policy in Oregon has given little attention to the significant and often specialized needs of this population. Migrant health clinics must often make up for the absence of general health services, especially in farming communities. Local migrant farm-worker clinics such as La Clinica del Cariño in Hood River, Salud de la Familia in Woodburn, the Virginia Garcia Memorial Health Center in

Cornelius, and La Clínica del Valle Family Health Care Center in Phoenix team up with local county health departments to meet ambulatory health-care needs in those communities. Urban areas also lack affordable and appropriate medical care for Hispanics despite the intense need for general medical care for young mothers and babies, the elderly with no families, persons who have AIDS or are HIV-positive, and those with alcohol and drug addiction problems.

The Hispanic community has continued to keep health care at the forefront of its social-policy agenda and is contributing to the state and national debate over health-care reform. Hispanic physicians and advocates working in migrant health-care clinics remain in contact with the Oregon Health Plan administrator in an attempt to influence any new health-care reforms and to insure that access for seasonal workers and their families is included. The main challenge now seems to be to hang on to the existing local health-care networks in the hope of improving access to them through the adoption of universal coverage. However, if some seasonal agriculture workers are excluded from mandated coverage and the benefits of health-care reform, as occurred in Washington state, the ability to provide even the most basic care will be critically undermined. With more than 70 percent of the seasonal agricultural work force made up of Hispanics, the Hispanic community is keeping a close watch on developments related to this health-policy challenge.

CRIMINAL JUSTICE AND PUBLIC SAFETY

Criminal justice and public safety issues have recently begun to take on increasing importance within the Hispanic community. The rise of youth violence, drug-related crimes, and gang-motivated criminal activity are taking their toll. There is a disproportionate number of Hispanics arrested, convicted, and serving time. (Currently, Hispanics make up more than 10 percent of the state's total prison inmate population and almost 7 percent of the offenders in community services.) A significant number of these individuals are undocumented Mexican nationals who are most often incarcerated for their involvement with illegal drugs. The increasing number of Mexican national and other Hispanic criminal offenders has caused serious concern among community leaders. While such behaviors are not condoned by Hispanics, the crime brought into Hispanic neighborhoods and the negative image cast upon the entire community have brought renewed debate and investigation into the criminal justice system itself.

Community leaders and legal services advocates have pointed out that the entire criminal justice system, including local and state police departments, jails, prisons, and all levels of the court system, lack Spanish-speaking staff. Of the 49 management positions in the Oregon Judicial Department, none is filled by a Hispanic. Community members are also questioning whether language barriers and access to legal counsel could be affecting the disproportionate numbers of Hispanics arrested,

sentenced, and convicted. Language barriers, as well as reports that police are singling out individuals who wear "gang garb clothing" or are "Hispanic-looking," have resulted in serious allegations of unequal treatment. A stinging report released by the Oregon Supreme Court in 1992 specifically noted that: "minorities are more likely to be arrested, charged, convicted,

Judge Marco A. Hernández, Washington County District Court, and Lee Vasquez, Yamhill County sheriff, bring badly needed language skills and cultural understanding to the criminal justice system in Oregon. Hernández, who is of Mexican and Spanish descent, initially became a lawyer so he could work with migrants. Vasquez, who was a deputy for over twenty years after serving in Viet Nam, is heavily involved in the activities of both the Hispanic and Anglo communities.

Education can take many forms. The Miracle Theatre o Teatro Milagro, founded by Joe Gonzalez (left) and his wife Danielle Malan, often presents dramas that concern social issues affecting Hispanics. Right. While their parents work in the fields, these youngsters are literally given a "head start" on the skills that will help them improve their success rates in school.

put on probation, and incarcerated, and less likely to be released on bail in the adult system." Mirroring the concerns in the Hispanic community, the report also noted that many non-English-speaking minorities appearing in court do not comprehend what is going on because they do not understand the justice system, because interpreters are not present, or because interpreters are not qualified. This report went on to point out that there are also far too few Hispanic lawyers practicing in Oregon and that efforts to recruit Hispanic lawyers are inadequate. Finally it found that judges handling family law cases involving minorities often lack an understanding of the traditional and cultural practices of Hispanic families.

The need to address juvenile justice issues such as increasing youth violence, gangs, and drug use is currently the most pressing criminal-justice concern among Hispanics. However, just as in the adult judicial system, the juvenile justice system is fraught with inadequacies and irregularities that disproportionately affect Hispanic youth. The Supreme Court of Oregon's 1992 report revealed that Hispanic young people are more likely to be arrested, charged with delinquent acts, removed from their family's care and custody, remanded for trial as adults, found guilty of delinquent acts, and incarcerated. The evidence is staggering and as a result, the Hispanic community and state officials have turned to Hispanic school officials, correctional officers, lawyers, social workers, and police officers for assistance in developing tough but appropriate measures to deal proactively with these troubling issues and to sensitize and educate people who work in the system. (The City of Portland, for example, took steps to educate police officers about Hispanics.) The result of such discussions is the recognition that families, the school system, and law enforcement must form a

web of cooperation and understanding based on prevention and not just punishment.

IMMIGRATION

One of the longest standing and most pressing social policy issues facing the Oregon Hispanic community has been the negative public image of Hispanic migrant workers and the misperception that undocumented Hispanic immigrants are having a drastically negative impact on Oregon's economy. Most of the rhetoric fueling this debate has come from our neighbor to the south, California, where the current negative economic downturn has kept this issue at a high pitch. The debate has spilled over to Oregon and—especially in small coastal communities—is being played out against the backdrop of public concern over the unfortunate conditions faced by unemployed rural timber workers. In Oregon, the immigration question is quickly turning into a social policy issue with a high and negative profile threatening to polarize the Hispanic community and the general population. At the center of this debate is the fear that undocumented Mexican workers are taking jobs away from "real" Oregon residents, keeping the wage base low, over utilizing public-assistance programs and health-care services, and burdening our public education and legal systems. Undocumented immigrants, especially from Mexico, are of great concern to policy makers because these migrants come to this state in search of work. Some politicians have been quick to blame undocumented migrant workers for some of the state's budget problems. As a result, the Hispanic community is faced with the need to respond to allegations, however unjustified. This has not been an easy task. Some farm-worker labor unions quietly contend that the seemingly endless supply of Mexican workers recruited to work in the fields and farms has prevented them from successfully organizing agriculture workers and has given no incentive for farm owners to raise wages or provide adequate benefits. This is not the consensus of the larger Hispanic community, which is made up of many immigrants and children and grandchildren of immigrants. Now, in the wake of California's Proposition 187, which blocks access to social welfare services, and the Republican post-1994 election vow to block such services even for *legal* immigrants, the question of immigration reform is becoming an even hotter issue among Oregon's Hispanics.

EDUCATION

One of the most pressing social policy challenges for all Hispanics in Oregon continues to be education. Keeping young Hispanics active and successful in school represents our hope for the future. Unfortunately, Hispanic children in Oregon schools are dropping out at an unprecedented rate, and lack of scholastic achievement has too often characterized those who are fortunate enough to stay in school. In 1988 a panel of representatives from Hispanic organizations across the state declared this issue to be the most critical one affecting Hispanics in Oregon. Their report called for information to help parents understand the school system, for implementation of Hispanic-specific retention programs, and for increased bilingual and English as a Second Language programs. During the same year a master plan was also developed by the Oregon Hispanic Affairs Commission. The goal was to make school districts ac-

One of the most critical problems facing Oregon's Hispanic youngsters is a high dropout rate and lack of scholastic achievement. Luis Machorro, multi-cultural/multi-ethnic specialist for the Portland Public Schools, is helping combat the problem by providing curriculum materials and guides to teachers in 92 district schools. The goal is to help teachers incorporate Spanish language and culture into their class work.

countable, especially for Hispanics, by influencing policy changes and parent involvement. In a subsequent report by the Commission, it was noted that

> *school dropout rates remained at the alarming rate of between 40 and 60 percent. Because of this condition the issue remains one of the community's top overall social policy priorities.*

Schools with a high number of seasonal agricultural workers have additional pressures. During peak harvest seasons it is not uncommon to have some schools increase their population by an additional 30 percent. Migrant students often speak little or no English and lack the academic background to keep pace with their non-migrant peers. These students require special attention from both a teaching and an administrative perspective. In recognition of this fact, the state school system and federal migrant programs are constantly involved in the development of policies that will improve the migrant students' learning environment. Bilingual teacher organizations are also working in the community to advocate on behalf of migrant students, demonstrating how the migrant and non-migrant segments of the Hispanic population work in the development of social policy.

¡Projecto Adelante! offers exciting possibilities for Maria Elena Campisteguy-Hawkins, executive director for the Oregon Council for Hispanic Advancement (OCHA)—and for the Hispanic students at Portland's Marshall High School. The program uses mediators to intervene with students, parents, and administrators to prevent expulsions and dropouts. Another OCHA program at the school provides job placements for youth and adults.

EMPLOYMENT

Since higher educational attainment usually translates into higher job status and income, Hispanics in Oregon find themselves at a distinct disadvantage. High dropout rates have the long-term effect of limiting employment opportunities and in-

Workers demonstrate at a rally sponsored by Pineros y Campesinos Unidos del Noroeste (PCUN), a ten-year-old, 4,000-member union of Northwest tree planters and farm workers. PCUN not only deals aggressively with the needs of the workers it represents but also builds leadership skills among farm workers and empowers their community. In May 1995 the union set a 17¢ per pound wage demand, pointing out that workers had been paid 10¢ to 12¢ per pound for the past ten years.

come and keeping many members of the community in various levels of perpetual poverty. Currently, Hispanic unemployment is running about 10 percent—almost double the rate for the general population. Employment and economic advancement programs for Hispanics, although limited in number, have been of vital importance to the progress of the community. The policy agenda has included targeted job-training programs; better wages and benefits for seasonal agricultural workers; increased opportunities for Hispanic women; small business development; and equitable hiring and promotion practices in private businesses and in local, state, and federal government. Unfortunately, both federal and state policies have been unable to keep pace with the high number of unemployed and under-employed Hispanics and the need to diversify the work force in key job categories and positions. With the Hispanic

work force expected to grow 74.4 percent in the next five years and migrant and seasonal farm workers keeping the $1,629,000,000 Oregon agricultural industry supplied with its labor, economic status and employment will continue to be key policy concerns.

HOW HISPANICS ARE INFLUENCING PUBLIC POLICY

The wide variety of key issues such as health care, criminal justice, immigration, employment, and education, coupled with a very diverse Hispanic community, has influenced the nature and extent of the debate and development of public policy. What may be of importance to one segment of the Hispanic population may not always be as crucial to another. Some issues have served to polarize the community into different public policy camps. For example, Hispanic leaders and most of the Hispanic community in Oregon have historically considered the plight of the migrant seasonal Hispanic population as part of *la causa*, (the cause). Maintaining a united front on this question has served to provide the Hispanic community with a sense of meaning, solidarity, and a definite social policy focus. However, this solidarity in no way insures universal agreement on the political process or strategy to be used when addressing any social policy concern.

The Hispanic community has traditionally used different forums and formats to communicate and mediate concerns. Public policy issues affecting Hispanics are discussed during everyday contacts among friends and family. Informal communication among members of the Hispanic community in the form of general discussions or just plain gossip serves to frame the issues and develop some type of community understanding and general consensus. On the more formal level, Oregon's network of social service agencies, church-sponsored advocacy groups, political organizations, and health-care agencies often addresses these issues via meetings, workshops, community celebrations, conferences, newsletters, newspapers, and radio programs. This also happens among the many Hispanic clubs such as MEChA (Movimiento Estudiantil Chicano de Aztlan) at high schools and university campuses and sometimes at places of employment. Here community leaders provide their opinions with two audiences in mind. Their work is the "social glue" that binds the Hispanic community and provides the foundation for the development of public policy. Hispanic leaders also attempt to reach members of the general public, especially public policy makers. Recently, several Hispanic organizations responded to the public's outcry for immigration reform by releasing information to the news media intended to dispel the misconceptions that undocumented migrant workers are a drain on the economy and prevent Oregonians from accessing much-needed services. These organizations were able to show that nationwide, immigrants paid $28 billion more in taxes than they used in services in 1992. Using an example closer to home, they indicated that in 1992 California's immigrants paid $30.7 billion in taxes to the state and used only $18.7 billion in government services. In this case, the California economy received $12 billion additional dollars directly from immigrant workers. Both formal and informal lobbying of this type is conducted in the hope of influencing the development of social policy affecting the Hispanic community. While this has been officially the task of Oregon's Commission on Hispanic Affairs, other Hispanic groups and organizations successfully direct their concerns to local and state law makers on an ad hoc basis.

The loosely connected formal network of migrant health centers and community clinics, federally funded bilingual education programs, local clubs and organizations such as the Oregon Council for Hispanic Advancement and the Oregon Human Development Corporation, church groups, and the Oregon Commission on Hispanic Affairs all serve to bring social policy issues to the public's attention and broker them to the policy makers in state and local government. As the Hispanic community grows and matures, new strategies will be developed that will allow the system to utilize its growing numbers, especially its professionals, business owners, and politicians.

Juan Prats, founder (in 1982) and publisher of El Hispanic News, *a statewide publication for the Hispanic community.*

Any discussion of the development and implementation of social policy must acknowledge the ultimate role politics plays in transforming the social and economic needs of a community into appropriate, working, and effective public policies. Politics is the mechanism for bringing about the change that is needed to meet the social challenges facing Oregon's Hispanic community. In the past, local and state politics in Oregon have too often been inaccessible to Hispanics. We are finding now, however, that voting-age Hispanics in several districts have the potential to make up a significant and influential voting bloc. If numbers and trends are any indication, the increasing Hispanic population is poised to alter the political landscape of this state forever. As a result, politicians at all levels will be exposed to the increasingly visible Hispanic community, and social policy concerns and ma-

Manuel Castañeda, president of Pro-Landscape in Aloha, is host of Foro Abierto, *a monthly Spanish-language program that deals with health, money management, gangs, and other timely topics. The program is usually taped at Centro Cultural in Cornelius.*

Centro Cultural, in Cornelius, is the result of grassroots efforts by Hispanic families to establish a cultural and community center, and volunteer efforts continue to make it a strong organization. Here, the community celebrates Centro's 15th anniversary in 1987.

jor social policy issues affecting that community will inevitably take on a higher priority. Political empowerment work first started in 1955 by the Oregon Council of Churches (*see page 48*) can now be transformed into effective political action.

Oregon's Hispanic community is working to capture this political momentum. To be effective, Hispanic leaders will need to focus with laser accuracy on the salient policy issues and implement an aggressive political crusade. They will need to build on the work done by community advocates on issues like voter registration; strengthen coalition politics among Mexican Americans, Puerto Ricans, Cubans, and other Hispanics; achieve meaningful representation in all political parties; and encourage local political action. In addition, it is im-

perative that migrant Hispanic policy issues continue to be combined with the policy concerns of non-migrant Hispanics.

There is no doubt that Oregon, as well as the rest of the country, is undergoing a Hispanization that will translate into an increased awareness of Hispanic needs and major, if subtle, changes in social policies. Hispanic leaders and community members will persist in their efforts to better their lives and create a social and political environment that will facilitate their goals. The political strength needed to impact social policy changes for Hispanics will come first from that resource which is most impacted by social changes—the women, men, and children who make up the Hispanic community.

10

SPANISH LANGUAGE RIGHTS AND LAW IN OREGON

BY STEVEN W. BENDER

*As of 1994 eighteen states had either declared English
to be the official state language or prohibited the use
by government of languages other than English.
Most of these state policies, enacted as statutes or as amendments
to state constitutions, were adopted in the mid-1980s
in response to the urgings of national organizations such as U.S. English.*

This Official English or English-Only movement aims its arguments and proposals primarily at Hispanic immigrants — newcomers who are accused of learning English more slowly than past immigrant groups, or, even more harshly, of refusing to learn English altogether. English-Only proponents argue that providing bilingual government services is tantamount to telling Spanish-speaking immigrants that they need not learn English because their basic needs will be accommodated—in their native language—by the government, at taxpayer expense. The government services targeted for abolition by proponents of Official English and English-Only laws include bilingual 911 emergency services, bilingual public transportation schedules, translators in public hospitals, foreign language books in public libraries, and bilingual education.

These presuppositions of the English-Only movement are refuted, however, by recent sociological and educational research: Hispanics do, in fact, learn English as fast or faster than earlier immigrant groups from German, Italian, Jewish, and other backgrounds. Moreover, a recent study of Hispanic immigrants found that 98 percent believe that their children must learn to speak perfect English in order to be successful in America. Finally, no Hispanic organization suggests that English is unnecessary and none encourages Spanish-speaking immigrants to refuse to learn English. Indeed, these immigrants, while exhibiting none of the recalcitrance of which they are accused, are likely to find that the English-language acquisition programs designed to help them are overbooked and underfunded.

Several states have recently resisted the misguided effort to designate English as their official state language. In 1994 the governors of Delaware and Maryland vetoed such legislation. Although Oregon has thus far resisted the current national English-Only movement, Oregon law predating this movement has long mandated the use of English in certain situations. Oregon's constitutional convention in 1857 adopted a resolution that "all laws of the state of Oregon, and all official writings, and the executive, legislative and judicial proceedings, shall be conducted, preserved and published in no other than the English language." Although not submitted to voters as part of Oregon's Constitution and thus not becoming part of Oregon's laws, this resolution set the tone for later legislation. Oregon's legislature ultimately adopted legislation that requires that all writings in Oregon court proceedings and all public records be in English. From 1924 until 1974, Oregon's Constitution required that a citizen be able to read and write English in order to vote in any election. In addition, the right to vote in school district elections has been conditioned separately—since a 1948 initiative petition—on the citizen's ability to read and write in English. Although this initiative has never been repealed, federal voting rights law enacted in 1970 likely nullifies this discriminatory requirement.

Despite this regrettable record, Oregon's two landmark contributions to the national struggle for tolerance of other languages and cultures indicate its emerging commitment to linguistic diversity. The first of these contributions grew out of a conflict at a Forest Grove tavern where, in the early

1970s, Spanish-speaking customers were asked to sit at private tables away from the bar. At the time, Forest Grove had a population of only 8,500 people with more than 2,000 Mexican-Americans. In 1972 several Chicano customers were instructed by the bartender to either take a booth or leave the premises. These customers sued the bartender and the tavern owners under a federal civil rights statute that gives all persons the same right to make and enforce contracts as is enjoyed by "white citizens."

The tavern owners claimed in that lawsuit that their discriminatory seating policy stemmed from concerns that Chicano customers sitting at the bar might talk in Spanish about white customers; they attempted to justify it as necessary to keep the peace. However, in the reported decision of *Hernandez v. Erlenbusch*, an Oregon federal court judge concluded that the tavern's enforcement of its language policy against these Spanish-speaking customers amounted to "patent racial discrimination against Mexican-Americans" in violation of that federal civil rights law and entitled them to compensation. Judge James Burns likened the impact of

the tavern's policy to the indignities suffered by African-Americans, and concluded that:

Just as [federal law] forbids banishing blacks to the back of the bus so as not to arouse the racial animosity of the preferred white passengers, it also forbids ordering Spanish-speaking patrons to the "back booth or out" to avoid antagonizing English-speaking [patrons].

Judge Burns refused to uphold the tavern's policy as a legitimate peacekeeping measure. He concluded that:

The lame justification that a discriminatory policy helps preserve the peace is as unacceptable in barrooms as it was in buses. Catering to prejudice out of fear of provoking greater prejudice only perpetuates racism.

The state's second landmark contribution to linguistic tolerance occurred sixteen years later when Oregon joined the handful of states with symbolic legislation encouraging rather than stifling the use of diverse languages in government affairs. Adopted in 1989, Senate Joint Resolution 16 declared that the use of diverse languages in business, government, and private affairs is "encouraged and protected

At a migrant summer school program, students practice speaking English.

65th Oregon Legislative Assembly—1989 Regular Session
Senate Joint Resolution 16

Whereas the diverse ethnic and linguistic communities have contributed to the social and economic prosperity of Oregon; and

Whereas it is the welcomed responsibility and opportunity of Oregon to respect and facilitate the efforts of all cultural, ethnic and linguistic segments of the population to become full participants in our community; and

Whereas Oregon's economic well-being depends heavily on foreign trade and international exchange and one out of five jobs is directly linked to foreign trade and international exchange; and

Whereas we wish to protect and promote the multilingual nature of communication that currently exists in Oregon and to build trust and understanding; and

Whereas English is already the predominant language of Oregon and legislation imposing English as the official language of Oregon impairs our pluralistic ideals; and

Whereas our federal courts have recognized that English-only rules can have an adverse impact on protected groups and constitutes discrimination; now therefore,

Be it resolved by the Legislative Assembly of the State of Oregon:

That the use of diverse languages in business, government, and private affairs, and the presence of diverse cultures is welcomed, encouraged and protected in Oregon.

Adopted by the Senate, March 15, 1989
Adopted by the House May 8, 1989

in Oregon." Moreover, the Joint Resolution recognized that Official English legislation "impairs our pluralistic ideals" and constitutes discrimination against protected groups. In 1971 Oregon's legislature had embraced the same multilingual tolerance when—to allow for bilingual education—it amended Oregon law requiring educational instruction only in English.

Despite Oregon's notable contributions to tolerance of linguistic diversity, English-Only advocates have been active in the state. Legislation introduced in the Oregon legislature in 1991 and 1993 sought to declare English the official language in Oregon. The 1993 proposal, if enacted, would have prohibited the legislature from making any law that "diminishes or ignores" the status of English as the state's official language. As a result, the legislation would have called into question existing statutes that provide protections and services for non-English speakers. For example, what effect would such a law have on Oregon's requirement that rent-to-own dealers provide foreign language disclosures of costs and terms whenever they conduct any part of a transaction in a language other than English? Even though both the 1991 and 1993 English-language bills failed to win legislative approval, English-Only proponents will likely introduce similar proposals in subsequent legislative sessions. It is thus likely that Spanish-speakers in Oregon will face continuing challenges to their lifeblood of language. In the meantime, Oregon workers who are Spanish-speakers were

dealt a severe blow by the federal Ninth Circuit's decision in *Garcia v. Spun Steak Company*. In this case the court decided to ignore a federal agency guideline that requires employers to demonstrate a business justification for English-Only rules in the workplace. Instead, the court forced employees to prove the existence of a discriminatory workplace environment. If they cannot meet this difficult burden, the language ban is valid regardless of whether it has any business pur-

Programs designed to teach migrant children English are often in demand, but many are underfunded.

81

pose. This decision stemmed from an employment discrimination case that arose in California, but the court's decision is binding on the federal courts of all of the states in the Ninth Circuit, including Oregon.

In the private sphere of restaurants and taverns, Spanish-speaking customers in Oregon continue to suffer unlawful indignities. In 1990 three women were ejected from a Eugene tavern for speaking Spanish. They ultimately settled their lawsuit against the tavern brought under an Oregon statute prohibiting discrimination on the basis of race, religion, sex, marital status, color, or national origin in places of public accommodation. In 1992 a lawsuit based on the *Hernandez* (Forest Grove) case was filed in Oregon following a Hillsboro tavern owner's refusal to allow two Chicano customers to speak Spanish in his bar. As observed by Judge Burns in his *Hernandez* decision, incidents of this nature and the lawsuits that stem from them are a "sad reminder that significant racially discriminatory attitudes still remain" in Oregon.

Oregon's law, like our attitudes toward others, remains in a state of flux. At the same time, the ethnic and linguistic make-up of the state has entered a period of radical change. As Oregon's demographics change with the coming of the next century, it is up to Oregonians to determine whether Oregon will succumb to the anti-Hispanic sentiment that has held sway in eighteen other states or continue to embrace the tolerance for a multilingual citizenry reflected in Senate Joint Resolution 16.

11

HISPANIC BUSINESSES IN OREGON: A GROWING FORCE

BY KENT PATTERSON

*Most grocery shoppers don't expect to find
a stuffed armadillo eyeing them from an overhead shelf,
but La Tiendita ("the little store") in Eugene isn't
just a place to pick up a loaf of bread and a carton of milk.
It's a bit of Latin America.*

Crammed into one bay of a commercial building, La Tiendita strains at the seams. Displays hold souvenir flags of the Latin American nations, and piñatas protected in plastic wrappings hang inches over customers' heads. Shelves of Spanish- and English-language videos cover one wall, while hats, Spanish movie posters, and bunches of dried peppers cover the others. La Tiendita is like a Spanish version of the old general store. It sells candles set in painted jars and jalapeños by the gallon. Along with everything else, it's a mini-restaurant, with two tables and a window serving up "Taco Locos." Customers coming in on Saturday can get Salvadoran "*pupusas*," the specialty of the house.

A BRIDGE BETWEEN CULTURES

"I want my store to serve as a bridge between cultures," says founder and owner Oscar Hernandez. He means a bridge not only between Hispanics and Anglos, but between the various cultures usually but not too accurately lumped together as "Hispanic." A friendly man with a quick smile, Hernandez was born in El Salvador and educated at the University of Oregon. As he talks, he divides his attention between the interview and his small daughter playing in the store's narrow aisles. Every few minutes she wants to be held, so he picks her up until she gets bored with all the adult talk and gets down again.

According to Hernandez, La Tiendita has annual sales around $170,000—small change compared to grocery stores like Safeway and Waremart. All employees are family members working together. In fact, one reason Hernandez founded the business was to provide employment that would keep the extended family together. Small as it is, La Tiendita serves the approximately 7,000 Hispanics in Lane County as a commu-

nity center. It's a place where new immigrants can go to find out about housing, government agencies, and job opportunities. Anglo students learning Spanish drop in to try out yesterday's lesson and rent videos more up to date—and more entertaining—than any they're likely to get in school. Last, but certainly not least, it's the only place in town to get a genuine Taco Loco.

In addition to being a bridge between cultures, La Tiendita offers a good example of how Hispanic people work. That's not

For the family of Oscar Hernandez (second from right), La Tiendita is a bridge between cultures. The family comes from El Salvador.

Richard Herrera, a Mexican American from Klamath Falls, owns and operates Richard Herrera About Hair, a full-service salon in Portland. In 1992 Oregon Business Magazine named his establishment one of the ten best places to work in Oregon.

Esther Puentes is president of Interface Network, Inc., a firm that offers diversity training to businesses, nonprofit organizations, and schools nationally and internationally. Puentes also serves on the state board of higher education.

to say that all Hispanic-owned enterprises are like La Tiendita. Far from it. Small businesses are as individual as fingerprints. A business reflects its owner's business style as surely as a painting reflects the artist's. But La Tiendita does typify a wave of entrepreneurial enterprise that has gathered force in Oregon's Hispanic community in the past few years. Given time, Hispanic enterprise may change the face of the greater community of Oregon.

Like the majority of new Hispanic businesses, La Tiendita is family centered, small, and retail. (Most manufacturing requires a large capital investment, and that's not often available for startups.) It's also a restaurant, which makes it even more typical.

GAINING A FOOTHOLD

According to U. S. census figures, persons describing themselves as Hispanics make up roughly 4.5 percent of Oregon's population. Based on population movements of the past, this percentage is projected to grow to 8.1 by 2020.

Of course the U.S. census crystal ball isn't any clearer than anyone else's. The actual figures may vary—and probably will. But from 1982 to 1987, Hispanic businesses in Oregon grew from 1,022 to 1,598, a rate of 31.7 percent. Current census figures are not yet available, but according to Bruno Amicci, president and founder of the Hispanic Chamber of Commerce in Portland, Hispanics currently own approximately 2,000 busi-

nesses in Oregon. In the Northwest as a whole, Amicci says, Hispanics spend about $29 billion annually. In the nation, the magazine *Hispanic Business* estimates Hispanics make up 9 percent of the entire population and possess a "buying power" of $185 billion. Yet in the Fortune 500 list of the largest corporations, Hispanics hold less than one percent of executive positions, though that percentage is climbing.

Given such numbers, there's little wonder that Hispanics are finding new opportunities in business. Some visionaries have seen all Hispanics banding together in a block under a single leadership, but Amicci has his doubts. "Leading Hispanics is like herding cats," he says. "We are not mono-cultural and you cannot lump us all in a box. I'm Argentine. I'm very different from a Mexican, who is also very different from a Cuban. We have shared family values, a shared cultural history, and a shared language, but there's no monolithic block."

NETWORKING OPPORTUNITIES

In 1993 Amicci founded the Oregon chapter of the Hispanic Chamber of Commerce in order to give Hispanic business persons the same advantages of networking and mutual support enjoyed by others. "Most Hispanic businesses, like most small non-Hispanic businesses, have just plodded along without the benefits of an organized chamber," Amicci says. Currently, the membership of the Hispanic Chamber of Commerce is about equally divided between Hispanics

Joe Esparza, owner of Esparza's Tex-Mex Cafe, came to Oregon in 1986 and established an eatery that quickly became immensely popular with Portlanders. In 1992-93 The Oregonian *named it the city's Restaurant of the Year.*

Jose Cruz, Jr. believes in taking risks. After spending his youth in migrant camps, he earned degrees in humanities and urban planning. Now he owns the import-export firm Cruz & Associates, which deals in fine woods, marble, and coffee.

and non-Hispanics, which Amicci sees as being right. The essence of networking is to include as many diverse people as possible. "Good business benefits everyone," he says.

The power behind the chamber and other groups that are springing up around the state is the recent influx of Hispanic professionals into Oregon. "When I came to Portland in 1981, very rarely would I meet a Hispanic professional. Now I meet a lot of them. They're moving up from California, New Mexico, Arizona, and they're middle class people," Amicci says. Hispanic professionals are moving for precisely the same reason as other professionals: Oregon is a nice place to live.

Amicci is himself a good example of the wave of Hispanic professionals. After working for Hewlett-Packard, he founded the Triad Technology Group, a computer consulting and flexible staffing company. "I provide consulting and temporary staff," he says. A successful businessman himself, Amicci is very optimistic about the future of Hispanic business in Oregon.

Others still see problems. According to Maria Elena Campisteguy-Hawkins, executive director of the Oregon Council for Hispanic Advancement, some of the biggest problems are the barriers faced by Hispanic youth. "We are trying to reverse the dropout rate for Hispanics, which is almost double the rate for other populations," Campisteguy-Hawkins says. "I think there's economic reasons. Some quit school so they can go to work and help support their families. Hispanic parents

are usually very supportive of education, so it's not that they're being told at home education's not important. Another aspect is that there hasn't been a lot of support in schools. Parents are not involved in the school system because they feel they do not belong there."

PREPARING YOUTH TO ENTER THE WORK PLACE

For the past ten years, the Council for Hispanic Advancement has worked to help Hispanic youth with a variety of programs. The Oregon Leadership Program trains youth and young adults. Taking seven months to complete, the program includes modules on culture, careers, team building, and others. "We've had over 450 graduates, and all of them have continued on through high school and on to some form of higher education," says Campisteguy-Hawkins.

Recently the Council got funding from Tektronix for a professional track in high technology. "We will be adding tracks in banking and financial services, and exploring different professions," says Campisteguy-Hawkins.

To help Hispanics find work, the council has an "employment bank." "This will be a business, and local corporations can buy a membership," says Campisteguy-Hawkins. A computerized data bank will help match applicants and employers. "All the major companies in this town have called me saying we don't know where to find qualified Hispanic candidates.

I tell them you don't find them, you develop them." Few companies, she says, are willing to take the time to train new workers—even if the worker has good general skills.

A special problem for Hispanics is that they have a different cultural outlook than most workers. "We're a little different in the interview process. I was always taught not to talk about myself, to talk about the family, 'we' instead of 'I,'" says Campisteguy-Hawkins. Born in Uruguay, where employment frequently comes through family networking, she emphasized her family when she faced interviewers in the United States. "I don't think that was what they wanted to hear," she laughs.

Hispanic women especially may have difficulty knowing exactly how to answer questions about their own abilities. What they perceive merely as polite modesty may be interpreted as a lack of qualifications by non-Hispanic interviewers.

HELPING BUSINESSES GET STARTED

Until recently, Hispanics in general and Hispanic women in particular had few places to go to learn appropriate business behavior. Grace Gallegos, president and owner of Impact Business Consultants, now provides services in marketing, management, and finance. "We specialize in providing services to small minority- and woman-owned businesses," Gallegos says. Impact employs 50 people full-time, with an additional six part-timers, and has offices in Salt Lake City, Phoenix, Tucson, and Seattle as well as Portland.

A former farm worker of Mexican-American background, Gallegos knows how hard it is to work one's way up from below. "I happen to be the kind of person that when I see adversity or negative kinds of things which impact me, I make it a point to take negative situations and make them positive," she says. "It took a lot of guts and a belief in the fact that I had a service to deliver."

With the increase of service organizations like Impact, Gallegos believes it's now easier to found a minority- or woman-owned business than at any time in the past, but problems remain. "Language sometimes becomes a very crucial issue. No question that English is necessary. Maybe it shouldn't be if you're willing to work, but English is a barrier," she says.

The biggest barrier of all, of course, is capital.

Francisco "Pancho" Rodriguez (right) and his wife Carmen started their bakery in Nyssa in 1964. Their oldest son, Marco (left), now manages the bakery. His wife Becky (holding their daughter Victoria) and other family members also work in the business. Rodriguez Bakery products are distributed widely in eastern Oregon and Idaho.

"There's a very strong desire for ownership in the Hispanic community, but expansion is tough. It requires money," Gallegos says. At a time when even established businesses with a successful record find difficulty in getting loans, new businesses must step to last place in line at the bank. Minority- or woman-owned businesses frequently are one step behind that. Then, too, minority businesses are not immune to the problems that plague all businesses. It's a dismal fact that the majority of all startups fail after a year or two—usually due to lack of capital.

But Gallegos emphasizes that "business is business." The problems faced by a Hispanic woman trying to start her own store are precisely the same as those faced by an Anglo man trying to start his. "Getting started is a matter of do we have the right product, do we have enough capital—the factors are the same," she says. They're just a little bit tougher for minorities and women. "It takes perseverance, energy, drive, and commitment. I chose to do that with my life, and I think anyone who's willing to make those kinds of commitments will naturally succeed. We live in a pioneer state. The opportunities are there."

As the largest city in Oregon, Portland naturally has the biggest concentration of Hispanic businesses. However, a smaller but very active Hispanic concentration is growing in southern Oregon.

Ike Apodaca founded Hispana Industries in Central Point, Oregon, in 1991. He's now president with his wife, Christy, as owner. Hispana offers a number of services: confidential document destruction, maintenance and landscaping, and security.

"We serve mostly large corporations," Apodaca says. He likes to concentrate efforts on services that corporations will always need. "You can't have a bank without alarms. You always have to have the building cleaned," he says. Apodaca's own background includes a degree in business administration from UCLA.

Like many others, Apodaca moved to Oregon for the quality of life the state offers. He points out that many of today's Hispanics are professional people seeking a better place to live and raise their families.

One of Apodaca's goals in founding Hispana was to provide permanent employment for seasonal workers. Hispana now employs 25 people, many of them former seasonal workers.

In addition to running Hispana, Apodaca spends time advising local Hispanics who are interested in starting their own businesses. He agrees with Grace Gallegos that the major hurdle for any new business is finding capital. As a woman-owned business, Hispana Industries managed to get a Small Business Administration (SBA) loan. Even so, the company ran a year before the loan came through. Many startups simply don't have that much time.

In the past, Apodaca says, the Small Business Administration has not served minorities well. The SBA recently promised to increase the percentage of loans it gives to minority

Former agricultural worker David Solorio, shown with his son David, now owns Solorio's Jalisco Videos in Medford. The store stocks a large selection of Spanish-language videos.

businesses and probably will. Still, competition for these loans remains tight.

"The advice I give to new entrepreneurs is that they must present an air-tight case for themselves," Apodaca says. This means a well-thought-out business plan plus solid and realistic financial estimates. Part of the problem, he says, are new federal regulations designed to curb the carelessness of the savings and loan industry of the 1980s.

The large Spanish-speaking population of Woodburn provides plenty of customers for Casa de Mexico, which specializes in Mexican-style clothing and goods. Clerk Maria Luis (above) speaks only Spanish.

Hilda Galavíz-Stoller and her family once lived at the Eola labor camp (now a private equestrian boarding farm) where she attended dances at the camp dance hall (right). Today, she has her own law firm in Dundee and takes on cases for migrant workers.

Tino Ornelas, owner of Onelas Enterprises, Inc. in Hillsboro, does contract manufacturing for high-tech firms. He established a fund at Forest Grove High School to help Hispanic students improve their English and in other ways prepare them to succeed.

It's very tough, but Apodaca says he sees five or six people a year with ideas that make him sit up and take notice. One man came in and asked one question: "What is there for entertainment for Spanish-speaking people in this area?" Apodaca had to agree that there wasn't much. The man wanted to start a video rental business. Of course, there were many video rentals in the area, but none for the Spanish market. "He started out with 100 movies; now he's got over 3,500 titles," says Apodaca. "He's computerized and organized just as well as any chain video rental store."

As an example of the Hispanic family approach, he cites five brothers who worked together to found one Mexican restaurant. They started it for the first brother, worked together to get it going, then started another for the next brother and so forth. Now all five have their own restaurant. It's a perfect example of how cooperation can make a little capital go a long way.

It's a story Apodaca likes to tell, a story that demonstrates the strength of Hispanics' will to better themselves. The problems are there, but so are the solutions.

TODAY'S LATINO UNIVERSITY STUDENTS: IDENTITY, DREAMS, AND STRUGGLES

BY MARY ROMERO AND DONNA WONG

For much of Oregon's history, Latinos have been nearly invisible—
as students, administrators, and faculty and as a subject of study.
However in the last few decades, the establishment of student organizations,
student affairs offices, and course offerings on the Latino experience
have made the presence of this group more visible.

The future leadership of the Latino community in Oregon lies, in large degree, with its students—with the strength of their ethnic-group identity, their dreams, and their struggles for improved socio-economic status, political representation, and race relations. In this chapter we profile twelve Latino students who were enrolled at the University of Oregon during the 1993-94 school year. Their stories typify the breadth of experience and the variety of social backgrounds that Latinos bring to higher education in the state.

While a few of Oregon's Latino students represent the second and third generations in their families to attend college, most represent the first. This is true of the students we interviewed, some of whom are also the first in their families to graduate from high school. Most of Oregon's Latino students are of Mexican descent, although an increasing number have Central and South American cultural backgrounds.

Some of these students have a biracial or multiracial background, and most come from families that are bilingual. Their parents' occupations range from migrant worker to professional.

THE STUDENTS

Isaac Alonso

Isaac Alonso moved to Oregon from California when he was seven and has lived in Eugene most of his life. His parents are Mexican and Spanish, his stepfather white. Isaac received a scholarship to the University of Oregon, where he majored in journalism and Spanish literature. He began law school at Harvard in the fall of 1994.

Lydia Lerma

When we interviewed Lydia Lerma, she was a senior majoring in history. Several generations of her family lived in Texas and in the last generation began migrating to the Northwest to work in the fields. When her family made their final trip to the Northwest and settled in Oregon, Lydia was five months old. She is the first high school graduate in her family and the first college graduate. Her career aspirations involve working in the area of migrant labor law.

Gavin Gonzales

Gavin Gonzales was born in Portland and grew up in Klamath Falls. His mother is French Canadian and his father Mexican American. Although his parents and siblings have attended some college, Gavin was the first in his family to graduate. When we interviewed him, he was a senior majoring in English and creative writing. He is interested in looking into opportunities in journalism and news writing.

Luz Maria Ochoa immigrated to the U.S. from El Salvador eight years ago. Like many Salvadorans escaping political persecution, Luz's parents were unable to find employment suitable to their work experience and education. Consequently, Luz hopes to return one day to El Salvador with her parents. She is currently a senior majoring in architecture and plans to go to graduate school.

Sven Orozco is currently a junior majoring in cultural anthropology with an emphasis on indigenous cultures in Mexico. He and his twin brother Jack were born in Kodiak, Alaska. He

Sven Orozco

has lived in a total of twenty-three places stretching from Alaska into Mexico. His role model is his mother, who is a certified midwife. While at the university, he has served as an acting co-director of MEChA, a Latino student organization.

Adela Rios's parents were born in Durango, Mexico, but they raised their eight children in Oregon. Following in the footsteps of her older sister, Adela decided to stay close to her family and attend college in Oregon. After graduating in the spring of 1994 with a degree in business, she planned to pursue a career in international business, working in the area of trade between Mexico and the United States.

Hector Rios is a Mexican immigrant who came to Oregon as a migrant worker. His primary and secondary school years were spent in and out of different schools following the seasonal work. He eventually dropped out of school and began

Hector Rios

working in the fields and in restaurants and packing houses. While working full time he heard about the High School Equivalency Program (HEP) at the University of Oregon. He got his high school diploma and applied to the university. He is currently a senior majoring in business. His interests are in the area of business and law, and he plans to provide services to bilingual clients. In the meantime, he uses his own personal story to encourage other migrant workers in Oregon to get a college education.

Liz Rodriguez is a senior majoring in sociology and minoring in Spanish. Her parents are second-generation Americans, born in Texas. After years doing migrant labor, they eventually settled in Oregon and raised their daughter and son. While attending the university, Liz has been active in recruiting students from farm-labor backgrounds and has served as a tutor in the High School Equivalency Program. Last summer she accepted an internship to work with the Northwest tree planter farm union. Liz plans to use her bilingual skills as a social worker or school counselor in the Latino community.

Raquel Rodriguez is a junior majoring in English. Her parents are both from California, but they raised their five sons and two daughters in Klamath Falls. As the youngest in the family, Raquel finds encouragement from her mother's example of earning a GED late in life. Before transferring to the University of Oregon, Raquel earned an associate degree at the Oregon Institute of Technology. She plans to pursue a career in advertising.

Fabiola Roldan arrived with his family from Mexico City in 1980. His mother, sister, and brother live in Salem. Bilingual education was important in making the transition and in achieving his goal of attending college. He is currently a senior majoring in finance and Spanish. He hopes to participate in an exchange program and intends to acquire international experience in business before pursuing graduate studies.

Jose Romero is a second-generation college student whose parents and older sister all graduated from the University of Oregon. Although he attended high school in Beaverton, he was born in Eugene. His passion is to build a career in television broadcasting. While at the university he worked as a campus TV show host. Jose graduated in 1994 with a degree in journalism.

Joe Valencia

Joe Valencia is a senior graduating with a double major in business and Spanish. His mother is a Mexican immigrant and his father is half Mexican American and half white. Joe grew up on a farm in Myrtle Point. He began his college education at a community college and later transferred to the university. Joe plans to combine his interests in business and Spanish to provide bilingual business consulting to the Latino community.

Rick Vasquez spent most of his life in Texas, attending school in El Paso. Unlike most Latino students in Oregon, Rick grew up in a predominately Mexican community along the Mexican-U.S. border. While having close ties to Mexico, his family members are not immigrants but rather trace their roots to communities that became U.S. territory after the Mexican American War. Rick's commitment to higher education was partially instilled by his father, who returned to school after he retired and earned an associate degree. Many of his four brothers and three sisters are attending college or professional school. While attending the university, Rick has worked with bilingual children in the Eugene 4J school district. He majors in English and creative writing and has published his poetry in the anthology *Where Dreams Begin*.

COMMON EXPERIENCES

All of these students identify themselves as Chicano, Mexican American, or Latino. At the same time, they recognize generational differences with their parents. For example, Adela Rios described the difficulty of growing up in a Euro-American dominated community while being forced to adhere to a Mexican culture at home. Like many Latino youth, her challenge was finding an ethnic consciousness that would reflect her experiences in both cultures. As she put it:

> *Even though the times are changing, my parents were still very focused on Mexican culture. I had a hard time because I didn't know where they were coming from. I couldn't relate to them. We grew apart, but after coming to college and reflecting back on growing up Mexican I have better communication and I understand my parents a lot better.*

Although her parents were bilingual and she heard Spanish spoken among adults, the dominant language she and her siblings adopted was the one they heard at school, and they all became monolingual English speakers. Neither of her parents had more than a grade school education and worked hard, as a custodian and as a cannery worker, to provide for their eight children. Adela learned a strong work ethic from her father:

Both formally through their own organization, MEChA, and informally, Latino students support one another.

It was tough growing up because my father did have to work sometimes two jobs to just support the family. My father has a very strong work ethic value—if you want money you have to work. So when I was as young as ten years old, he would take us early in the morning to the strawberry fields and we had to pick strawberries.

This work ethic provided many Latino students with the strength to study and work for long hours throughout their undergraduate careers.

Unlike many of their parents, most of the Latino students did not grow up in a predominately Latino neighborhood, but experienced sharp cultural divisions between home and school. Liz Rodriguez described the division:

I always knew about my culture, my family, but it was kept at home or with relatives when we went to visit. But as far as school went, I never really intermixed the two. So my home life and school life were really separated.

For many Latino college students, a strong ethnic conscious-

ness was an identity developed at the university. Latino students attending high school in Oregon uniformly describe themselves as the only Latino in the class and frequently the only Mexican family on the block or in the community. For instance Adela Rios described the typical small town in Oregon:

When I was growing up the only other Mexican family or Latinos were cousins or friends of the family. We were really close. It was a very small Latino population. If they weren't family, blood relatives, we treated them like family.

Some of the students recalled racial incidents with classmates and teachers, while others described their social world as exclusively white and felt that no distinctions were made. The following quotes illustrate the regional, class, and cultural tolerance they encountered:

I grew up living in a small community and never really felt any racism towards me. The community was so small, it was like a family community. But at the same time they were very closed minded. The rule was, "all Mexicans are

According to the 1990 census, Latinos comprise more than 5 percent of the state's population between the ages of 18 and 24, but they have only 2.4 percent of its high school graduates. This population is under represented in colleges and universities. In the fall of 1993, Latino students made up 2.8 percent (1,320) of all the undergraduates in the Oregon state system of higher education—up from 2 percent (1,216) in the fall of 1990 and 1 percent (655) in the fall of 1980. However, during this period, Latinos experienced the largest enrollment increase (86 percent) of any ethnic group.

Oregon's increases are substantially larger than the 50 percent increase for Latinos registered nationwide, and—interestingly—the Latino student population is evenly split between men and women (269 men and 260 women in 1981 and 533 men and 540 women in 1990).

The number of bachelors degrees awarded to Latino students has been steadily increasing since 1980. In 1980-81, sixty Latino students were awarded an undergraduate degree, but by 1990-91, the number had increased to 119, a 62.8 percent increase. In 1980-81, most of these degrees were awarded in business (24 percent), social sciences (23.3 percent), and education (20 percent). In 1990-91, the major fields were the social sciences (24.2 percent), business (16 percent) and humanities/fine arts (15 percent).

According to a 1992 survey of high school juniors, the three most important factors in choosing a college were academic reputation, program choice, and cost. Nearly three quarters (74.1 percent) of Latino juniors identified as college bound listed Oregon State University as their first choice, followed by out-of-state universities. Their third choice was the University of Oregon. Interestingly, in actual enrollment, the University of Oregon registered the largest Latino enrollment (350), followed by Oregon State University (337) and Portland State University (251).

Liz Rodriguez and her friend Raquel Rodriguez work on an assignment at the university's computer center.

among Latino students and the lack of Latino faculty in higher education, finding role models was not always easy. For many of the students, parents served this function. Liz Rodriguez identified her parents and her best friend, Maria, as her role models:

> Maria showed me the ropes and how to do things and how not to do things at the university. She went to early orientation registration program with me and helped me along with things like that. I made the adjustment really well.... My parents were always telling me that I could do anything I wanted to do and become anything I wanted to. My parents wanted me to be an independent person. I had a choice. I had an opportunity and I could go to college. They always told me to do it and if I needed help with finances, we could always figure out a way. That was really encouraging to me. I could make it on my own without feeling like I had to be taken care of.

Sven Orozco similarly identified his mother as a major figure in his life:

> My mom went to work in midwifery and teaching. This year she is the first certified Chicana midwife in the state of Oregon. She's always been supportive, but she never went to college. My mom has been really supportive in keeping culture important in our life. It affects me in a lot of ways and that's where I find my strength.

Her mother provided Lydia Lerma's strength, but her mother's educational background limited the kind of help she could provide:

> My mom was really adamant about having me work hard....I remember all she ever told us was "all I want from you is to get an education." We didn't have to work; we didn't have to have after-school jobs. She worked very very hard. She just wanted us to finish school. She was

bad but not you because you're my friend." I never felt racism or discrimination because of course I was different.

That's not the kind of place that I would raise children. I heard the term "spic" quite a bit. A lot of the discrimination was the jokes people —in bad jokes people made.

My little brother and I were the only Mexicans in the entire school. We had a lot to learn about Euro-Americans and they had a lot to learn about Latinos. They had all these stereotypes and I had my own stereotypes about them so it was a culture shock.

I didn't feel discriminated against when I was growing up. I just felt like everyone else.

Given the number of first-generation college students found

really supportive in a way.....Not having parents who can tell me, "This is what you've got to do to make it through college with a decent transcript and a good GPA"—that's a big problem for me. Our parents didn't go to college and can't tell us, "Hey you've got to take this class, and take this class, and take this class to prepare you for these 400-level classes."

One of the most important sources of support named by these students was their own student organization. All the campuses have a Latino student organization, association, or club that brings students together for a variety of social, cultural, and political activities. Since the mid-1960s Latinos have organized student groups—the majority of which eventually changed their name to MEChA (Movimiento Estudiantil Chicano de Aztlan). MEChA is now the oldest and most established student organization in the country, holding annual meetings at the national and local levels, as well as participating in the National Association for Chicano Studies. The Chicano Student Union, the first Latino student organization at the University of Oregon, began in 1964 and eventually changed its name to MEChA. Today, that organization networks with chapters throughout the country and actively participates in annual conferences. National conferences have offered students like Liz Rodriguez additional learning opportunities:

MEChA students go to the national conferences every year, and every year we go to a different state and meet other students and see what's going on in other parts of the country and are exposed to different issues. It just opened my eyes a lot and helped me to be more open minded.

Political activities have included organizing to hire more Latino faculty, to increase student services, and to establish a multicultural curriculum. Latino student organizations have been an important vehicle in bringing to the attention of the university community local and national issues affecting the Latino community.

Latino student organizations are particularly important in Oregon because colleges or universities in the state are predominately white institutions. MEChA, like other Latino student organizations, provides an environment for learning about Latino culture and community. As well as offering support to address issues they face as Latino students, this office is frequently the only place on campus where Latino students can interact or know that they will not be the only Latino in the room. Raquel Rodriguez, Liz Rodriguez, and Luz Maria Ochoa acknowledged the comradeship and support they found in MEChA:

We come from the same backgrounds. We talk about the same things.

It gave me a lot of encouragement to see other students that I could relate to in the same situation. MEChA is one place where I feel comfortable, where I can just be myself and I don't have to explain myself to other people.

I feel comfortable they (other Latino students) are experiencing similar things and we can speak Spanish.

Jose Romero also sought out other Latino students through the organization:

Being involved in MEChA is a good thing because I've been able to develop a lot of good relationships. I've found support in a lot of the friendships and relationships that I've built with other Chicano students here.

Adela Rios described her participation in MEChA:

In my second term, I got involved in MEChA. I really felt the support there and the closeness of the family that I had never felt before [in college]. I educated myself and learned a lot about my culture and heritage. I got my pride back and that's when I started identifying myself as Chicana. MEChA was my strong support in the university.

Over the years, MEChA has changed in keeping with the needs of a changing student population. Efforts have been made

When Latino students like Lydia Lerma plan their future education and careers, they often make choices that will help other Latinos. Lydia, the first high school and college graduate in her family, plans to work in the area of migrant labor law.

to include other Latino groups and broaden organizational goals beyond a Chicano agenda. Women have also gained a stronger voice and have developed programs aimed at their specific interests and needs. All of these student activities have increased the university's success in recruiting and retaining Latino students.

A profile of these Latino students would not be complete without mentioning the one common theme that linked their accounts about college life and their future plans. All of the students shared a desire to tie their career goals in with their culture and strong ethnic identity. Even students majoring in business identified international trade or bilingual services as an area in which they wanted to develop expertise. For instance, Hector Rios explained his desire to work with the community, saying, "I just want to be able to pay back some of what I've gotten in these years to the community, to my community. I want to be able to make a difference." Similarly, Luz Maria Ochoa included community interests in her plans to be an ar-chitect, as she looks forward to working with people needing low-cost housing.

Jose Romero planned to follow his parents' and older sister's footsteps in combining a career with community service:

> I've been one of the lucky ones just because I've always had a strong educational background. I figure when I graduate and I get myself going in my career, I want to be able to do a lot of what my parents do. They're community people—they help out in the community and that's what I want to do. I mean whether it be financially or giving speeches or advice, I'd be more than willing to be able to do that in order to help some of our people and other people advance. So in my future is community involvement.

Young Latino college students like these represent the hopes and dreams of their community. They will become the Latino leaders in the future. While they have had different experiences than their elders, they retain a strong ethnic identity and a commitment to a better future.

EXPRESSIONS OF OUR CULTURE

Hispanic artists are achieving recognition for their contributions to the
Oregon art scene—contributions that often draw inspiration from their cultural roots.
Some of these artists carry on folk traditions from their homelands,
while others push the boundaries of modern artistic expression
in the visual and performing arts. In communities like Cornelius,
Woodburn, Hermiston, Eugene, and Portland celebrations and festivals
feature folk music, dance, food, religious observances, and ceremonies.
Regardless of the messages they bring or the forms they take,
these expressions of culture add vibrancy and meaning to all of our lives.

NUESTRAS EXPRESIONES CULTURALES

Artistas hispanos están logrando ser reconocidos
por sus aportaciones al arte del estado de Oregon—aportaciones que
muchas veces emanan de sus propias raíces culturales.
Muchos de estos artistas traen consigo las tradiciones folklóricas de su
tierra natal, mientras que otros exploran las fronteras de la expresión
artística moderna tanto en las bellas artes como en el teatro.
En comunidades como Cornelius, Woodburn, Hermiston, Eugene, y Portland
las fiestas y festivales tienen como atractivo la música folklórica,
danzas y comida así como también ceremonias y ritos religiosos.
Independientemente del mensaje que portan o de la forma que toman,
estas expresiones culturales enriquecen nuestras vidas y le dan más significado.

13

RAIZ, RAMA Y FLOR
ARTISTS OF
LATIN-AMERICAN DESCENT
IN OREGON

BY CHERYL HARTUP

Throughout Latin America, art is a very visible, instructive
presence in the everyday lives of ordinary people.
In large cities, monumental artworks line the streets, fill churches
and schools, and adorn the walls of nearly every public building.

In the countryside and in urban centers, the ruins of ancient civilizations display some of the most spectacular sculptural forms known to humankind. The colorful garments that people wear and the decorations for village and town festivals have descended from traditions that reach back centuries, as do the totemic items that abound in households, markets, and cemeteries. Latino artists who have moved to the Pacific Northwest have brought with them this common emphasis on the public, celebratory nature of art as well as the cultural traditions of their various societies. Their work involves a variety of styles, themes, imagery, and materials. Some of the artists exhibit nationally, while others share what they do only with family and friends. Many of these artists teach and play active roles in their communities, and some have contributed to the state's renowned public art program.

Throughout the 1980s and 90s, the Hispanic population in Oregon has grown dramatically, and there have been greater opportunities for exhibitions of Latino art. This does not mean that works by local Latin-American artists are highly visible, but exposure is the beginning of a deeper understanding of Latin-American cultural life.

The eight artists highlighted in this chapter cover a broad spectrum, geographically and artistically. Some live in small towns and some in metropolitan areas. Their work ranges from "high" art to folk art, examples of which have been displayed in museums. These individuals by no means comprise a representative sampling of artists of Latin-American descent presently working in Oregon, but they do have something important in common. They have all traveled some distance from their homelands yet maintain a deep respect for their cultural traditions, mainly through the medium of their art. Cultural memory, in fact, is the thread that connects the diverse works discussed in this chapter.

Folk art, or *arte popular*, is widely practiced throughout Latin America. Since pre-Hispanic times, folk artists have helped to establish and maintain the cultural traditions of their people through the decorative, ceremonial, and utilitarian objects they make. In this way they play a vital role as chroniclers of the community.

In Oregon, Latin American folk artists—many from Mexico—serve as caretakers of artistic traditions from their hometowns. As such, they provide an important link between the past and present and a reaffirmation of their community's Latino identity.

Some folk artists produce work for a small circle of intimates, while others make objects that are marketed to the general public. Eva Castellanoz, a wax flower maker from Nyssa, and Dagoberto Morales Durán, a straw weaver who lives in Medford, each take a different approach.

Both Eva and Dagoberto are from Mexico and work parttime at their specialties. Eva is mainly a *curandera* or folk healer, but for over thirty years she has also made wax bouquets and headpieces for weddings and *quinceañeras* (coming-out parties for fifteen year-old girls). Dagoberto works as a cook in a restaurant, and spends his free time making straw ornaments to supply shops around Medford.

Eva was born in Guanajuato, Mexico, of an Aztec father and a mother who is Otomí. Her name in Nahuatl, the native language of the Aztecs, means magical child. She has lived in Nyssa since 1959, when only about five Mexican families were settled there. Now, she says, Nyssa is about eighty percent Hispanic. Eva recalls an impoverished childhood, but one that was artistically rich. In her family, art was a way of life. For example, when her father was not working as a migrant farm laborer he carved and painted wood furniture. He also carved statues of saints, and both her parents wrote and sang *corridos*, or Mexican ballads.

Eva returned to Guanajuato when she was twenty-five and saw a man in the street making wax flowers, an important part of many Mexican communal ceremonies — baptisms, holy communions, weddings, funerals, and the Day of the Dead. Although she only watched the man for a short time, she became convinced she could learn his craft. On returning to Nyssa, she taught herself to make wax flowers and was soon creating floor-length bouquets. She now works in a *casita*, or studio, she built next to her house and named "Studio Genesis—Where Beautiful Things Happen."

To make her flowers, Eva generally uses crepe paper for the petals, which she paints with tempera and dips in hot wax. With this technique she can produce elaborate arrangements of roses, lilies, calla lilies, and orchids. She also makes *coronas*, or headpieces for brides. Traditionally, all Mexican *coronas* were comprised of orange blossoms—small, closed white buds that symbolize purity and chastity. However, now brides request a wide variety of flowers.

To Eva, making wax flowers is a spiritual act as well as a physical task. While she is forming her flowers, she prays for the new couple, the young woman entering adult life, or the newborn baby. She feels honored to have participated in these special events, and she believes that the person carrying her bouquet or wearing her *corona* will transform the inanimate flowers, giving them life and making them beautiful.

Eva makes flowers for eight to twelve events a year. While friends have encouraged her to market her work outside Nyssa, she insists on working with clients she knows personally, and she believes in charging people what they can afford.

In 1989 she received a National Endowment for the Arts award as a Master Traditional Artist, and in 1994 she received the Presidential Award. She freely teaches her craft as a way to encourage others in the practice of traditional Mexican art; recently one of her granddaughters participated in an apprenticeship program sponsored by the Oregon Folk Arts Program.

For Eva Castellanoz (also pictured on page 96), the art of making wax flowers is a spiritual act, involving prayers for the people who are the recipients of her cornonas *and bridal bouquets.*

Dagoberto Morales Durán, a fourth-generation craftsman, is teaching his niece, Faviola Morales Chavez, the age-old Mexican tradition of straw weaving.

Dagoberto Morales Durán also believes strongly in preserving Mexican folk art traditions in the United States. He, too, teaches his craft, mainly to school children, and is proud to be working in an age-old tradition. Dagoberto was born in 1963 in the small town of San Jerónimo by Lake Pátzcuaro in the state of Michoacán, Mexico. Unlike Eva, who stumbled on a folk art tradition, Dagoberto is a fourth-generation craftsman who at the age of five learned to make straw decorations from his mother. This is a major industry for his native village and for many other towns nearby. Over half the residents of San Jerónimo, both men and women, weave straw into ornaments that are used to adorn churches and homes. Families sell their wares to local tourists or to middlemen who market them in the big cities.

When he entered college in Mexico, Dagoberto stopped weaving. However, after he came to the United States in the early 1980s, he began to weave again as a way to keep in contact with his family and his community back in Mexico. He also wanted to demonstrate to North American acquaintances that Mexicans are not just migrant workers, but that many are master artisans who draw on rich cultural backgrounds.

Dagoberto uses a variety of natural materials. He finds tule or large bulrushes locally, but his straw comes from either Yreka, California, or Mexico. He prefers the Mexican straw because it is long and fine, and therefore easier to handle. Sometimes his mother sends him a box of straw, or friends bring it across the border. Dagoberto also uses palm leaves, cattail reeds, and wheat and rye for weaving very fine details.

He presently markets his work in Medford and hopes to expand his venues around the state. In the fall and winter, especially near the holidays when things get very busy, he asks his wife and their relatives to help weave and decorate the ornaments. He makes many styles: baskets, bells, trees, candy canes, angels, pine cones, stars, and cornucopias. He also weaves larger, more elaborate figures like Christ on the cross, *La Virgen de la Salud* (The Virgin of Health)—the patron saint of Pátzcuaro—and peasants playing instruments or balancing jars on their heads. Dagoberto believes that each object he makes has a unique personality. No matter how hard he tries, no two ornaments turn out alike. When he visits his hometown, Dagoberto is keenly interested in the materials people are using and the objects they weave. Occasionally he experiments. He once bowed to a request to produce a likeness of the popular TV dinosaur "Barney" for a friend's child. However, like Eva Castellanoz, he prefers to remain true to traditional styles.

The radiance that gives Latin-American folk art its sense of celebration and playfulness often finds its way into painting and sculpture. This is decidedly the case with Portland artist Margarita Leon, whose larger-than-life wood-branch sculptures seem to dance and fly from the floor. She paints her figures in festive colors with shiny gold accents and gives them exuberant poses. Walking into a roomful of her works is like catching a Caribbean carnival in mid-procession.

Margarita has two distinct bodies of work: whimsical kinetic characters she paints with bright colors and quiet figures made of sticks that are nailed together, sanded smooth, and left unpainted. The artist feels that these two styles represent her two personalities—her energetic, extroverted, playful self and the one that is quiet, internal, and intellectual.

Margarita begins making her more lively figures by choosing a log from a large pile in her studio. She uses a chain saw to quickly carve out big chunks, shaping the torso and head. Then arms, hands, legs, toes, neck, and hair are made of sticks in which she sees a certain character or unusual form. "They demand to be made into something," she says. The last step—painting the twisted, intertwined bodies—is the most challenging, and the part that excites and frustrates her the most. She keeps at it, applying layer after layer of different colors, until everything looks right.

The figures vary in height from three to seven feet and are usually free-standing. Because she has always been intrigued by how people speak with their hands, the hands of her pieces

La Virgen de la Salud (The Virgin of Health), one of Dagoberto Morales Durán's more elaborate straw creations.

are often outsized, to emphasize the power and spirituality of gesture.

Margarita was born in Maracaibo, Venezuela and knew at an early age that she wanted to be an artist. When she was about three years old, she went with her family to see the museum of the great Simón Bolívar, liberator of South America. On display were some of his toys and some of the clothes he wore as a child. When Margarita returned home, she gathered up some of her things and gave them to her mother, saying, "This is for my museum." A little later her father gave her a camera, and the two of them developed photographs in a darkroom in her house. She also had her own studio where she drew.

Margarita attended college in New York and Boston and enrolled at the Pacific Northwest College of Art when she came to Portland in 1981. She had arrived as a painter, but she found that she kept putting three-dimensional objects onto her paintings, which were becoming so large she needed a ladder to paint them. She enjoyed the physicality of assembling these masses and decided to change her major to sculpture.

Saints, angels, and devils are Margarita's current obsessions. One of her angels has the head of Medusa, with wild hair standing on end and two sets of large-handed long arms that wrap around its body. It is a mischievous angel, a trickster, bright gold with spots of color and rather frightening to imagine in motion. More comforting is a tall guardian angel that has a children's prayer in Spanish winding around its sinewy body. There is another figure with candy-apple spirals on its chest, perhaps representing human souls it has caught with its many outstretched blue arms.

Oscar Flores-Fiol's studio in Eagle Creek, Oregon, is full of light. Large windows look out onto trees, rolling hills, and distant mountains. But rather than painting this spectacular view, the artist has created impressionistic landscapes that come out of memory, imagination, and romantic nostalgia—a tropical paradise with a French twist. Lining the walls of his studio are freshly painted canvases in a virtual kaleidoscope of color.

Oscar is a painter with an unabashed taste for the florid. He was raised on a large rural estate outside of Piura in north-

In her Northwest Portland studio, Venezuelan-born artist Margarita Leon transforms blocks of wood and tree branches into whimsical, larger-than-life sculptures. Her studio doubles as an art school for children and some adults.

ern Peru. He grew up in what he calls "a little paradise" of thick vegetation, palm trees, and other tropical flora and fauna, and memories of this lush environment are evident in his paintings. Arts and crafts are widely practiced in the Piura region, and Oscar would like to someday return to his hometown to open an art school and work with the people to protect their environment from pollution and disease.

Oscar came to the United States for a college education. In 1977 he received a fine arts degree from Portland State University. After graduation he traveled in Europe and Latin America for seven years, struggling against the dominance of minimal and conceptual art in the 1960s and 70s and eventually developing his own personal style. Although he has accumulated an impressive collection of pre-Hispanic figurines and textiles from Ecuador and Peru, it is his many books on Impressionism and Post-Impressionism that inspire Oscar the most. His heroes are Renoir, Bonnard, Cézanne, Van Gogh, Toulouse-Lautrec, and Gauguin (whose mother, he is quick to point out, was Peruvian).

Often Oscar's paintings depict tropical rain forests with birds and animals camouflaged by dense vegetation, but he also paints gardens and coastal inlets saturated by a strong light. As with Monet, a garden in one of Oscar's paintings might contain abundant irises and wild flowers, with a Chinese bridge in the background and a cool stream reflecting nature's brilliant colors. He also creates whimsical scenes that play off famous Impressionist or Post-Impressionist paintings. Renoir's young woman with a dog in *The Luncheon after the Boating Party*, 1881, drinks a glass of white wine by the ocean, and miniature master paintings such as Van Gogh's *Starry Night*, 1889, hang salon style on the walls of a fantastical house. Each square inch of Oscar's oil paintings present all the colors in the spectrum.

Transformation has been a dominant theme in Latin American art since pre-Hispanic times. Depictions of humans becoming animals or transporting themselves to another time or place decorate sculptures, weavings, and pottery throughout the Americas. For centuries ceremonial masks and costumes have been donned for magical purposes, to transform the wearer's face, body, and soul. The costumes and movements of Peruvian dancer Luciana Proaño evoke images of beasts, insects, and birds. Sometimes she appears as fire or the ocean. Her costumes envelope her body completely—with feathers, coral, or layers of tiny white shells, among many other objects—and by means of vigorous movements, postures, and expressions, she becomes an element of the natural world.

Luciana was born in Lima, and although she now resides in Oregon, she travels and dances in South America, Europe, and throughout the United States. Her performances and costuming are inspired by a variety of influences, including literature, painting, music, and encounters with other world cultures.

Luciana's costumes are as important to her as the dances themselves, and she appropriates objects from daily life to decorate them. She has used her great-grandmother's woven sash

The tropical paradise of his childhood home in Peru and the dappled scenes of the French Impressionists inspire many of the oil paintings that fill Oscar Flores-Fiol's studio in Eagle Creek.

for example, or placemats she recently served dinner on. She is inspired by the smells, sounds, and textures of such natural materials as prehistoric fish scales and African spider nests. For one costume she wove a body covering of large bird feathers and for another assembled coral she found along the beach.

Her costumes are both playful and dramatic and each one suggests a multitude of possibilities. In this way Luciana continually encourages her audiences to use their own associations and ideas. Her feather costume was made so that from the back she looked like a skeleton, while head-on she appeared to be a magnificent bird. With the addition of a traditional rainstick to her repertoire, she became a shaman in the forest.

For Luciana, transformation is integral to what she does as an artist. Her materials, even if made of modern plastics, become organic forms as she works them with her hands. Green nylon can be knit to resemble sea foam; props or costumes that have served for one performance can be added to, taken apart, or generally reinvented for another. And, of course, Luciana herself is transformed from human being to animal or even life-force when she puts on her creations.

Chicana artist Lynda Jasso-Thomas has been inspired by the sculpture, architecture, and pottery of her ancestors—the Maya, Olmec, Toltecs, and Aztecs of ancient Mesoamerica. Lynda is a mask-maker, but she doesn't simply follow traditional styles and techniques. Rather, she derives from these instruments of transformation their basic forms and expressions and the ritual beliefs they represent.

Like Luciana Proaño, Lynda uses mostly natural materials and colors. Black, white, brown, yellow, and red—colors often associated with the various "races" on earth—predominate in her most recent series of masks. Duality is an important theme

Luciana Proaño in "Where I Sense with My Feet", 1992-95. Costume made of pelican feathers, with spider cocoons for ankle shakers.

Lynda Jasso-Thomas, Afro-Maya 3, 1989, clay mask, 15 x 14 inches

Oscar Flores-Fiol, Red Bridge, *oil on canvas, 24 x 36 inches*

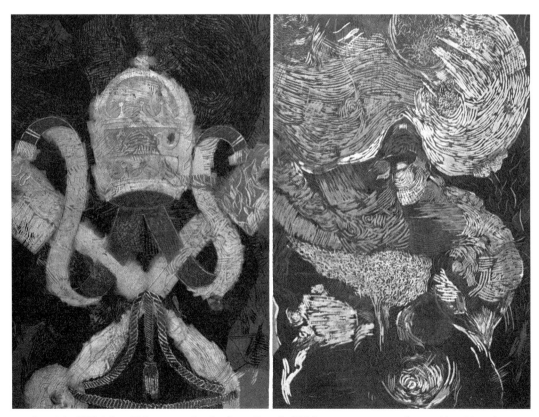

Patricia Villalobos Echeverría, La Lechera Papal, *1989, monoprint, vinyl-cut, 44 x 60 inches*

Margarita Leon, Sisters of the Maries Group, *1992, wood, acrylic paint, and gold leaf*

Francisco J. Rangel, Don José Silva, Cornelius, Oregon, August 1987, *color photograph*

in her work, as it was in pre-Hispanic art throughout Latin America.

Muerte mascara duality—death/life is small and black. The right side of the face represents life with a tongue sticking out, while the left side is a fleshless skull. This is a configuration of life and death that has adorned pre-Hispanic artifacts for centuries. Like many contemporary Latinos, Lynda shares the belief of

Lynda Jasso-Thomas, Racism

the Aztec poets who wrote that life on earth is a fleeting moment, a brief passage. Death in this view is an awakening from a dream, and humanity's true home is beyond the grave.

Ella que me llama (She Who Calls Me) is natural in color, with a smoothly curving surface and soft feathers surrounding a stylized woman's face. Two large hands cover the cheeks with outspread fingers. Hands appear on a number of Lynda's masks, representing power, healing, the act of embracing, and creativity.

Lynda's *Malinche* mask is a self-portrait, with closed eyes and filled-in nostrils and mouth. Feathers protrude from the mask's head and cheeks, and a long pre-Columbian style beaded necklace hangs below the chin. Malinche was Cortez's lover and interpreter when he came to the "New World," and many Mexicans view her as a traitor who was partly responsible for the genocide of her people. Her name in Mexico, even today, has strongly derogatory connotations.

But Malinche also embodies duality. She is protrayed by some Mexican muralists as the symbol of *mestizaje*—the Conquest-era mixture of Spanish and indigenous blood, culture, and religious beliefs. By naming a self-portrait *Malinche*, the artist seems to embrace the many conflicts of her cultural heritage. However, she says that ultimately she envisions a world where people help one another and work together.

While Lynda Jasso-Thomas looks to the ancient past for her sources, other artists choose to work in the present day. Photographer Francisco J. Rangel's portraits, for example, provide an immediate, detailed, and brightly hued account of Oregon's contemporary Latino culture. Unlike the bland flattery of studio portraiture, Francisco's photographs document the customs, accomplishments, and daily struggles of Hispanics living in Hillsboro, Cornelius, and Woodburn.

Francisco often takes his photographs in personal environments: a living room, a prison yard, a migrant laborer's cabin. The relaxed, self-assured expressions on the faces you see in these intimate spaces show how completely and personally the artist relates to his subjects.

Francisco does not care to move quickly in and out of situations, nor to intrude in people's lives. Perhaps this stems from his first job, when (at seventeen) he was asked to document a bilingual adult education program in rural Mexico. He spent a year in a small village with the Otomí, an indigenous group that lives in states north, south, and west of Mexico City. In his black-and-white portraits of people in their homes, in the streets, and in traditional rituals, Francisco's close-up look at the Otomí served to remind Mexicans of the rich variety of cultures within their own borders.

While there is socio-political content in Francisco's contemporary portraits, his focus is on the individual. He does not pigeonhole his subjects in any way but simply strives to capture their pride and dignity. The individual spirit of each photograph catches the viewer's attention, whether it is a farm worker on strike, a woman in front of city hall protesting the use of pesticides in the fields, or a young man sleeping in the trunk of his "bedmobile."

Some of Francisco's photographs also convey the importance of Catholicism—especially religious icons—in Chicano and Latino culture. In one photograph, a woman stands next to a shrine in her home, and a young man has pulled up his shirt to proudly reveal on his back a tattoo of the Virgin Mary surrounded by saints. In other photographs, Francisco documents public processions associated with religious holidays, and every December he and his wife and business partner Annette participate in a procession from Forest Grove to Cornelius in honor of the Virgin of Guadalupe.

The Virgin of Guadalupe is also a fixture in the work of Patricia Villalobos-Echeverría, but with a very different effect. In Patricia's prints, photographs, and mixed-media installations, the much-loved icon becomes a medium for questions about cultural hybridization, gender roles, and self-identity. Patricia was born in Memphis, Tennessee to parents from El Salvador, but she grew up in Managua, Nicaragua. When she was fourteen she came to the United States with her parents to escape Nicaragua's political unrest. Since then, she has lived in the U.S., occasionally visiting Nicaragua to see her mother, who returned. Currently she resides in Ashland and teaches at Southern Oregon State College.

During college and graduate school, Patricia was something of a cultural chameleon. Depending on the situation, she could pass as a "Latina" or a "Caucasian" by changing the way she talked and acted. She became intrigued by this power to reinvent herself and found it liberating. Then she began to look for a symbol she could use in her artwork to represent the synthesis of two cultures in a single entity.

  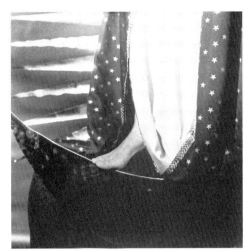

Patricia Villalobos-Echeverría, Guadalicue Series, *black and white photographs, 1994, 16 x 20 inches*

Patricia became fascinated with the Virgin of Guadalupe, a highly complex and controversial image. The Virgin of Guadalupe has long been seen as a traditional role model: woman as nurturer, protector, and comforter. She is said to have first appeared in 1531 in the outskirts of Mexico City near the shrine to Tonantzin, the Aztec earth-mother goddess. Every year on December 12, millions of people converge on the place where the Virgin first appeared. While a priest celebrates mass inside an enormous church, indigenous groups from all over Mexico dance traditional dances in the plaza outside the cathedral.

Many contemporary Chicana and Latina artists have appropriated the image of the Virgin. Often she is recast as an aggressive symbol of self-affirmation or liberation from oppression. However, Patricia recently completed a series of photographs, the *Guadalicue Series*, which, in part, show the artist dressed and posed as the Virgin at her most traditionally demure. In this image, Patricia finds a fitting repository for numerous identites: one indigenous, one European, one conventional, one iconoclastic, all essentially Latin American.

In addition to the docile image of the Virgin, Patricia's work also plays on the great Aztec stone sculpture of Coatlicue, "Goddess of the Serpent Skirt." (In Aztec cosmology, Coatlicue is the mother of Huitzilopochtli, cult god of the Aztecs, a war and hunting deity.) Two serpents' heads meet to form the goddess's face, and she wears a necklace of severed hearts and hands. Her own hands and feet are claws, and a large skull is at the center of her serpent skirt. In several photographs of the *Guadalicue Series*, Patricia turns to the role of the carnal, terri-

fying Coatlicue. She wears no costume in these pieces, but her body and face are tensely contorted to convey the awful power of the goddess. The artist states, "The power of La Virgen de Guadalupe is shared with Coatlicue: they are intimately linked, and their relationship is not merely relative but symbiotic; neither can exist without the other." In Patricia's version of these traditional figures, she has transformed powerful, archetypal images into a personal symbol that embodies all the conflicts of *mestizaje,* the blending of European and indigenous cultures.

There is a famous picture by the great twentieth-century Mexican photographer Manuel Alvarez Bravo called *Portrait of the Eternal,* which shows a woman looking into a hand-held mirror. Octavio Paz has written about this photograph in words that could also describe the work of Patricia Villalobos-Echeverría or any of the artists presented here. Paz writes:

The woman looks at herself and we look at her looking at herself. Perhaps that is what "the eternal" is: looking at oneself, being looked at, looking. . .Álvarez Bravo has not, of course, told us a story: he has shown us realites in rotation, momentary fixities. Everything links together and unlinks. Revelations of the instant but also instants of revelation.

— from "The Instant of Revelation" in *Essays on Mexican Art* by Octavio Paz, 1993

Note: *Many of the photographs in this book, including the cover, are the work of Francisco Rangel.*

14

CELEBRATIONS AND FESTIVALS

BY ELIZA BUCK AND NANCY NUSZ

*Community celebrations play an important role in the cultural life of all groups.
For immigrant populations living in the United States,
social, religious, and nationalistic celebrations often become more significant
than they were in their homelands.*

For Mexican-American communities, fiestas provide occasions for folks to get together to enjoy one another's company, to reinforce their ethnic and nationalistic pride, and to share a common love for the foods, music, and traditional activities. Large public fiestas also provide an opportunity for individual communities to showcase their traditions for the broader population. Oregon's Mexican communities have numerous public and private fiestas taking place around the state.

Woodburn's *Fiesta Mexicana* is one of the state's longest running Hispanic events. It began in 1964 when Woodburn merchants started a harvest celebration. Unlike other public Mexican fiestas in the state, *Fiesta Mexicana* was not planned

A mariachi band entertains at the Woodburn Fiesta in 1989. The annual event began in 1964 as a tribute to seasonal workers.

Traditional Mexican food is prepared by a group of women at an early fiesta, organized by Guanajuato exchange students at Southern Oregon State College and Pamela de la Torre (third from left) in Ashland.

tinue from early in the morning until late into the night.

From the 1940s, when Mexican workers were brought to Oregon for the Bracero Program, some communities like Medford, Hermiston, and Boardman had fiestas. During the 1980s and 1990s the number of Mexican immigrants and migrant workers in Oregon increased substantially and new residents in communities around the state began celebrating Mexican fiestas, including *Cinco de Mayo* (May 5) and *Dieciséis de Septiembre* (September 16), or *Día de Independencia* (Mexican Independence Day)—two national holidays in Mexico. Cinco de Mayo commemorates General Ignacio Zaragoza's victory over the French army outside the gates of Puebla, Mexico. In their 1993 program booklet, organizers of *Fiesta Latina* in Eugene, Oregon define the significance of this holiday as being one of morality: "*Cinco de Mayo* celebrates the struggle of a people determined to create their own future—a struggle common to many people of the world."

Dieciséis de Septiembre celebrates Mexico's independence from Spain in 1810 and is one of the most celebrated of all Mexican holidays. Similar to celebrations of the Fourth of July in the United States, merry-making includes picnics, parades, speeches, games, and patriotic songs. In Oregon, some Mexican Americans also celebrate this holiday with pageants and grand balls.

Each of these celebrations is the community's expression of being *Mejicano* while living in Jackson, Washington, Marion, Umatilla, and Morrow counties. These fiestas follow a similar format to that of the *Fiesta Mexicana* and include foods, *mariachi* music, dancing, and children's games. And although these cultural events are designed for Mexican communities, organizers hope that everyone from the larger community will feel welcome to join the festivities.

Since 1992 another type of Hispanic festival has taken place annually in Eugene—*Fiesta Latina*, organized by Adelante Sí

in conjunction with a Mexican holiday. Today, the Woodburn Latin American Club produces the event with city-wide support. It takes place in Legion Park and draws thousands of people over a three-day weekend in early August.

Fiesta Mexicana begins on Friday afternoon with a children's carnival, music, and various games. In the early evening, adults gather to watch soccer playoffs. Later at night, *Señorita Fiesta Mexicana*, Miss Mexican Festival, and her court formally open the festivities with a ribbon cutting. Folkloric dancing and boxing matches end the first day's events. On Saturday and Sunday live music, folkloric dance, games, and speeches con-

Two young girls in traditional costumes (left) sit atop a float in the 1993 Cornelius fiesta while a second group (right) poses on another float honoring the Virgin of Guadalupe.

Felicitas Saldaña (left) and Andrea Chavez-Schooler are long-time supporters of the Latin American Club in Woodburn. Today the club produces Fiesta Mexicana, a community festival that draws thousands each year.

Hispanic Organization of Lane County. Although it occurs on *Cinco de Mayo, Fiesta Latina* differs from the Mexican celebrations in that it includes all Latin cultures in the Eugene area. This pan-Latino focus reflects the demographic makeup of the various Latino communities. The larger population centers of Eugene, Salem, and Portland have more non-Mexican Hispanics than the rural towns.

Two important factors contribute to *Fiesta Latina's* special flavor. First, its organizing committee is comprised mostly of first- and second-generation Mexican Americans—many of them professional people who would like to broaden the public's perception of Latin Americans and their various cultures. Second, many of the performers showcased at *Fiesta Latina* are professional groups that perform folk and popular pan-Latin music—groups like Armonia Latina, Caliente, Sandunga, and Latin Expression. Many of the musicians are professionally trained, university educated, and live in Eugene or Portland.

Music is a vibrant, expressive form of traditional art in Mexican-American communities. There are very few occasions when there is not some form of music at the heart of the event, for no fiesta is complete without it. Most notable is *mariachi* music, which symbolically expresses a community's pride in being Mexican. Rural communities like Hermiston may not have a local *mariachi* band, so they must hire bands from Yakima, Washington and Hood River to play for special events. Consequently, there is a very active network of musicians who travel widely to perform throughout eastern Oregon and Washington and western Idaho.

Another form of traditional music popular with adults is *musica norteña*, which developed in the northern part of Mexico

and south Texas. It is a country music style that often uses guitars and the accordion. *Mariachi* and *norteño* groups play traditional songs such as *serenatas, cumbias, corridos,* and *rancheras.* The *corrido* is a type of folk song that follows a particular structure and generally tells a story, much like a ballad. Individuals write and sing *corridos,* some of which relate stories about events that happened in regions of Mexico and some of which describe episodes in the lives of people in Oregon.

Banda is another musical form typically heard at fiestas and is currently one of the most popular kinds of dance music among Mexican-American youth around the state. *Banda* music is so popular that promoters can arrange to bring big-name bands from Mexico for *grand bailes* (dance concerts). *Banda* music has inspired a popular dance style, complete with appropriate clothing. Couples wear fancy Western-style outfits including cowboy boots and hats and dance together in a tight embrace. The man leads the woman who arches her back in such a way that her head almost touches the ground. They move around the floor in fast spins and lunges.

Dance is a key element of fiestas. Many communities have a folkloric dance group which performs at all major events. *Grupo Folklórico Quetzalcoatle,* Hermiston's Mexican-American folk dance troupe, performs dances from regions around Mexico. Each dance has elaborate dresses from a particular region of Mexico. Dance director Pablo Garay regularly travels to Mexico to keep up his dance skills. He wants to keep the dances alive so that his people will not forget who they are, where they are from, and what cultural richness they bring from their home country. Folkloric dance is another way of presenting a community's ethnic pride and of teaching about the culture to the younger generations as well as to non-Mexicans.

Another popular folkloric dance group in Oregon is the *Ballet Folklórico de Woodburn.* Originally formed in 1991 by seven Mexican youth, the group has grown dramatically in members and popularity. With over a dozen

In the 1990s, banda *music swept Mexican communities across the United States. Banda originated in the Mexican state of Sinaloa on the Pacific coast in the 1930s and consisted of a large horn section and a big bass drum. Today, synthesizer keyboards usually create the horn section and electric guitars give* banda *a sound more reminiscent of rock and roll than of marching band music. Along with the music comes a distinctive dance style, a cross between a polka and a tango, and western style clothing with a northern Mexican flair.*

dancers, this group performs dances such as *La Bamba, Jarabe-Tapatío* (also known as the Mexican Hat Dance), and *Los Viejitos* (The Old Ones). The group dances at *Fiesta Mexicana* in Woodburn, Portland's annual *Cinco de Mayo* celebration on the waterfront, and events all over the state.

In addition to dance and music, celebrations often have certain craft traditions that are associated with them. For example, *piñatas* have long been a favorite of children and are most often associated with children's birthday parties. Colorful *piñatas* hang from the ceilings and windows of *tiendas* (Mexican stores) throughout the state. Wonderful animals, stars, guitars, and popular characters made out of balloons or cardboard, newspaper, crepe paper, and glue are part of the public celebrations. Outdoors the *piñata* hangs from a tree or pole to entice children into a game of luck. An adult pulls the rope from which the *piñata* hangs and everyone takes turns trying to break the *piñata* for its candies, trinkets, and coins. When the *piñata* finally breaks, treats rain down on the scrambling children. Piñata breaking is a standard event at all the *Cinco de Mayo* and *Dieciséis de Septiembre* celebrations.

Another less familiar craft tradition for fiestas is *cascarones*. Last year at Boardman's *Cinco de Mayo* celebration, ten-year-old Elvia Ayala sold *cascarones* that she and her family had made for the event. She explained that to prepare *cascarones*, her mother broke the pointed end off of eggs and removed the yolks. Family members then painted and filled them with confetti. Lastly, they glued a thin piece of paper over the opening. Children had great fun cracking the *cascarones* on the heads of unsuspecting friends.

Religious ceremonies also involve community festivities. Many of these observances mark seasonal, cyclical changes that affect people's lives. Our Lady of Angels Catholic Church in Hermiston celebrates *El Día de la Cosecha*, the harvest, with an outdoor mass. People bring fruits, vegetables, flowers, and home-made items to give thanks for a good harvest and individuals place their offerings in front of the altar during mass. The act of acknowledging the harvest has roots in ancient customs but it also gives spiritual value to the manual labor or employment of many of the community's members.

The Christmas season also brings traditional religious celebrations to Hispanic communities in Oregon. Beginning on December 12, the feast day of the Virgin of Guadalupe, an incarnation of Mary the Mother of God, parishioners from Catholic churches prepare for Christmas by performing *Las Posadas* or folk dramas. *Posadas* are re-enactments of Joseph and Mary's search for lodging in anticipation of the birth of the Christ Child. In Cornelius the community participates in traditional *Las Posadas* by having individuals dress as Mary and Joseph and wander from house to house asking for shelter. For nine consecutive nights, the entourage, including children dressed as angels and shepherds, goes door to door singing traditional songs asking for lodging. The occupants of the homes reply with songs of refusal. After the group has visited several homes,

Ballet Folklórico de Woodburn performs Danza de los Viejitos (dance of the old ones).This comical dance depicts the great energy and experience old men can bring to their traditional dance. Ballet Folklórico performs at festivals all over the state.

the residents of the final house invite the procession in for a party. Finally, on the Sunday before Christmas the party arrives at the Centro Cultural, where everyone participates in an elaborate celebration of dance, song, and theater called *la Pastorela*.

In *la Pastorela*, community members theatrically portray the mysteries of the Nativity, with angels, shepherds, and the devil depicting the forces of good and evil. After *la Pastorela*, everyone shares festive foods such as *buñuelos* (crispy sweet bread in syrup) and hot punch made of tea, citrus, tamarind, and jicama. To end the evening in an explosion of fun, children break open a *piñata* filled with fruit and candies.

Right. Los Tres Josés—José Sanchez, José Fuentes, and José Arreguin—play norteño *music at a going-away party for a notable Mexican-American businessman at Loli's Restaurant in Medford.*

Family ties and commitments play a major role in Hispanic communities. Extended families—parents, grandparents, aunts, uncles, and cousins— often live in close proximity and gather for significant events such as births, baptismals, communions, weddings, and deaths. These family celebrations are an integral part of the Mexican-American communities' cultural life.

Cumpleaños, or birthdays, are family celebrations that honor each person's membership in the group. The most important birthday in a Mexican-American girl's life is her fifteenth, or *quinceañera*, and to outsiders it may seem like a bigger affair than a wedding. The *quinceañera* is the marker that announces a girl's entry into womanhood, and many people from the community take part to make it a grand event. Family members and friends sponsor the big day by paying for assigned items: an aunt may purchase the shoes, an uncle may hire the band, a godparent might pay for the beverages. The rite-of-passage usually begins as a religious event with a Catholic Mass, fol-

lowed by a party. The attendees dress in formal attire and spend the evening dancing and socializing with extended family and other members in the community. Teens from the non-Mexican community also often attend the *quinceañera* to help celebrate a friend's big day.

El Día de las Madres, or Mother's Day, is a family celebration that has some religious as well as broader community aspects. In Mexican culture, mothers are symbolically connected to the Lady of Guadalupe and are therefore highly revered on their special day. *El Día de las Madres* is celebrated on May 10,

Religious observances can involve the whole community. In Cornelius (right), "The Passion of Christ" is reenacted each Easter season, as parishioners of St. Alexander's visit the stations of the cross in a procession that winds through the town. Below. A procession in honor of Our Lady of Guadalupe under rainy Forest Grove skies, 1984.

For young people, no tradition is quite so important as the quinceañera, which marks a teenage girl's passage into womanhood. The girls wear formal dresses and their escorts don tuxedos for the Catholic Mass and evening of dancing that mark the occasion.

regardless of the day on which it falls. In Mexico, beginning at midnight, small groups of musicians move through the streets of cities and villages serenading under the window of the women of the household. If a family member plays guitar and sings, he or she may do the honor, but family members customarily hire professional musicians to serenade their mother.

In Oregon, *El Dia de las Madres* continues to be an important fiesta time, but as *mariachi* musician Candelario Zamudio of Oregon City points out, the tradition of serenading is difficult to practice here because non-Mexican neighbors may not be sympathetic to the late-night festivities. Yet highly valued customs are not easily relinquished and people adapt to new circumstances in order to continue the tradition. For example, at Medford's *Cinco de Mayo* fiesta one year, the master of ceremonies asked for the eldest women and the women with the most children to come to the front of the audience to be honored by the whole community. After several rounds of applause and a presentation of awards, local singer José Arreguin sang a *serenata* to the mothers.

Latin fiestas proliferate around Oregon as the Hispanic population increases. Small communities of Hispanics from Central and South America also bring their traditions to Oregon. Antonio Centurion of Salem enchants audiences with the national instrument of his homeland, the Paraguayan harp. Neftali Rivera of Aloha enlivens many festivals and parties with the sounds of his native Puerto Rican guitar and traditional songs. Alfredo Muro of Lake Oswego creates the feeling of the Peruvian *peñas*, spontaneous music gatherings, of his childhood with friends in the greater Portland area. Irene Farrera of Eugene whips up excitement throughout the state with her tropical sounds inspired from her youth in Venezuela. The talents of many from traditional Latin backgrounds bring new flavors to Oregon.

As more Hispanic people arrive in Oregon, the traditional makeup of the various communities will continue to change. Old ways may be maintained by most, but some traditions will likely disappear from communities as younger generations become more Americanized. Whatever the future holds for Oregon, it is clear that the festive traditions of the peoples of Mexican and Hispanic heritages will continue to enrich our state's cultural life.

SOME OF OUR STORIES

*Courage, determination, and isolation have characterized the journeys
of newcomers to our state, from the Oregon Trail pioneers of the 1840s
to the immigrants and migrant workers of the 1990s.
Each has a story to tell—sometimes a story of hardship and degradation,
but often one of triumph and success.
Here, we meet the Mixtecs, the poorest of the agricultural workers
who make the annual journey from Mexico; a group of Mexican women
facing cultural change in Washington County;
and several men and women whose personal
stories and observations end this book.*

ALGUNAS
DE NUESTRAS HISTORIAS

*Valor, determinación, y aislamiento han caracterizado los viajes
de los que recién llegan a nuestro Estado, empezando con los pioneros
que siguieron el "Camino a Oregon" desde 1840 en adelante
hasta los inmigrantes y trabajadores migratorios de los años 90.
Cada uno tiene una historia—a veces una historia de sufrimiento y degradación,
pero con frecuencia una de triunfo y logro.
Aquí vemos a los Mixtecas, los campesinos mas pobres que hacen
un viaje anual desde México; a un grupo de mujeres mexicanas
que se enfrentan a un cambio cultural en el Condado de Washington;
y a varios hombres y mujeres cuyos recuentos
personales y observaciones ponen punto final a este libro.*

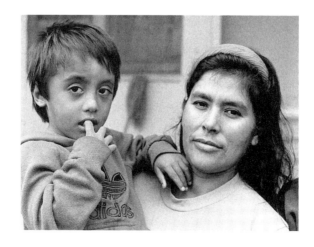

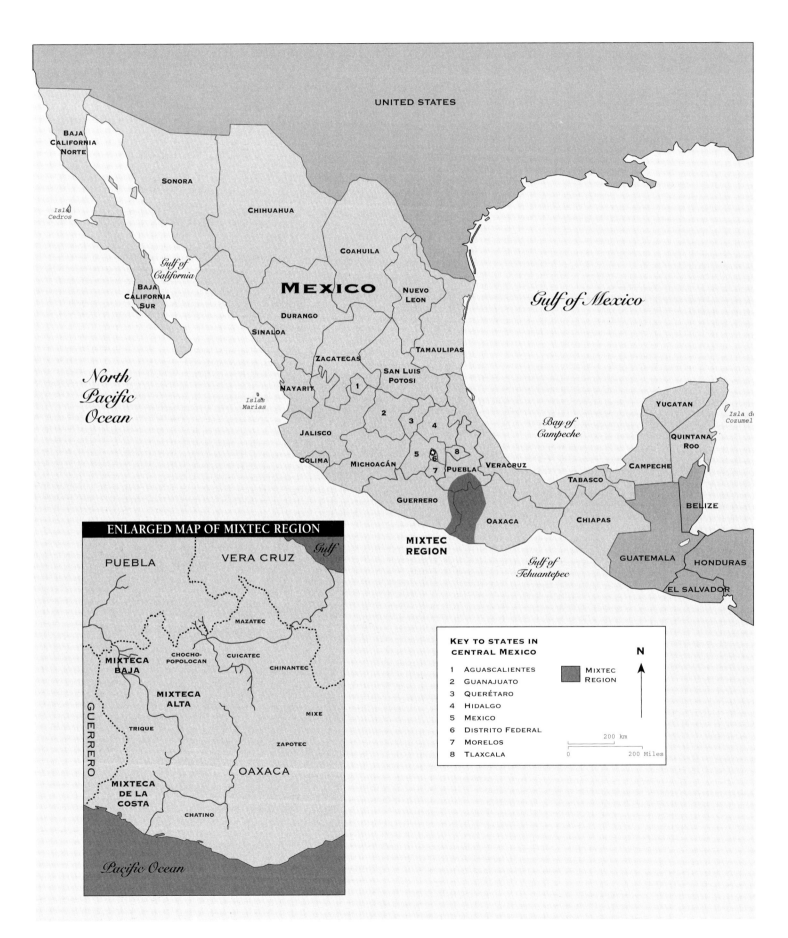

UNITED STATES

BAJA CALIFORNIA NORTE

SONORA

CHIHUAHUA

COAHUILA

Isla Cedros

Gulf of California

BAJA CALIFORNIA SUR

MEXICO

NUEVO LEON

Gulf of Mexico

DURANGO

SINALOA

TAMAULIPAS

North Pacific Ocean

ZACATECAS

SAN LUIS POTOSI

NAYARIT

Islas Marias

1

2

3

4

Bay of Campeche

YUCATAN

Isla de Cozumel

JALISCO

COLIMA

5

6

8

QUINTANA ROO

MICHOACÁN

7

PUEBLA

VERACRUZ

CAMPECHE

TABASCO

GUERRERO

BELIZE

MIXTEC REGION

OAXACA

CHIAPAS

Gulf of Tehuantepec

GUATEMALA

HONDURAS

EL SALVADOR

ENLARGED MAP OF MIXTEC REGION

PUEBLA

VERA CRUZ

Gulf

MAZATEC

MIXTECA BAJA

CHOCHO-POPOLOCAN

CUICATEC

CHINANTEC

MIXTECA ALTA

MIXE

GUERRERO

TRIQUE

ZAPOTEC

OAXACA

MIXTECA DE LA COSTA

CHATINO

Pacific Ocean

KEY TO STATES IN CENTRAL MEXICO

N

1 AGUASCALIENTES
2 GUANAJUATO
3 QUERÉTARO
4 HIDALGO
5 MEXICO
6 DISTRITO FEDERAL
7 MORELOS
8 TLAXCALA

MIXTEC REGION

200 km

0   200 Miles

THE MIXTECS'
ANNUAL 3,000-MILE JOURNEY

BY LOURDES DE LEÓN

*Since the 1960s Mixtecs have provided a cheap labor force
for the agricultural economy of California and Oregon.
The trajectory of their proud but tragic history has brought them
from the mountainous regions of southern Mexico
into American society as a distinctive ethnic group.*

In late 1986 a trial was held at Clackamas County, Oregon, in which Santiago Ventura Morales, a young Mixtec Indian from Oaxaca, Mexico, was convicted of murder and sentenced to life imprisonment. An expert evaluation of his case revealed that the court was unaware of Ventura's ethnic origin and expected that, as a Mexican national, he (and the Mixtec witnesses in the trial) would understand the Spanish court translator. Consider the following lines of the trial transcript:

> Court: *Would you translate what he said, please?*
> Interpreter: *That was Mestican, I don't understand.*
> Court: *You have to tell us what he says.*
> Interpreter: *It was Mestica words.*
> Court: *Very well.*
> District Attorney: *I would ask Ms. Roche to tell us whether she knows what those Mestica words are?*
> Interpreter: *No I don't.*

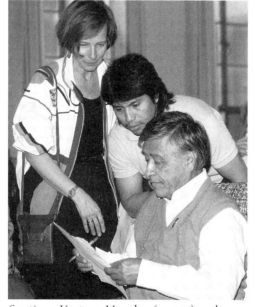

Santiago Ventura Morales (center) and Donna Grund Slepack, a woman who worked to get him freed, show Cesar Chavez Santiago's release papers.

Despite the interpreter's repeated complaints, the trial continued, with officials either dismissing the fact that the so-called "Mestica" words (a mispronunciation of Mixtec) were not Spanish or thinking that these words were just a variety of Spanish.

The court's ignorance of the linguistic and cultural background of the defendant and witnesses ultimately would have condemned the 18-year-old migrant worker to life in prison, had not the Santiago Freedom Committee—a group that included three jurors from his trial—intervened and had the case

reopened. In April 1991—after Ventura had been in jail for five years—the district attorney's office cited lack of evidence, a judge dismissed the charges against the prisoner, and he was freed. Ironically Ventura's unjust incarceration changed the course of his life. Once an unskilled migrant agricultural worker with minimal education, Ventura became a student of social work at the University of Portland, a trilingual political activist, and the Oregon leader of the workers' organization Frente Binacional Mixteco Zapoteco (Mixtec-Zapotec Binational Front).

The tragic ignorance of the court in Ventura's case mirrors the public's lack of understanding of the many non-Spanish speaking ethnic groups—Zapotecs, Tarascans, Triques, Huicholes, Mayans, and others—that make up Oregon's "Mexican" work force. Those groups are Hispanics because of their countries of origin (Mexico and Guatemala) but have a very different ethnic background from Spanish-speaking immigrants. In fact, their native tongues have no genetic relationship to Spanish, a language many of them can barely speak.

Today, they provide cheap labor in both Mexican and American agricultural settings, where their language and their educational shortcomings combine with their distinctive indigenous features to make them targets for prejudice and human rights abuses. In Mexico, Mixtecs are pejoratively called "Oaxacas" or "Indians." In Oregon they are referred to as "the little people."

LA MIXTECA

Mixtecs have historically been located in the region referred to as "La Mixteca," comprising the northern and western parts of Oaxaca and neighboring states of Guerrero and Puebla (see map on page 118). Mestizos (who are of mixed Spanish and Indian blood) are also present in the region but are concentrated in its few urban centers.

La Mixteca comprises three ecologically distinct areas: Mixteca Alta, Mixteca Baja, and Mixteca de la Costa. The three zones, which range from the high mountains of Oaxaca and eastern Guerrero to the Pacific coastal plain, have had slightly different histories and reflect both cultural and linguistic differences. In 1980 the Mixtec population in the area was approximately 450,000, but since then several thousand have migrated to other states in Mexico and a sizable migrant Mixtec population now exists in Baja California, California, and Oregon.

PRE-COLUMBIAN TIMES

Three thousand years before Christ, several groups settled down in the highland valleys of western Oaxaca. There in Nuu Ñuma, "the land of the clouds," they developed what a modern humanist, Alfonso Caso, has called "one of the most exquisite cultures of Ancient America." It was a culture that—contrary to the belief of Mexico's early historians—had a complex written history. These ancient ones were ancestors of both the Mixtec and Zapotec cultures of today.

Although most of the ancient manuscripts were burned at the time of the Spanish conquest, the surviving Mixtec codices date as far back as 692 A.D. Their content is historical and genealogical, showing births, marriages, deaths, political events, wars, conquests, alliances, and religious fiestas of Mixtec dynasties. The manuscripts show clear features of a writing system with ideographic and phonetic symbols, which were also found carved in sculptures; engraved in stone, wood, or bone; and painted in pottery.

The ideographs indicate names and surnames of individuals; rank; place names; dates, including year and day; and representations of the sun, moon, stars, geographic localities, births, battles, sacrifices, animals, vegetables, houses, and weapons.

The Mixtec writing system was originally deciphered by Alfonso Caso, who found correlations between symbols in archaeological sites and ritual objects and in the Mixtecs' manu-

CODEX NUTTALL

Originating from what is now the state of Oaxaca, the Codex Nuttall is a pre-Conquest handpainted book that depicts the sacred history of the Mixtec through pictures and hieroglyphs. Over a white gesso background, the figures are drawn in rich earth tones. They show animals and the births of kings, marriages, wars, and other major events. The figures are shown in elaborate costumes and in ceremonial or dramatic postures that can be read by those who understand the visual clues.

The ideograph from Codex Nuttall reproduced here illustrates the ingenuity of the Mixtec writing system. The upper drawing pictures "the lord male 8 Deer 'Tiger's Claw' and the lady female 13 'Serpent of Flowers,' who is offering him a bowl of chocolate, symbolic of marriage." Their names refer to the day they were born and are depicted at the base of the drawing. (Note the deer's head, tiger's claw, and the eight circles under the man and the serpent with thirteen circles in the center, under the bowl of chocolate.) The date of their marriage, the day 12 Serpent of the year 13 Cane, is also recorded and would be A. D. 1051 in our calendar.

The second drawing shows the birth of two sons, "male 4 Dog 'Tame Coyote' in the year 7 Rabbit, A.D. 1058, and male 4 Crocodile Serpent Ball of Fire' two years later in 9 Stone, A. D. 1060."

scripts and maps made before the conquest. At the time of the conquest, the Mixtecs continued writing, sometimes using both the Mixtec and European calendar systems. This correlation provided clues to deciphering the Mixtec calendar and writing systems.

The Mixtecs' ancestors also developed a particular political system known as *cacicazgo*—a pyramid with the *cacique* (political boss) at the pinnacle, the nobility below, and landless taxpayers and slaves at the bottom. This political system had profound influences on other Mesoamerican societies.

THE COLONIAL PERIOD

Before the Spanish conquest, La Mixteca was never united into a single political entity but had several major autonomous ruling centers. During the four decades that preceded the Spanish conquest, the greater part of Mixteca Alta was under the political domination of the Aztecs, who were more interested in acquiring tribute than in dominating the Mixtec area physically.

The basic social structure of the Mixtec kingdoms—similar to that of feudal Europe—was retained after the Spanish conquest. The Spanish were recipients of the Aztec tribute through a system called the *encomienda*, by which Indian communities owed goods, labor, and other services to the Spanish crown.

During Spanish colonial times, as Carol Zabin, Michael Kearney, Anna Garcia, and their colleagues have pointed out,

> *there was a significant change from an agricultural economy to one based on raising cattle and wheat—both new elements imported from Castile. Spanish entrepreneurs developed the cochineal and silk industries. Both cochineal—a red dye obtained from an insect that grew on a cactus—and silk found a good market in Europe, and for a brief period La Mixteca was the foremost silk-producing area in the world.*

The changes introduced by the Spanish economy generated increasing deforestation of the Mixtecs' mountainous terrain, which in turn had severe ecological consequences: impoverishment of the soil, a decrease in precipitation, and an alarming degree of erosion. By the end of the eighteenth century, the ecology of the region was dramatically altered. In a document from 1706, the local governments of the area complained that they could not raise the money to pay their tributes because the Indians could not raise corn and were leaving the area. Within two centuries, La Mixteca, one of New Spain's richest regions in the sixteenth century, had nearly become a deserted land.

FROM COLONIAL TIMES
TO THE TWENTIETH CENTURY

For those Mixtecs who remained in their eroded mountain homeland, Mexico's colonial period brought intensified disputes over village boundaries and land rights. Ancestral lines

...in the Year and the day of Darkness...before there were days or years, the world was in chaos and confusion and the earth was covered with water, lime and moss....The creator's parents appeared in the world with human shape, the God 2 Deer "Lion's Snake"..., who with their great wisdom and power founded palaces and magnificent crafts, by the town of Apoala that in their language meant "the place where the heavens were...." There they stayed for centuries with great pleasure while the world was still submerged in chaos and darkness.

—An Ancient Mixtec Myth,
recorded by Alfonso Caso

At the time of the Conquest, the Mixtecs worshipped the forces and elements of nature: the wind, rain, sun, moon, flowers, stones, caves. The sacred natural elements were referred to with a special pronoun: *yaa* (deity), which is still used in some Mixtec dialects.

The natural forces were represented as images that the Spanish indiscriminately classified as *idolos* (idols) and systematically destroyed, to be replaced by Christian imagery. Four centuries later, the Mixtec language and culture still retain traces of this religious representation.

As Ronald Spores has shown, historical events and characters were identified on a calendar established through astronomical observation. Each day of the year had a name, and scribes indicated each day with a different sign. The year consisted of eighteen months of twenty days and another month of five days. Every four years the additional month contained six days in order to account for six hours gained every year in the 356-day calendar. The six-day month was known as the "useless month." Each cycle of fifty-two years was divided into four components of thirteen years each, and each component was associated with one of the four cardinal directions. The association to the heavenly direction foretold good or bad fortune.

of authority, fortified by alignments with the ruling party, gave political and economic power to *caciques* and local bosses.

Today, Mixtecs are based in small villages and hamlets that retain traditional patterns of subsistence, politics, cultural practices, religious beliefs, and language. These self-contained communities jealously guard their land and natural resources. Although outside marriages now occur, especially between members of non-adjacent villages, most Mixtec marry someone from the village where they were born. Ties to the village are also maintained through religious and political obligations that involve contributions and communal work. These ritual commitments apply both to resident and non-resident Mixtecs and include participation in the major fiesta for the village's patron saint.

Where language and literacy are concerned, the 1990 Mexican census indicates that monolingual Mixtec speakers have declined, few indigenous children finish elementary school, and full literacy in Spanish is minimal. The situation is worse among women, who have less education. Although the post-revolutionary government has implemented several measures to provide bilingual elementary education in La Mixteca and other indigenous areas, it has failed due to a lack of both resources and political consistency. The results are very low literacy, the use of Mixtec in most social contexts, and a limited knowledge of Spanish.

Mixtecs—like other Mesoamerican groups—are still "people of corn," and corn, beans, and squash are their main foods. However, due to a scarcity of land and to heavy erosion, most households cannot produce enough corn to live on. Some supplement their farming with crafts, such as the weaving of palm into bags, mats, and hats for sale to a government agency or at the weekly market. However, a skilled weaver can produce only two or three hats a day, which bring a mere thirty cents each.

MIGRATION: THE ONLY OPTION

Under these circumstances, Mixtecs have been forced to migrate in order to survive. The statistics concerning this migration are startling. According to Michael Kearney, writing in 1986,

> Between 1960 and 1970, the rate of depopulation from the Mixteca exceeded that of the state as a whole....It has been calculated that in some districts, the rate of permanent out-migration might reach 50 percent.

Some of the Mixtecs move permanently to urban areas like Mexico City and Oaxaca City, where they are underemployed and work as street vendors, masons, and domestic workers.

Scenes from Santiago Ventura Morales's home village in Mexico. Top and bottom. Villagers wear colorful costumes to celebrate the Fiesta of San Miguel, a festival honoring their patron saint. Left center. A Mixtec woman tends to her planting. Right center. Another woman makes corn dough.

Others take up work throughout the Mexican Republic: harvesting cane in the Gulf Coast, picking cotton in Chiapas, picking tomatoes in Sinaloa and Baja California. The commercial production of tomatoes in the northwest of Mexico since the 1960s has become increasingly dependent on the labor of tens of thousands of Mixtec people.

Among both girls and boys, twelve is the age for initiating the long trek. Girls accompany their father and older brothers to do the cooking and housework and often to share in the agricultural work.

In the 1960s Mixtecs started coming to the United States, where they worked mainly in the tomato fields of San Diego County and the citrus groves of Riverside, California. (During the 1940s and 50s some Mixtecs had worked in the U.S. as *braceros*, or contract laborers.) However, the economic crisis in Mexico during the 1980s contributed to an increase in migration into California and other areas of the United States, such as Oregon, Washington, Idaho, and Florida. Today, the 3,000-mile trek north is made every year by thousands, who come up the west coast of Mexico and the United States following the ripening crops.

The pattern of following crops and going back home is conventionally referred to as "circular migration" and involves a highly complex structure of relations and support along the migratory routes. In one situation that is by no means unique, a young Mixtec man was able to send his dead father's body from San Diego to his Oaxacan village thanks to the support of a network of fellow migrants.

Through the Mixtecs' migration, the subsistence economy of La Mixteca and the sophisticated agricultural economy of the Californias and Oregon are also linked, resulting in a relationship of interdependence. The sending region depends on the cash generated in the North, while the economy of the developed regions depends on the cheap labor provided by the migrants.

MIXTECS IN CALIFORNIA AND OREGON

Recent research indicates that California now produces more than half the fresh fruit, vegetables, and nuts grown in the United States, and more than 60 percent of the processed vegetables. As increasing competition in the global market for this $18 billion-per-year industry has forced California growers to seek cheaper sources of labor, Mixtecs have been replacing *mestizo* migrant farmworkers, who in turn had replaced Chinese, Japanese, Filipino, East Asian, and other earlier migrants.

Mixtecs in California are mainly concentrated in San Diego, San Joaquin, Madera, Fresno, Kern, Tulare, and Riverside counties. Yet most also take seasonal jobs in Oregon, Washington, and Mexico.

Mixtecs in Oregon are largely invisible. Some 5,000 of them live in Clackamas, Multnomah, and Marion counties and smaller numbers live in Umatilla, Yamhill, Lane, and Polk counties. These communities represent branches of the California

enclaves—linked by home-village networks. There are other communities that have additional connections with countrymen of the same Mixteca Baja area who attend the same churches (Seventh Day Adventist, Jehovah's Witness, and other Protestant groups).

Those who are in Oregon work primarily in agriculture—in the fields, in canneries and nurseries, or in tree-planting operations. Programa Hispano estimates that of the 30,000 seasonal migrants at work in Multnomah and north Clackamas counties during the peak harvest time, a large percentage are Mixtecs.

Research in Oregon strawberry camps reveals that, in fact, growers consider the "little people" more productive than other workers. They can stand twelve-hour days and will work with-

Mixtecs call their mother tongue *tùnhun-dahvi*, which means "language of the poor people." The Mixtec language is related neither to Spanish nor to the two major Indian languages: *Náhuatl*, spoken by the Aztecs, and Mayan, spoken by the Mayans of the south of Mexico. Today, as the result of a long process of diversification, the language has five major dialect areas and further variations within each dialect. Local dialect differences are fiercely maintained to preserve community boundaries, which are often threatened by longstanding land disputes between neighboring villages.

This tendency to protect local dialects has thwarted attempts to create a standard language for Mixtec-Spanish bilingual education. By contrast, attempts to define a pan-Mixtec identity, based on culture and language, have met with some success in U.S. labor camps. Even without such attempts, Mixtec migrants in Oregon, who come mainly from the Mixteca Baja, can understand one another fairly easily.

out rest until the harvest is finished, which can take several weeks. These laborers are pushed to harvest at the rate of the fastest picker, which can mean up to 800 or 900 pounds a day. Those who produce under that rate may make less than minimum wage and may be fired, to be replaced by the waiting surplus of unemployed workers. By using Mixtecs, farmers can complete the harvest in a shorter time, with fewer workers, and at a lower cost.

Not surprisingly, Mixtecs have now begun to replace *mestizo* workers, although the strengthening of Mixtec labor organizations is now deterring labor contractors from hiring Mixtecs who come from the same village in Mexico. Some contractors and foremen try to break old village networks by hiring young single males from a mixed pool of workers. When they do, they relieve the owners of their responsibilities for having families in the labor camps, and they prevent workers from organizing themselves on the basis of previous working experience in the same camp.

In spite of the difficulties involved in agricultural work, that work offers more opportunities for Mixtecs than they find in urban areas, where competition for jobs and cultural and communication barriers are greater. This tendency has been noted in general as a migration pattern by Richard C. Jones, who also points out that "their penetration of northern cities is slower, proceeding as kinship and cultural ties are built up." As one Mixtec man in Woodburn said, "*Mestizos* have better chances to work in restaurants or bars in the cities because they are good looking. We are always kept apart in the camps."

Access to jobs is usually through labor contractors (*contratistas*) or their foremen (*mayordomos*). The 1992 Or-

A young Mixtec worker gets a ride to Cornelius so he can attend mass. However, some Mixtecs in this country adopt new religions.

egon strawberry crop report by Robert Mason and Tim Cross at Oregon State University indicates that 88 percent of growers use labor contractors to recruit workers.

Contractors recruit and hire crews of workers for each season and are the point of contact between English-speaking growers and the workers. These contractors are usually bilingual Mexican-Americans or established immigrants with the ability to negotiate with the English-speaking sector and the workers. Foremen are usually Spanish-speaking *mestizos*, who supervise the work, provide tools, and transport and pay the workers. Although a few Mixtecs have been foremen, they tend to attract workers from their hometowns and have therefore begun to be replaced by *mestizos* who can break the village networks in Oregon's labor camps.

Foremen and labor contractors are often the only contacts Mixtecs have with North American society, and those who speak little Spanish are unable to express themselves to anyone outside their cultural group. This situation not only reinforces the insularity of Mixtecs in Anglo-American society but reproduces the pattern of subordination to *mestizos* that exists in Mexico.

The dependence of the workers is reinforced by strict rules of social life in the camps. In many camps, workers are not allowed to have external visitors and are kept locked up during rest periods.

With the labor contractor system, the workers rarely know who they are harvesting for. In such circumstances, it is not surprising that Mixtecs are likely to be victims of all kinds of abuses: low wages, work overloads, poor living conditions, and life-endangering duties such as the application of pesticides.

This pattern can be broken if a family member (for example an older school child) is bilingual or trilingual and can help the family gain access to social agencies, legal assistance, and a flow of information. Also, the adoption of a new religion (such as Jehovah's Witness or Seventh Day Adventist) by some families may have the effect of breaking ties and ritual obligations to the Mixtec community. Mixtecs who adopt new religions are indoctrinated by Spanish-speaking missionaries, who promise them a new life of redemption, modernization, and assimilation into mainstream society. The introduction of literacy skills in Spanish through Bible reading is a strong incentive to become better educated.

Access to education and a new social support network is hard to reject. As one Mixtec man—a Jehovah's Witness—said, "I never went to school and hardly knew how to write my name.

Now I am reading the Bible. Now we can understand who we really are and why we all speak many languages."

Even in Mexico, Mixtecs who move to the city are adopting new community ties and obligations and experiencing a new independence. According to Leticia Irene Mendez, those who move to Mexico City begin to look on those at home in the village as "rurals" or "inferiors." As they learn Spanish, they become further removed from their traditional culture. In contrast, Mixtecs in the U.S. whose jobs are rural can maintain their native language at home and in several spheres of their social life.

In fact, as Michael Kearney and Carol Nagegast argue, migration and settlement in the United States seems to reinforce the natural borders of the Mixtec community and to build a pan-Mixtec identity not present in the Mixteca region. In California, several Mixtec organizations based on village affiliation flourished in California in the 1980s, providing legal advice and support to migrants and connections with sister organizations in Mexico. In the 1990s, these several organizations have become part of the Binational Mixtec-Zapotec Front, which operates in both the U.S. and Mexico. The creation and expansion of such grassroots groups reveals a growing awareness of Mixtecs as a large distinct group with political potential.

CONCLUSION

The insertion of Mixtecs into West Coast agriculture in this country has initiated a new cycle of poverty (as reported by the California Institute for Rural Studies), but it has also started a new cycle of history for a people who have both a proud and a tragic history. The migratory experience has brought Mixtecs to the surface of American and Mexican society. It has given them the historical option to resist and persist as a distinctive community defined by its cultural past and by its political and ethnic potential.

Note: *Some aspects of the research concerning Mixtecs in Oregon, mentioned in this chapter, were carried out in collaboration with Santiago Ventura Morales. An evaluation of linguistic anomalies in Ventura's trial was done by the author and John Haviland. The studies of Mixtecs in Oregon strawberry fields were conducted by the author, John Haviland, Santiago Ventura Morales, and the late Bernardo Cruz. The author also wishes to acknowledge The Santiago Ventura Freedom Committee, the Mixtec community in Oregon, and the people of San Miguel Cuevas, Mexico.*

HONEYMOON IN OREGON: REFLECTIONS ON CULTURAL CHANGE

BY SUSAN U. CABELLO

"We came to Oregon in February, just the two of us.
We came because he has resident status.
He can enter the U.S. legally, and he's been working here for many years.
When he's employed, things go well for him.
That is one reason why we decided to come."

Newlyweds and young mothers, the wives of Mexican workers accepting the challenge of adventure and embarking on a new life, are some of Washington County's most recently arrived residents. Often their husbands come first, seeking employment that will allow them to support their families and retain the small parcels of land some of them or their parents own in Mexico. Following the migrant cycle, they labor seven months in the U. S. and then return to their villages in Mexico for the other five. Eventually, they marry their childhood sweethearts and return with them to Oregon. These wives find themselves in a strange land, unable to speak English, forced by circumstances to bear and rear their children far from the support of their families. Their journey north is a story of hardships, valor, humor, and tragedy. Their communication with those at home is limited by their status as illegals.

Other newcomers have been in the U.S. ten to fifteen years, working in California, Arizona, and other areas. As jobs there become scarce, they travel farther north, hoping to find more favorable conditions for housing and employment.

Both groups of women were raised in a different culture and cherish a different set of cultural norms. In the U.S. they discover racism and limited economic opportunity. Life in the North is confusing, exhilarating, startling, exhausting, and sometimes boring. Since it is the wives and mothers who in large part preserve and pass on cultural values, they are faced with the ill-defined task of interpreting American norms for their children. Often they possess only minimal literacy skills to help them adapt to life in their new land. As they embrace the American dream, they can choose to accept or reject differ-

ent aspects of our lifestyle. When their children become fluent in English, they become the translators, the interpreters of lifestyles, and the cultural cushion for the family.

These Mexican women are part of a massive migration north, swelled by the entrance of a million workers into the Mexican work force each year. Writer Carlos Monsiváis observed while lecturing at Pacific University in 1992, "I doubt there is a single family in Mexico that doesn't have at least one relative in the United States." Their children have now raised the Hispanic enrollment in some Washington County elementary schools to as high as 40 percent. These children with radiant smiles and shining black eyes will transform the future face of Oregon.

The women we will meet in this chapter range in age from twenty-three to thirty-seven. When I interviewed them in preparation for writing the chapter, they had been in the U.S. for four months to fifteen years. Many, but not all, come from El Albareño, San Bernardo, Zinapécuaro—rural villages and towns in the state of Michoacán. All come from large families of five to twelve children. Their parents and grandparents were *ejidatarios*, the recipients of a tract of land of six hectares (about 15 acres) from the government. They planted corn, beans, sorghum, garbanzos, and wheat and raised a variety of farm animals: pigs, chickens, goats, turkeys, and cows.

Most of these young women married in their mid-teens and began their families in Mexico. But at this point their lives diverged from the pattern followed by their mothers and grandmothers. Frequently their husbands returned to jobs in the United States, and the new brides spent the first years of their marriage living with their husbands' families. Often, one or two children were born in Mexico before the imperative to re-unite the family impelled the women to uproot themselves and take on the dangers of migration. Rosa remembers her mother's advice: "Look, *m'hija* (my daughter), if one day your husband wants you to go, you must."

For these women, the desire to strengthen the family unit is the impetus to undertake a journey of thousands of miles. Not a single person interviewed initially crossed the border legally. They entered through a variety of points: Tijuana, Mexicali, San Luis, and Nogales, after a long bus trip from central Mexico. While some crossings were relatively uneventful, others were more hazardous. Each crossing is a potential encounter with death or failure, given the nature of the predators who stalk the border to take advantage of the innocent and the increased surveillance efforts of the INS, known to migrants as *la migra.*

The perils of the crossing are followed by the sometimes startling discovery that life in the United States is not at all what the women imagined it would be. The picture that friends and relatives have painted has exaggerated the gains and minimized the losses. Everyone comes prepared to work hard. The commitment to the odyssey includes a clause about hard work, but the United States of the mind is quite different from the one across the border, and eager anticipation folds quickly into a sense of disillusionment. Angélica remembers the imagined United States:

> People make a lot of money there. You'll be able to buy a good car, all the clothes that make you look nice, and I don't know what all else. But they only tell you the good part. They never mention the sacrifices you have to make to acquire those things.

Marta focuses on the transition time, when one is waiting and waiting. In the house the days pass in monotonous similarity.

> They don't tell you about what happens from the first day you get here, until you get a job; how...if things go well for you, maybe in a week or two you'll be working. But if not, months may pass with no job, and you have a lot of problems—no place to live, no money for food or clothing.

The interviews are replete with evidence that attests to an extended period of culture shock. Each woman must find a way to deal with feelings of isolation, loneliness, and occasionally severe depression. With no preparation, they are plunged into a perplexing environment in which their limited or non-existent English circumscribes whom they can talk to and impinges on their freedom of movement. When Rosa arrived, she lived on Vermont Street in San Jose. There were no other Mexican families in the neighborhood. "I never went out. If I went out, it was with my husband. I was certain I would get lost."

Suddenly, familiar support systems have disappeared. Young women who would have benefited from the wisdom of mothers and grandmothers when their children are infants are cut off from that sense of security and warmth and find that materialism is a poor substitute. Many women report bouts of crying and despair. One even sought medical assistance and was told she was having a nervous breakdown. Lucía, who has only been in this country a few months, dwells most on the older children she has left behind. Asked what advice she might give others, she responds:

> I have a brother-in-law here who says he thinks he'll bring his wife next year. I tell him: "If you bring your wife, bring your children, too, because one suffers a lot." During the day I'm fine, but at night it really bothers me. I think about whether they might be sick. I wouldn't want anyone to come and leave their children behind.

Two important keys to survival in a new land are adequate housing and full-time employment, but Marta paints a dramatic picture of what happens when work is not steady:

> I control the money, but it doesn't make any difference because there's no stability. He doesn't receive a fixed wage, and he never earns the same amount. It depends on where he's working. Until now we've never had to do without, but right now there isn't much work, and he's been laid off and I say, "Ay! If he doesn't get work by next week, we won't even have money for food."

As these women have gradually established themselves, they have begun to embrace the American dream of owning their own homes, but not all realize that dream. Lucía has found that without two salaries, she and her husband can't save any money. Angélica, as a single parent, has had many different kinds of jobs.

In most cases housing is occupied by more than one family, a survival tactic generally frowned upon and misunderstood by North Americans. Still, several salaries pay the rent more easily than one. Angélica explains, "One is always on the lookout for people who are serious and responsible with whom one might live and rent an apartment." Rosa, Marta, and Lucía all share their living spaces with another family. Julia lives in a duplex with all her in-laws, who followed her and her husband to Oregon.

Multi-family living arrangements are, however, more than a matter of practical necessity. John Condon reports in *Good Neighbors* (1985) that Mexicans exhibit greater group loyalty than the Japanese. "Families are extended beyond blood-lines through the institution of *compadrazgo*, godfather relationships. To be a godparent is often much more than an honor; it is a means of becoming part of a vast network of relationships, through which advice or loans or favors may be sought and granted." One would not think of turning away one's relatives, especially in a strange land. Lucía relates how some distant cousins helped them, when they lost their housing. "We didn't know anyone, but then it turned out this lady, Juana, was a relative of my husband through her husband, and we came to live with them."

Gloria and her husband found another solution to the housing dilemma. They bought a mobile home.

A desire to unite the family impels many women to follow their husbands to Oregon for what they hope will be a better life.

We've had it for two years. Before we bought it, we had a lot of problems, because sometimes you can stay a long time in an apartment, but sometimes the owner wants to fix them up or something. You have to move out, and when you have children, it's hard to be going around looking for a new place.

Behind her words looms the specter of housing discrimination, a problem alluded to by some of the women.

Starting a new life north of the border plunges family traditions into a crucible of change. The redefinition of women's roles, however, begins in Mexico, as a consequence of the migrant cycle. Wives who are left alone to cope with family matters begin to broaden the areas of their jurisdiction and assume more responsibility. Lucía comments, "I am the mother and the father. When he is gone, I make all the decisions."

In the United States, as many wives join the work force they have greater economic independence and more freedom of movement, and the family may need to redistribute responsibilities in the home. Traveling from one part of the country to another also introduces them to different life styles and opportunities. Sometimes these changes are easily accepted by the spouse and sometimes they are resisted. Rosa worked in an electronics assembly plant in California for five years. "And my husband didn't like it that I would get home at ten o'clock at night. I would say to him. 'Well, look, I always come home with money in my purse.'"

Since coming to Oregon, Rosa has augmented her family's income by selling cosmetics door-to-door in the Hispanic community for the Jaffra Company. Through her part-time business Rosa has made many new friends and vastly expanded her horizons. "When they know me, they call me Doña Rosa." Now, Rosa dreams of getting a driver's license and one day having her own car.

In this new environment the subordinate role of women may become an irritation. Julia resents the control her husband exercises over her life.

A lot of people say that machismo doesn't exist any more, but I think that it does because there are some men who think they aren't macho (domineering), but I think they shouldn't be the way they are. For that reason we don't always agree. The decisions aren't made by both of us. They always have to be made just by him. And if I want to do something and he won't let me, either I'm left wishing or I have to do it secretly and hope he doesn't realize.

This same problem, the need to defer to male authority in the family, caused Irma and her husband to separate. She came to Oregon with two of their children and the other two stayed with their father in California.

Another major difference which couples encounter in the U.S. is the general level of information about sexuality and birth control. For many women there is a virtual revolution in knowledge, and for the first time, women are in a position to take control of their bodies. Gloria and Lucía first learned about contraception in Mexico, after their first children were born. Other women learn here. All the women envision smaller families than their parents had. Lucía says her family is complete with the three children she has. Gloria had her tubes tied after the birth of her fourth child. This procedure was an option she learned about at the Virginia Garcia Clinic during the prenatal care period of her last pregnancy. Marta also plans to limit the size of her family. "Once we have two children, my husband will have a vasectomy. We've talked about it, and we think that is the best thing to do." Rosa sums up the vast generational differences that exist. "My mother told us the stork brought babies, and we were never curious the way children are today. My nine-year-old daughter says to me, 'Mamá, when I get married, I'm only going to have two.'"

Raising children in the United States is difficult. Families are smaller and siblings are fewer, but one is removed from the like-mindedness of one's village, where every adult is a surrogate parent and identical principles of obedience and respect are held by all. American parents are perceived as way too permissive with their children and there is a general misunderstanding about the parents' right to discipline. A great deal of emphasis has been placed by schools and social agencies on avoiding child abuse, and parents feel their hands are tied. Angélica expresses the typical complaint:

In Mexico...if I see that my son is getting into trouble, I can hit him, without any problem. Nobody will say anything. But not here. "If you hit me, I'll call the police." That's the first thing he says to me. And that's bad. It's bad because you can't do what you want with your own children. Because they're your children. You want the best for them. If I hit him, it's because he needs it. Because you can't just let children do whatever they want....

Rosa also laments what she considers to be the erosion of parental authority and asserts that if her children want to do something she doesn't like, there's no way to stop them. "We weren't raised that way," she says indignantly. "All you can do here is give them advice." Four of the women interviewed have

Some women leave their children behind when they go north to seek work. Reunions in their home villages are bittersweet and serve to underscore the vast differences between the women's two homes. Yet economic necessity often drives them back to Oregon.

children enrolled in Oregon public schools. Their attitude toward education is one of reverence. Says Rosa: "I would like my children to study always because that is what makes you worth more." Angélica hopes that her son will be able to attend school long enough to become a professional, perhaps a lawyer. Yet all of the women have a rather hazy understanding of what is involved in higher education and how one proceeds from secondary school to a university education. The more typical response to the inquiry about how many years they envisioned their children attending school was: "for as long as they want to." Framed against the experience of the mothers, that might not mean earning even a high school diploma.

All of the mothers are concerned with the daily academic progress of their children and their children's happiness in the school environment. "When they have a problem at school," says Irma of her daughters, "they don't want to go. The younger one has trouble with math. Now that she's getting help, she's learning, and she's not so terrified." Many problems are rooted in the language barrier and are eloquent testimony to the fact that submersion in a second language, when advanced cognitive skills are not yet in place in the first, is a slow and painful process. "Sometimes they don't understand what it is in Spanish that the teachers are saying in English." All the mothers have occasionally gone to conferences with their children's teachers and are grateful to the special English-as-a-second-language teachers for the extra help extended to their children. "A little while ago I went to a conference with my son's teacher, and she told me he was behind in math and reading. Now he has a Migrant Ed teacher and he's catching up." Their comments point to the growing need for real bilingual education in Oregon's schools.

For each of the mothers, their children are the focus of their lives and what is most dear to them. In February of 1991, a tragedy took place in Yuma, Arizona. Angélica lost her niece, who had only been in this country for a month, and Irma lost her oldest daughter. The girls, one fifteen years old and one thirteen, were walking along the highway with two friends, playing at being brave while they waited for the school bus. The driver of the car that hit them said he didn't see them. Angélica finds that hard to believe. "I think, we all think, that he wanted to scare them, so they'd run, but the car got out of control and he couldn't stop." Irma remembers being called, still in her bathrobe, seeing her daughter stretched out on the pavement, lying very still. The authorities found the girls at fault for not getting out of the way. They became one more roadside fatality of migration, and the mothers were left to struggle with the meaning of their grief. Angélica views the whole episode more critically and wonders if there are racist prejudices at work. "If it had happened that a Mexican had killed some American girls, it wouldn't have been left at that. But since it was the opposite, that's how things stayed."

All of the women were baptized Roman Catholic in Mexico and attended mass regularly when they were small. Many con-

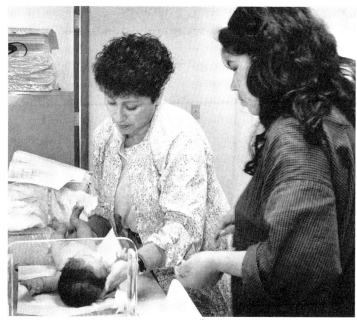

In Oregon, many Mexican women encounter information about family planning for the first time. Through clinics like Virginia Garcia Memorial Health Center in Cornelius they also have access to good, inexpensive health care for their children.

tinue to do so here. Marta notices that the physical aspect of the churches is different, although the service is the same. "The churches are very decorated there and have a lot of images, painted with lustrous color, which invites you more to worship." Lucía has a sustaining faith and feels protected. "The Holy Spirit gets me out of the scrapes I get into." Other women no longer attend mass regularly but follow a Christian ethic. "I don't think I have to go to church or to confession to believe in God. If I have done something wrong, I ask God for forgiveness in my conscience and to act in such a way that the same thing doesn't happen again."

Rosa's case is different. Rosa became a Seventh Day Adventist. Part of her conversion is tied up with what for her is the miracle of literacy and part with the real help that her new church has given her in holding her family together and raising her children. When her father became ill and died, she was overcome with depression. Unable to return to Mexico for the funeral, she had to deal with her emotions far from her family.

I was crying all the time. And I said to myself, "Ay, my children are still very small and I'm going to die. What will become of them?" And I began to pray. The only thing I knew was the Lord's Prayer, and I would say to Jesus: "You, who are so good, you who can do anything, take these awful thoughts from my head."

Gradually she became calmer and then she heard an inner voice that told her "You need to read the Bible." With her own savings, Rosa went out and bought herself a Bible in Spanish. Her husband was scornful. "You don't even know how to read," he said, but little by little she learned. She would open her

Bible and ask her oldest daughter, "What does it say here?" First she was able to recognize names like Mark and Luke and then little by little she learned more. Now she finds that reading the Bible is a great source of strength and consolation to her. "In the Catholic Church," she says, "they never told us to read the Scriptures."

What do Oregon's newest residents think about their new home? In general, Oregon is perceived as an infinitely more attractive place to live in than California. Marta reports that her husband likes the climate, the vegetation, the flowers, even the rain. It's not as cold as Chicago and not as hot as California. Rosa says she and her husband chose Cornelius because it's peaceful. Others came because they heard there was more help available and the cost of living was cheaper. Irma says that's probably not so, "but we did come out ahead because here we met more people who were willing to give us a hand." Lucía hopes that Oregon will become her permanent home. "I like it because it's peaceful. There aren't a lot of *cholillos* (gangs of kids) that go around at night keeping people awake. It's not like that in California."

As the honeymoon comes to an end, what does the future hold for these women? Some imagine they will return to Mexico, with cash ringing in their pockets. Marta expects to work for about four years and then go back. Rosa would prefer to live in Mexico to be closer to her mother and come only during the work season, but her expectations are more grounded in reality. "Our dream is to buy a house here. If we die, then we'll have something to leave our children." Most of the women mention a home, a steady job, and being able to speak English well. Angélica sums up their comments: "I always long for Mexico, but I think it's true that here, although the jobs are harder, one lives better. Here one has things one could never have in Mexico." As their first experiences in Oregon blend into the future, the United States of the mind is replaced by the Mexico of the mind, a country to which they will likely return only for occasional visits.

LISTENING
TO THE PEOPLE

*To understand a people, you must listen to their voices, their stories.
In 1992 the Oregon Council for the Humanities undertook an
ambitious oral history project to record the recollections
of Hispanic residents from towns and cities around the state.
Those who were interviewed represent a number of countries and backgrounds
and have lived in the state for decades, their careers and volunteer work
woven into the fabric of their community life. Here, we present a sampling
of their stories, which echo the themes introduced earlier in this book.*

MARY THIEL
Mexican, Nyssa

We came in the year 1929. As a child in the coal mines I remember snow—that we had to work out paths from one house to the other so the kids wouldn't get lost, because we were way up in the mountains. Of course, at that time we were very much into a growing family of small children. We had a tragedy in our family, where my brother who was just younger than I had a heart tear. Nobody knew quite how it happened, and the doctor did not share that with my father, so from there we went to Twin Falls in order to take Frankie to a doctor there. My father was told that Frankie would die anyway, that there was nothing they could do for him. I believe that was when the suffering for us started, because when we were in the coal mines we had food and clothing and a roof over our heads.

We went into agricultural work. We couldn't speak any English whatsoever, and of course, there was the terrible tragedy of my brother and how our family felt about him. People weren't as giving. There was nothing. So one man kind of brought us under his wing, if that's what you want to call it, but it ended up that he would leave us out in people's barns without their permission with no heat, no food, nothing. If you got sick, you got sick. There was just nothing.

I remember having abscessed teeth and earaches, and you just suffered your way through them. It was very sad times for my mother and also for my father, because my father was trying to find something and didn't appear to be able to find anything for a long time. The last thing I remember in the Twin

Falls area was that this man dropped us off in a manger of straw and there was still snow on the floor. That was in Jerome. That had to be one of the really low points in our life.

From there we went to Twin Falls, and we were able to work in the sugar beets there for the sugar company. I personally started thinning beets at the age of nine. There was no age requirement; you started early with your family, you ended up late. Fortunately, we went to St. Edwards, the academy there, and my mother did the altar cloths and different things that they needed—in order to pay for our tuition.

The little sisters at St. Edwards decided that they would teach us how to speak English, and so after school we went to the convent and they worked with us. And they saw that we had food. They would send little packages home with us all the time. And they would also help us with clothing. I think if it wasn't for the little nuns there, I don't know what would have happened to us. And slowly we started speaking English and feeling a little bit more secure. From Twin Falls we came to Jamison, Oregon and thinned beets there for a few years, and then still went back to Twin Falls. We thinned beets for small farmers who are still well known over into the Jamison area. We thinned beets for Lester Hammack who is a commissioner for the county court; we thinned beets for the McGoritys; we thinned beets for the Thomas Boston family. So we thinned beets for a lot of those old timers over in that area. And we still went back to Twin Falls. My mother decided that we should settle and not go back, so we stayed more or less in that area.

It's quite a transition when you stop to think that we were a migrating family actually from Mexico. We were all born—

all the children through me were born in Arandas, Jalisco, Mexico. My mother was born there, my father was born there, my grandmother was born there. It was a small village at the time. Now I understand it is humongous. So it was quite a transition, and then all of a sudden, you know, you are trying to stay in an area and work, and really, there was no work for the Mexican families at that time except in the summer. If you didn't save what you earned in the summer for the winter, you experienced some very hard times.

When I went to school there at Jamison, it was just a little old country school that is there no longer. I think there were three classrooms. From there I went to high school at Vale, Oregon, and I was still a migrant, you know, I was still doing the usual task of a migrant, thinning beets and hoeing beets and onions and all of the agricultural labor that we were noted for. Our family of the four girls and myself was known as a crew. We were hired as a crew to do a lot of work and had quite a reputation.

My mother became very ill and we were told she had pneumonia. But she had tuberculosis and ended up in a tuberculosis hospital at The Dalles, Oregon. She was healed and ready to come back but she got a blood clot in her leg and she died, and I was only 13 or 14 at the time. So actually we were a family that was being raised by a single dad and we laugh about it now. It was orphans raising orphans. We were very close and we depended on each other. We had to be a tightknit family.

I got sick in my junior year, entering into the senior year in high school, and managed to still stay in school and graduate out of high school, but I was still doing agricultural field work and at times clerking in the stores and ushering in the theater. And one day I went to work out in the field and I didn't quite make it. I got really sick again and the doctor just didn't give me any choices. He referred me a young attorney who needed a secretary and had no money, and we kind of made a deal—that he would train me and then I would work for him. It turned out to be a fairly good trade because he really did train me. The doctor told me that I could no longer work out in the fields, that agricultural work was just out of my life, that I had to find something else. And if it wasn't for his persistence I don't think I would have made the change, but he wouldn't take no for an answer.

This was in Vale, Oregon. Vale used to be a truly Western town. It used to be a town that catered to the cattlemen. The Vale Hotel was a meeting point for all of them. They had humongous rodeos. During the Fourth of July that town would just boom. It was the meeting place for a lot of the western people. I don't remember real painful times in Vale. We were one of I think only two Mexican families there, and the focus was not on us so very much. It was when other families started coming that people started focusing on the Mexican people. I think that when people started really coming more and more was maybe 1940, '41, '42. During the war years, during the time of the *braceros*, they imported a lot of Mexican people

In 1983 Governor Vic Atiyeh appointed Mary Thiel (third from left) to the state Commission on Hispanic Affairs. She served on the commission for eight years.

from Oaxaca. They imported a lot of what they call *braceros* from Mexico in the early forties to do the work while everybody was away at war. I supervised men out in those fields when they brought the Oaxaqueños to thin beets.

There used to be a lot of farm housing at that time. Farmers had houses for their crews. They weren't the best of houses but there was some kind of housing—there were little labor camps but the little labor camps were on farms, they weren't like big labor camps. There were labor camps at Nyssa and there were camps at Ontario and Payette, but not at Vale. A lot of little farm labor camps.

I thought Vale was booming more than Nyssa. And then Nyssa went through a booming stage, and then all of a sudden it died down, you know. But at one time there was a lot activity at Nyssa. In Nyssa I lived—well, it was before my mother died and a little bit after my mother died, so I lived in Nyssa probably around 1940-41. After I was married, I lived in Adrian, Oregon. There was more focus on the Mexican-American people and I felt the discrimination a lot more in Adrian. I remember being deeply hurt by things people said and did. I tried not to show that except that I'd go home and cry. But that's where I think the cultural shock happened to me.

In Adrian there was a labor camp. I wasn't working at that time so I held English classes at the Adrian labor camp. I asked them if they couldn't help me, loan me one of the rooms there, and we set up classes, we set up stores, we set up a doctor's office, we set up jails. We set up role-playing areas so that we could learn, we could teach them how to go and ask for services in the doctor's office. We taught them how to dial a telephone. A lot of people were afraid of phones because they didn't have them, it wasn't part of their life style, so they didn't know how to use them and we taught them how to use them. How to go buy their groceries and count their change. What their rights were. That they should ask for help so they would know how to work within the system.

So I had something going. And then the ministerial association wanted to do it, so I backed out and they took over, but they didn't do it for very long. I don't know what happened, they just didn't do it. So I just backed off on that score.

What I think that people don't realize was that migrants that come in from another country have no resources and suffer a lot. There was no food, no medical help. If you got sick, you died if it was a disease that would take your life. In fact, we lost three that way. They got sick and all you did was try to take care of them the best you could. We did go to a doctor. The doctors would tell you if you didn't have the money, they wouldn't take you. We did take a baby to a doctor with measles, and my mother didn't know how to bring the fever down and things of that nature, and the doctor turned her away. So she brought the baby back and it died that night. So, people just didn't have the resources that they have now.

One good thing that came out of it was you became good neighbors. If we had a little food and somebody next door to us didn't have any, we always shared, and they would share with us. There was a lot of sharing that went on. My mother would make maybe a big kettle of soup with one chicken and put everything in it, and then we'd take little bowls of it to the others. There was a lot of helping each other. You became a very good neighbor.

I'm Catholic and I think the churches were more involved in the people thing. The priests were more at your house, seeing how you were and how you were getting along. Even Monsignor Kaiser from Twin Falls would come with a blanket or so, wondering how you were. No matter how humble your house was, they'd stay and have a cup of coffee with you, or else, if you were eating, you would invite them, and it was more of a very comfortable, camaraderie kind of a thing, that just really helped you survive, I think. I have reflected a lot on the things that happened to me and how if it hadn't been for somebody, I'd have never made it, through sickness, through whatever, because there is always somebody there that believed in you maybe a little bit.

One who believed in me a lot was the principal of the Vale high school. His name was John Conway. I always thought I couldn't, and he always knew I could. Sometimes I got mad at him because he pushed me so hard, and he would ignore my anger and keep pushing. So I don't think you ever do anything alone. I always think that there is somebody, and your belief that there is a God, and your belief that no matter how tough times are for you that the only way it could go is up.

I've had a lot of wonderful people around me. My family. I think all of those things count for me, for me they count a lot. And yes, there is a lot of discrimination yet, there is. It is more sophisticated, more subtle, but it's there. I used to get so angry about it that I consumed myself with anger and fought it. And now my feelings are that it's just one more person to educate. They've got to know that I'm okay. And if I'm okay with myself that they need to be okay with themselves.

I feel that the culture is very, very important because it is your beginning. And it doesn't have to be your end. If you retain your culture, you're building some other things on that. And after all, you know, culture is your family, your country, your language, it's all the emotional, spiritual things of each one of us.

As far as my culture is concerned, I never think about it not fitting into my life. And the reason I don't is because I'm very traditional. But I know that there's different steps of assimilation. There's different steps of acculturation, that maybe I'm traditional but we don't all stay there. We go through different phases of acculturation. I can be a part of that transition, but when it comes to crunch and when it comes to my family, I always get very traditional. I always remember that I want my daughter not to seriously date until she's 16, and if my kids are sick I still fall apart and want to be with them, and all that.

My husband has never interfered with that. And fortunately he's Catholic, so that's no problem. The food—he loves the food. He doesn't care if I speak Spanish. He never tells me, "don't use that language." He encourages me to use it. So my family has not been a barrier.

But the cultural shock that I go through and went through was that my children were not as traditional as I was. That they would get mouthy, that once in a while the four-letter word would come out, and I almost died when I first heard it in my house. So, what I'm trying to say is that my cultural shock is watching my children transition into the Anglo culture and maybe not keep the values of the traditional Mexican

Mary Thiel at her home, 1995.

135

culture. I think that would be it. But being married to a blockheaded German who was born in the Dakotas has not been a barrier. For some reason he didn't bother about stopping me about this and that. He encourages me.

When I really got involved in working with Mexican people beyond the one-to-one favors that you do for people, was when I went to work for the Employment Division. And I knew that I would be gone from home, that I'd have to be involved in a lot of training and long hours away from home and what have you. So I discussed that with my husband. I didn't want him to say yes, I could do it, and then try to have him limit me. So he thought it over for about three days and he told me that if I wanted to do it, to go ahead. But he wanted me to make a commitment to do the best job possible for the people and not to take advantage of them and use my job as a way of my getting ahead for me personally. That if I wanted to focus on serving the people, that's what I needed to focus on, not on myself.

I asked him if he knew what he was saying, and he said, yes, that it meant that I'd be gone away from home and a lot of different things. So, basically I think that he freed me up to do a lot of things. The other thing is that I griped a lot, I griped about lack of education, I griped about lack of food, lack of housing. It seemed to me like I always had something that I was dealing with.

And you can't always just gripe, you have to be part of the solution.

ROSARIO MARTINEZ
Mexican, Adrian

I am Rosario Quintero Martinez. I was born in New Mexico in 1918 during World War I. My father was a miner and used to earn a good salary. I remember that we always had a fairly decent home and good cars. My mother never worked outside the home. I went to school in New Mexico the first year and then I went to Arizona. I didn't like the schools in Arizona because we were segregated. I went there until I was in about the sixth grade. All the Mexicans and blacks would go to school together, and the whites, the Anglos, would go to a separate school. This made me feel bad—inferior. When the Depression first started, we moved from Arizona and I was very happy to leave that place.

My husband and his cousin heard about beet thinning in Adrian and that you could make good money here. So he decided that he wanted to come. We had a little old car and that we had packed full of stuff. On the very top I had packed the ironing board. I had to take that with us because I didn't know how to iron without one. I just couldn't leave my ironing board. When we got here, it was late at night so we had to find an orchard to sleep in, in our car. My six-month-old woke early in the morning and wanted his bottle, but we didn't have any milk. We had to drive into Nyssa and find a restaurant that was open early in the morning so we could buy milk. After we went back and talked to the farm owner, we learned that the house he had promised us was occupied, so for the first couple of days we had to stay in the pump house. It was tiny and we had to sleep on the floor, but we had a little stove to cook on.

Here in Adrian we were treated very well because we adopted the Anglo way of life. We did this very quickly because there were no other Mexicans. We just adopted their ways, the Anglo ways. Now, in Nyssa I noticed that not all the Mexicans were welcome. I remembered that there were two places in Nyssa that had signs that said "No dogs and no Mexicans allowed." One of them was the smoke shop, the other one I don't remember. But I remember that when the Anglo people used to see the Mexicans, they used to turn their faces at them or make an ugly face towards them. I think it was the "Pastime"—the Pastime Tavern that had the other sign, and it said "No dogs or Mexicans allowed."

ARMANDO LAGUARDIA
Cuban
Educational Consultant, Assistant Professor, Portland

I was born in Cuba and grew up in Yaguajay. I lived in that town until I was 13 years old. Then in 1960, one year after the revolution, I moved to my grandmother's house in La Habana for two years while I waited for my application to leave the country to be processed. We had to evacuate our home, because the rebels bombed the town. Even before that—since 1955—there was a strong guerilla movement and warfare going on. Every night they would cut off the power and there would be shootings. I saw dead people when I was only 9 or 10. My parents didn't come to the United States until I was a junior in college and married.

Cuba is a strange place because it has a mix of Catholic and African religion. My parents were not very religious and didn't go to church very often, but if you had asked them they would have said they were Catholics but also believed in the Ifateria African religion. They had more religious traditions oriented toward the Ifa than toward the Catholic Church. Our big celebration was the Three Kings Day (Día de los Reyes). This is when we received presents—it was Christmas Day for us. This was cool because one of the kings was black, so it was like an identification thing for me as a kid. You would open your gifts very early on the sixth of January. We would go to church and eat a lot of traditional food. The family would get together to celebrate.

Before I came to the United States, I knew the system they had for Cuban refugees. I knew who I had to ask for in the airport. He was an agent of the American Welfare who would pick up all the kids under 18 and put them in a refugee camp outside of Miami. I went to a famous camp called Matacumbe. There were about 500 kids, and you had to stay there until

Armando Laguardia teaches at the Washington State University, Vancouver. He also has his own educational consulting business.

they found you a foster home somewhere in the country. When I came, I had in mind that I was only going to stay for six months because I thought Castro wasn't going to last.

I was sent to Portland with five other black Cuban kids, and I grew up here with a Cuban couple. The five of us kids went to the same home, but we were all strangers when we arrived. The parents of three of the children came and took them away from the foster home, and because it wasn't economically feasible to keep the home going anymore, the two of us who were left were sent to another home. I was in three foster homes before I finished high school. By the time I was 18 and finishing my senior year, they allowed me to move out on my own. I really wanted to get away from those foster homes, so I spent half of my senior year living on my own with a roommate and attending school.

I attended Cleveland High School because it was the only one with an ESL program in the city. After two years, the people at the foster home I was in transferred me to Jefferson and I graduated from there. I had a small, tight-knit group of friends, all of us good fighters who would protect one another. We all had paper routes to make money because we were all obsessed

with getting our parents out of Cuba. I never played sports because I had to go to work. Actually, one of my foster parents stole the money I had saved before they left town so I had to start all over again. I could never save all that money. My parents ended up getting out eight years later. Because my father was a doctor, they wouldn't let him leave. In Jefferson High School—I guess because I was a fairly nice kid—one of my counselors recommended me to a federal program that allowed me to attend Portland State University and Macalester College and got me started in my profession. I think that due to this counselor I am what I am today, because all the other guys who didn't go to school have been in the penitentiary and all the Cuban guys who came with me have had much rougher times than the ones who went to school.

However, there was also a woman English teacher at Jefferson High School who told me I shouldn't plan on going to college. She said, "You are not going anywhere." That was when I was trying to learn English. Usually I was a very good student and I was once elected student body president. That English teacher had told other people the same thing—even very intelligent students.

I got a bachelor's degree in romance languages and I have a master's degree in curriculum and instruction in education. Now I'm getting a doctorate in higher education administration from Portland State.

Teachers and counselors were interested in social action and were interested in changing the pattern of poor kids and minority or "colored kids" who had not been able to attend the University of Oregon. They motivated me and helped me get interested in the education profession, so my work there in Eugene, from the time I was a sophomore in college, involved being an assistant counselor, an assistant teacher in the High School Equivalency and Upper Bound programs. Eventually they had a whole career ladder within those programs. We actually ran the programs and learned our skills by working in them. We were getting paid. I was being paid for being a teacher at the time I was a sophomore. I taught math and English to migrant kids, mostly Chicano kids, all over the state and California. Eventually I went into counseling and was running my own counseling group in that program and in the Upper Bound one.

At the time I got to the University of Oregon, they had open discrimination in the fraternities and sororities. There were around fifteen black students in the whole school, and most of them were athletes. We spent our time there fighting a political battle in the institution to gain respect for the needs of the students of color.

MARIA LUISA BARAGLI DE BEVINGTON
Argentinian
Teacher at Lincoln High School, Portland

When I was a child in Argentina, we always lived with our grandparents, and we were always doing something in the kitchen. In winter time I would come back from school and my grandmother would be in the kitchen baking. As soon as I opened the door, I could smell what she was baking and feel the warmth at home. I was also close to my grandfather. He would come and pick me up from school and always had something in his pocket for me. He was Italian and loved the big ships, so we would go for walks from our house to the dock and watch the ships.

In 1962, when I was 13 years old, we moved to the United States. My father worked for Pan American in Buenos Aires and had several friends who had come to live in the States. It wasn't unusual for someone from Argentina to come to Miami, New York, or Los Angeles to stay, and because my father worked for the airline we could get tickets very cheap. By paying only $10 we could come to the States.

My mom was the one who wanted to make the change because she didn't see a very good future for us in Argentina. My parents had talked about it for some time, but my father didn't want to leave. A neighbor came to live in Portland and

Armando Laguardia (third from left, front), long an advocate for the Hispanic community, joins other Hispanic leaders for a 1980 noontime rally at Terry Schrunk Plaza in Portland. From left, Gail Castillo, Betty Andrews, Mr. Ramirez, Laguardia, José Calderon, Kay Toran, Vicente Garza, Luis Alvarez, Raul Soto, Sonny Montez, Lavar Gonzalez, José Romero, and Lina Garcia-Seabold.

would write to my father and ask him to come over. He said he would help him find a job. In those years, it wasn't too difficult to get your visa. If you had a good prospect for a job, there wouldn't be any problem at all.

My father, mother, eldest sister, and I moved to Portland, but my parents had in mind moving only for two years.

The first year was very difficult for me, mainly because of the language. My teacher gave me all Fs. No one taught me English—only a lady who was a speech therapist would sit with me in front of a mirror and would teach me how to move my mouth and where to put my tongue to get the correct sounds. The other thing I didn't like from that school was that there was a group of boys who were too violent. They knew that I didn't speak much English, and every time I would walk in front of them they would say things to me and swear all the time. I felt different from them and was different. I had long hair and did it in a certain way; my mother would sew my clothing, so it was completely different from what the other kids wore; my dad would come and pick me up from the parties or any other activity in school and we would walk home. Besides me, there were about five Greek girls in school, and I became friends with one of them. After forming this friendship, I started to feel better. She really helped me and my English improved a lot.

After a few months of living in an apartment, we moved. My mother was working already. My father worked only part time because he had problems with his English. A lady offered to share her house with us (this lady was very religious). I moved to another school and things were a lot better there. People were very nice. They even elected me as a candidate for a state girls' organization and I won. I had to prepare a speech, which I did with the help of a friend. My speech was about immigrants and their experiences.

When I was nineteen years old, I went back to Argentina on my own. All the family was waiting for me at the airport with big banners saying, "Welcome, Ana María." I stayed there for about three months. When I came back to Portland, I started studying at Portland State and working as well. The following year I went back to Argentina and got a job in the Avon factory in Buenos Aires as a bilingual secretary. I stayed there for about six months and decided to come back to the States and study. What worried me was that I had my parents in Portland and felt like I was cut in half. One half was in Argentina because I liked several things about it, and the other half was in Portland where my parents were.

However, I liked the people in Argentina. You meet people and they become your friends. They are always concerned about you and want to know how you are. They invite you out and you feel part of the group immediately. In Argentina, I could feel I had connections everywhere.

People here live more isolated lives. When you want to see people, you have to phone and make an appointment and they always have to check their calendars. Sometimes they can't see you until next week because they are already booked. In Argentina, even though people are busy or just leaving, they always have time for you.

I also like the neighborhoods in Argentina. In every neighborhood there is a coffee place, a park, an ice cream place where people gather. When I came back to Portland, I felt lonely here. I made friends, but they were all individual friendships. I got depressed very easily and I think it was due to the lack of "group" feeling. I felt that I didn't belong. Today I feel that I still don't have a group. I have lots of friends but each in their own world. Sometimes I try to get all of them together, but I find it difficult to do this.

Maria Luisa Baragli de Bevington

Now I am a teacher and there are several Hispanics in the school where I teach. Whereas I was discriminated against when I was in school, I think that now we have another problem. I think discrimination now could be due to the things that happened in the past with the students' parents. Maybe they were ashamed of being what they were, so the children are not proud of their culture and, as a consequence, do not work as they should in school. They miss class, don't do their work, don't take responsibility for what is important in order to progress in life. We also have discipline problems with them. We have to find a way to give them back their pride: pride in themselves, their history, and their families.

CELIA D. MARISCAL
Mexican
Juanita's Fine Foods, Hood River

My family came to Oregon in 1964 with about $200. In those days that was quite a lot of money. For us it was like a vacation. After we arrived in Hood River, my dad took off to visit orchard-owner friends. My mom said we were only staying a short time because my dad couldn't find work for us. No one wanted to employ such a large family—we were almost thirteen at that time, plus my mom and dad equals fifteen. At night we'd sleep in the orchards. It was so peaceful then and no one would bother you. You could sleep wherever and everyone was friendly. During the day we'd go to a park. We'd cook there and bathe in the river, but the water was very cold because it came from Mt. Hood. We did that for about a week and a half and then we found a man who had a two-story house where we could stay. The only thing available was the green bean harvest, which paid in cash daily. We loved it because our family had never worked out in the fields. We went one day and we made lots of money with the whole family. That evening we went to the store and bought chicken and vegetables and my mom fixed us a good dinner. We were real happy but we still wanted to go back to California.

One day my mom went to the "welfare office" to see if they'd help us with money to return to California. They said yes, to come back the next day and they'd give us the money. However, at that time my dad found work year round. My mom and dad must have discussed it while we were sleeping, because the next day they asked us kids and we all said yes and then no. During this time, my mom called my godmother in our home town in California, and she told my mom that there had been an earthquake and that our house had been completely destroyed. So we stayed in Oregon in the same house for about three years. Then my dad wanted to move because there really wasn't year-round work for him but he had to be "on-call" because we had free housing. So, my dad heard about a couple that needed a foreman for year-round work. Apparently the previous foreman had been stealing a lot of fruit from these orchards and this couple was looking for a better manager. The owners also provided us with a house that had lights, water, everything. The whole family was included in the decision making at all times, so when my dad asked what we thought we all said yes. Everyone was very friendly. We easily made friends with other schoolmates and we were happy. Actually, we were the only Mexican family in this whole valley. Later another family, the Ibarras, came. So we stayed and there were only two families here, us and the Ibarras.

My mom and dad went to work. When the harvest was on, my dad was the foreman; at other times he'd drive tractor, and during the harvest my mom would pick fruit. Mom always loved working outside. At night she'd go to work in the packing warehouse. During the day I was in school, but at night I'd take care of the family because I was the oldest. My mom always worked very hard and long hours. By the age of 16, I was a little more advanced than my classmates and much more mature (maybe being the oldest in the family contributed to this). So then I decided I didn't want to continue in school. I spoke with my counselor and told her I wanted to work in an office. My dad

never liked for us to work in the fields. So she said I could try for my GED. I passed my GED at 16, and my counselor got me a secretarial job with the Forest Service. I worked there about two years, and when I turned 18 they offered me a job as a manager of an office because I was bilingual at a time when there was a large influx of *braceros* who had no one to help them. As manager of this office, I also worked with the police, lawyers, and doctors in the valley whenever they needed me to interpret.

As time passed, the rest of my siblings grew up and began to graduate from school. The first one was Luís, who always loved school. He was very popular and was student body president. He is now the president of our company.

I was the first of my family to marry. I married Santos Mariscal, who is from Mexico. My brother Gonzalo was next; he married when he was 16, too young. I was 21 years old when I married. Then the others started to marry. My sister Virginia was next. In that year there were three of us that got married. José became manager of the Chevron station, and Alfonso worked for him.

Family members who work in Juanita's Fine Foods include (from left) Gracy Viramontes, Joe B. Dominguez, Maggie Ybarra, Christy Weekly, Celia D. Mariscal, Luís B. Dominguez, Juanita Dominguez (for whom Juanita's is named, holding a picture of her late husband Antonio C. Dominguez), Gonzalo B. Dominguez, Rosemary Serrano, Rey B. Dominguez, Carmen Vandenbos, and Virginia Kirby. Not pictured are Al B. Dominguez, Fred B. Dominguez, and Lena Herrera.

We kept on growing and I had my first son, Julián. Then I went to work at the Rehabilitation Center, working with the retarded.

In time, my brothers and sisters got together and discussed the possibility of starting our own business. My mom had always dreamed of owning her own business. She'd worked in Blythe, California in a tortilla factory owned by my godmother, Luz Rodríguez. However, I didn't have any savings since I had just purchased my home and the rest of the family had very little money saved either. My brother Gonzalo was in the service and we all decided that we just didn't have the money for a business.

We discussed our business for a year or two until we finally decided to go ahead and see how we'd do. In 1969 we opened a small place on 12th Street in Hood River (it was only 20 feet x 10 feet) and bought a very small machine on the installment plan. During the day we'd all work at our jobs and at night we'd work in the tortilla factory. I was pregnant at the time and I had to quit my job, so I started to do baby sitting during the day. At night we made our tortillas—about 30 boxes. Since I was the only one who didn't work during the day I would take the tortillas out to the stores to try and sell them. At that time the only competition was Reser's (another tortilla factory). Nightly we worked until about 10:30 or 11:00. In time, as we kept selling, we'd run out of *masa* (corn tortilla mix) and my brother would go to California in a van to buy it so we could make more tortillas. They'd bring about 30 to 50 sacks and we'd have enough for a whole month. The first year our profit was about $2,000. We didn't know about business or commercial dealings. Luís (who owned a store) was the only one, but the rest of us didn't know a thing. For us, $2,000 profit was good.

The second year was better. We sold more to the workers. By the third year we all had to quit our day jobs and moved from the 12th Street location into a larger place that my brother Luís found. We all decided to buy the place, and if the business didn't prosper we'd all pay the difference out of our own pockets. After three years, we moved again. We bought a place like a large garage and for us it was an immense place. We bought a larger tortilla machine. We used to pack and count our tortillas by hand. After a while we had to order our *masa* by the truckload, a semi would come and deliver to us on a monthly basis. We kept on making more tortillas as the demand grew. We also started spreading out further with our sales. From Hood River, we went to Portland, from Portland to Salem, and we kept branching out.

Luís was the president of our company, so his job was to go out and find new stores for us to sell to. One Albertson's nearby would ask him why he didn't go to Albertson's in Portland, and the Albertson's in Portland would tell him to go to the Albertson's in Salem. So that is how we kept on going further and further out. Then since he was already in Salem, he'd go and call on other stores in that area and that's how we kept

growing. After about five years we needed an even bigger place so we had to move and expand again. This time we moved to Industrial Street. There the cannery rented out a bigger place to us. Here we decided to make flour (wheat) tortillas. We bought another machine to make these flour tortillas, so now we had two machines. We made tortillas all day, all of us. Now we all had to leave any other jobs we had in order to work in the tortilla factory. Luís was always on his own, or rather, he had free time because he was the owner of his own store. José and my mom were the next to come on full time at the factory. We also hired a few employees. By the time we moved from Industrial Street, the demand for tortillas was so great we were delivering very far. With more workers coming into the area, the demand was immense. This happened within two to three years. My brothers and sisters started to question why we didn't make tortillas for other companies. Now we were working eighteen to twenty hours daily. I now had only three to four hours to sleep, shower, and go right back to the tortilla factory.

My brothers-in-law have always been supportive of my sisters, and my husband really helped me out. Daily he'd pick up the children at day care, feed them, and put them to bed. I had a sitter that came into our home so she'd take care of the baths the next day. This sitter really helped me out with my family. Now we were so busy that we had to have a day and night shift at work. We had a five-year lease on this place with the option of buying. We realized that this place was adequate for us because now the semis were delivering to us two times a week. We started having more business and now we started making "chips;" we now had the machinery to make chips.

About two years later we suffered a fire at the tortilla factory. This was publicized all over on radio, TV, and newspapers. It wasn't really a big fire. What happened was that the oil used in making the chips caught fire. Thank God no one was hurt, and none of the machinery was lost.

Oh, we had a lot of work cleaning up the place. You know, it was the day before New Year's and we had many festive plans but we had to scratch the *fiestas* and do the cleaning. We asked our employees if they would help. It wasn't mandatory but everyone pitched in and we got it all cleaned up so we could open up the next day. We were so lucky. Not even our supplies were damaged. Actually, it was a matter of cleaning up all the water used in putting out the fire. So we went on making tortillas and making chips. Now we decided that this place was really too small. It was too difficult for the semis to make their deliveries. They had to go through town and this was difficult for them. We knew of a place that was for sale but we doubted we could actually buy it. The next year was very profitable for us; we made a lot of money. Now, after about nine or ten years, we were making about $4 million a year. I guess we bought this place for over half a million dollars. We've been here three years and the value is now at least a million dollars—that's what it's appraised at. Of course, now we have adequate machinery: we have three machines for corn tortillas, two for flour and chips. Right now we're the biggest factory in the Pacific Northwest and in the nation. We also deliver and sell canned goods imported from Mexico. We have a huge warehouse for storage. I believe this location is where we'll stay. I live across the street. We're comfortable here and it's adequate for our company. Most of our family lives around here. One of my sisters lives in Hood River.

We haven't had any negative response from our community. As a matter of fact, someone is always looking out for us. If it's off hours and someone is here, they'll call me and let me know. They help us watch our business. Now we employ sixty people. This includes our truck drivers. We have three semis that go out daily to four states: Montana, Washington, Oregon, and Iowa. I hear that even in Kansas our tortilla sells. This could be because we sell to many private wholesalers so they buy our products and we don't know where they sell them. So they could go anywhere. We have an agreement with Juanita's in California (they sell *menudo* and other products)—they don't sell tortillas in Oregon and we don't sell them in California. We do sell their other products here. Now someone told us they saw our products, a bag of *chicharrones* (thick, crisp fried pork skin) in California, but again, we sell to others and they sell on their private label, like Safeway and others.

We employ workers year round, and we pay good wages. We're always looking for ways to better conditions for our workers. Right now, we're looking into insurance benefits for our workers. We're exploring different companies, different packages. We realize that our employees are important to our company. Without them we just couldn't do it all.

Being a Mexican-American woman has enabled me to do anything an Anglo woman can do, but in some ways more, because a Mexican-American woman relates to her grandparents and ancestors. We don't live our lives in the "fast lane," which enables us to live healthier. We are very close to Our Lady of Guadalupe through our religion, and we believe that She helps us throughout our lives. Being Mexican or Mexican American does not keep a woman from being whatever she desires. She doesn't have to be dependent on a man but can be successful on her own. Here in our company my brothers respect my decisions because I am the oldest. They don't treat me with any less value because I'm a woman.

ANA OLARIZ DE MORGAN
Mexican, Medford

My name is Ana Olariz de Morgan and I was born in 1917 in Morelia, Michoacán. We migrated to the U.S. when I was age 5—to Santa Ana, California. Religious wars in Mexico brought the family to the U.S. on a train. I began my education in Santa Ana Catholic and public schools. I was married on

Ana Olariz de Morgan

February 3, 1943, and we moved to Medford because my husband wanted to fish. We made one trip over to Medford so I could see the valley, and although it was beautiful I guess my heart was still in California.

As a little girl I grew up among the orange, lemon, walnut, and avocado groves. California was so beautiful then—not crowded. I still have a soft spot for California to this day. But when your husband says "I go," you follow. We moved here December 3, 1943. It was very cold. My husband had built a 24-foot trailer, and we moved everything we owned in that trailer. We had a 1936 Studebaker with which we pulled that trailer. I felt I was in heaven with that car.

We arrived here very late in the evening. Highway 99 had a service station on the outskirts of Medford. My husband asked the service station attendant if we could put up a tent for the night close by. The attendant said sure, and even though it was very cold we were quite comfortable in our little tent. The next day we went to my sister-in-law's. We stayed for two weeks before we could rent a cabin in what was a housing project for soldiers during the war. The project was empty at this time and the cabins were rented to people who needed them. We were there for some time, and then we bought a little house. We opened up a Signal Oil service station. We sold gas, my husband serviced and overhauled cars, and I helped him out at the station daily. We were always busy but we just weren't making enough money.

Five years later my husband came to me to tell me he was going into the logging business with one of our customers, and I said I was going back to California—if he wanted to stay here and get killed, okay, but I was going back. He didn't know a thing about the woods or logging. The customer, Mr. Provost, and my husband founded the company Morgan and Provost, and in 1948 they started logging. We borrowed money on the house and sold 300 acres of virgin timber. We had a bulldozer and Mr. Provost put up the rest of the money. We bought a cabin just below Wolf Creek at a place called Bald Ridge, about 4,000 feet high. We were up so high you could see for miles, all of the Medford area. I had everything I needed at the cabin, but every Saturday we'd come into Medford to buy groceries for the following week and to do the laundry.

When we first came to Medford, I never saw any Hispanic faces—not until the early 1970s. Then I became acquainted with Felípe and Elizabeth Reyes. We visited and my husband enjoyed their company. When Elizabeth was going to give birth to her second child, I went to the hospital to interpret for her. No, I never saw any Hispanics and if any black people came to town they were not allowed to spend the night. That was horrible. It was sad. I had a friend, Mary Kelly, who was a newspaper reporter up north, and she used to tell us about the Ku Klux Klan here in Jackson County and how they hated Catholics. I never encountered any negative response personally, but since the age of 12 I've always been in the environment of the white culture. I never had a problem in the malls, stores, or anywhere.

When we first came to Oregon, I looked for the Catholic Church. I bought this house and my husband knew why—because it was so close to the church. I felt at home in Oregon when I saw the beautiful church. My friend used to call me "Little Orphan Annie," but I didn't mind. I had peace in my heart because of my strong faith.

My children went to St. Mary's Academy, and I was involved in Altar Society and participated in their luncheons and worked in their rummage sales. When my son was an infant, I used to take him over to the convent and show him to the sisters and tell them that one of these years he was going to school there and to save him a corner in one of the classrooms. I told them my husband wasn't Catholic but I wanted my son in Catholic school. My husband wanted to know about cost, and I told him it would cost whatever he could give. What I did was save a little from our grocery money and use it to pay the tuition. I paid $74 a year—I managed that every year.

I felt my place was with my children when they came home from school. The cookie jar was always full and their friends always came over. My husband traveled, so I was always home for the children. After my husband died, I went to work at Providence Hospital. I volunteered for eight years at the information desk. For the church, I ministered to the elderly—took them communion or whatever they needed. Sister Mary would get the names for me. It's just wonderful, it's very rewarding,

Elizabeth and Felipe Reyes, Medford

it's a pleasure to be of service. You know, I don't feel my life story is very interesting but it has been a good life for me.

ROSARIO SALAZAR-COLLET
Bolivian
Pathologist's Assistant, Clackamas

The year I graduated (this was the late 1960s) there was a big revolution in my country. We had revolutions almost every year. Because of the revolution, they closed the university. This would happen constantly because we had a lot of changes of governments in these years. My older brother was given a chance by my mom's brother, who was a doctor here, to come to the States and live with him and my aunt in West Virginia. He offered to pay for the tickets and support my brother, but he wasn't interested in leaving the country at that time. I think one reason was that at that time, in Bolivia, people didn't like the "Yankees." They had the idea that they were taking over the world.

I remember I travelled in July and it was very hot and humid and I was wearing a coat. At the airport I saw my cousins were not wearing any shoes and were wearing hardly any clothes. I didn't get a very good impression, because I was so conservative and in Bolivia it is just not proper not to wear shoes when you go outside the house.

After I arrived in Virginia, I went to a Catholic school—St. Joseph—and then I went to Marshall University the next fall. I wasn't happy with my English so I decided to stop speaking Spanish, and in three months—with the help of a nun who was an English teacher in the high school—I learned to speak English.

Living with another family, even though they were relatives, wasn't easy. I didn't really know them as I had not met them until I came here. It was very hard to get adjusted. I only have my sister here in Portland. She lived with us while she went to her junior and senior years and went to Portland State and now she is attending graduate school. She is going to be a math teacher. I have two children, who are learning to speak Spanish. My son spent two months in Bolivia when he was four years old and really learned to speak Spanish. We go back every other year. When we are there, he is pretty fluent, but when we come back he has a harder time but he understands a lot. I always pray in Spanish.

I know there are families left that have the same values that we do and they want their children to be raised just right, be able to have a close family. I also think that we have a lot of children coming from broken families. I hear my son saying, "So and so has to spend the weekend with her mother or with her father" or "they are going to visit their dad this summer because they haven't seen him for months," and it is very tough.

CRISTINA DE LA CRUZ VENDRELL
Mexican, Nyssa

I was born in Juárez, Mexico on December 15, 1912. When I was three months old, my family left Mexico and moved to El Paso, Texas. I was one of four children. We lived in many places, including Las Vegas, Nevada and Ogden, Utah. I attended public school in Las Vegas, Nevada. I started first grade when I was almost ten years old and completed the ninth grade at the age of seventeen. My late husband, Mr. Luís H. Vendrell, was born in León, Mexico, on June 21, 1906. Luís and his mother came to the United States when he was about twelve years old in order to escape the Mexican Revolution. After several years they returned to Mexico. When Luís was sixteen they were recruited by the sugar factory in Idaho Falls to thin and haul sugar beets. I met Luís in Idaho Falls in 1931, and we were married in Blackfoot, Idaho, in 1932. Besides farm labor, Luís worked in the copper mines in Bingham, Utah. He also worked as a high-scaler in the construction of Hoover Dam. Luís and I came to live in Nyssa in 1944 with our five children: Oralia, Luís Jr., Marsela, Christina, and Virginia. The last of our eight children—Rosa, Rudolf, and Dolores—were born in Nyssa.

Luís first worked as a farm laborer in Nyssa. He was then hired by the sugar company in Nyssa to recruit Mexican farm laborers from many states in the U.S. and from the northern state of Mexico. Later, he was hired as a labor dispatcher by the Oregon State Employment Division. Luís was the contact between employers and farm laborers. The employers consisted of the area farmers, who would contact Luís requesting a specific number of farm laborers for a diversity of farm labor jobs. Or Luís would contact the employers on behalf of the farm

laborers seeking employment. For many years Luís also organized Mexican-American fire-fighting crews for the Bureau of Land Management.

Luís volunteered his service as an interpreter whenever someone needed assistance. He would interpret for medical appointments, banking negotiations, and purchasing of insurance, automobiles, and homes. Luís would help people study for citizenship and the Oregon driver's license by translating the study manuals and questioning them about the material. He also served as an interpreter during many court trials for an individual, a lawyer, or the court itself. Luís was a self-educated man. He retired from the Oregon State Employment Service in 1971 but continued to help anyone whenever the need arose. I dedicated myself to being a housewife and raising our eight children.

After all our children were grown and on their own, I worked at a packing shed. Then I worked at the Extension Service in the nutritional division. I would make home visits and take a history of the family's eating habits. My job involved advising families what foods they should eat, what they should add to their diets to make them well balanced, and how to prepare a variety of recipes in their homes. Later I worked with the Health Division of the Extension Service making home visits and recording medical histories and medical needs. When I found individuals with medical problems, I would refer them to a doctor. I would assist with transportation and interpreting services. After retiring, I volunteered my services for several years, driving and interpreting for the state Welfare Department.

In 1953 I was instrumental in organizing the *Siempre Adelante* (Always Forward) organization. It started because a white boy ran over Jimmy Mares near an overpass. The boy had said that he was going to kill a Mexican that night and he did. They didn't press any charges against him. They didn't even keep him in jail. He had been drinking, and he was driving real fast. It was so terrible: half of Jimmy Mares' body was left where the underpass begins and the other half was way off by the lower part of the underpass. That's why we started the *Siempre Adelante*—so that the people, the Mexican people in the community, could get together and ask for justice. This organization continued to function until the late 1970s and provided cohesiveness within the Mexican community of Nyssa. It was an organization that fortified pride in our heritage and in our hopes for the future. *Siempre Adelante* held dances that served as fund raisers and social events. We are proud that for many years the organization granted scholarships for students of Mexican descent who were graduating from Nyssa High School. Luís and I were also members of the PTA board. Luís belonged to other organizations such as Knights of Columbus and Kiwanis. He served as a member of the Oregon State Migrant Advisory Board and in the Oregon Human Development organization. Our children attended Nyssa public schools. Oralia is working at the Nyssa Memorial Hospital in the nursing field. Luís Jr. is employed as a high school counselor in

Cristina de la Cruz Vendrell (seated) with daughters Oralia (left) Christina, and great-grandson John.

Nampa, Idaho. Marsela is working as a secretary at the Veterans Administration Hospital in Boise, Idaho. Christina Mejia is employed by the Nyssa school district as a third-grade teacher. Virginia Barientos lives in Texas and is raising her family of seven children. Rudolf Vendrell is teaching and coaching in Newburg, Oregon. Dolores Cornwell is employed by GI Joe's in Portland, Oregon. My husband passed away July 19, 1981.

ROGER IPARRAGUIRRE
Peruvian
Businessman, North Bend

I was born in Peru in a small town with a population of about 3,000. We left Peru because the government took our land and that's all we had. Almost all my brothers and sisters came to the States. This was in 1974, when the government started to confiscate lands.

When the government took our land we were left with nothing. All we could do was talk with my brother, who was living in the States already, to see what chance there was we could join him. My brother came to the States, Los Angeles, with the intention of studying medicine, but he never did. He fell in love at work, married an Oregonian, and moved north to Coos Bay.

We arrived in Coos Bay in 1978. I came with my wife and our three children who were eight, seven, and three years old. The move was really hard for us, especially for me as I wasn't used to hard work. I started working for the Toyota dealership, washing cars, and got paid $2.45 an hour. I worked there for about two or three months. Afterwards, a lady friend, who spoke some Spanish, found me a job as janitor in a high school and then I started making $5.00 an hour. After a few months of this, my brother found me a job in a lumber mill and I got paid $8.00 an hour. After a couple of days of hard work, I wanted to go back home—it was too hard and I was in pain. Tired as I was, I was also aware that when you decide to come here, you come ready to work and try to succeed. I didn't last too long in this job at the lumber mill because it closed down, but I was one of the last workers that they let go before they closed. After this I decided to go to school to study electronics. I went to a community college for two years and earned two degrees in electronics, finishing in 1983. I worked while I studied.

My wife found a part-time job as an assistant in the school of the First Presbyterian Church. She also had a job helping a woman in a second-hand clothing store. This helped a lot. My kids also helped by delivering papers. Now my wife provides child care in our home. She has between ten and twelve children per day and teaches them Spanish as well.

After I finished school, I started fixing television sets and afterwards I found a job in a fishing company fixing electronic equipment. I guess I have been lucky because I still receive equipment to be fixed from different parts of the States and Canada. After the fishing company closed down, I started working with satellites. I started with my brother-in-law with computers at home. Then we rented a place and started our business. Then I had a chance to buy this satellite business, so by then we had two businesses—computers and satellites. Business is going well now. I have bought some land in a business area that is expanding and I am planning to build a club—a high class club.

In Coos Bay I made good friends from the beginning. At first, it was very difficult, partly because of the food: very different, but you learn and get used to it. One thing I missed was getting together with family and friends. When we get together in Peru, we dance, sing, and make jokes. but I find that we can't do that here, because people's way of thinking is completely different. I continue having my Latin way of thinking, so I don't get too involved with the American culture. It is difficult for me to adapt, but my wife did really fast. She likes the American music and everything. However, we still celebrate birthdays, Christmas, Mother's Day like in Peru.

When we came I only spoke a little English. In Peru I had had a teacher who was always telling me that I was going to regret not doing well in English class, and my answer was "Why, if I am never going to go the United States?" and he would say, "You never know." When I moved to Oregon, I went to college to take English classes for about six months. Now my English is not bad, but I still have a lot of problems with pronunciation.

All my children are bilingual; we speak Spanish at home. One of them is 24 years old. He is studying to be a lawyer. My daughter is studying international business administration. The last one is 11 years old and is going to junior high school. We Latins believe in the family unit and I don't see it here. We find that our children have a lot of friends who have a lot of problems, and their parents don't want to help them.

ALBERTO MIRANDA
Costa Rican,
Custom Roasting, Eugene

I came from San José, Costa Rica, which at the time was a small town where everybody knew one another. My father belonged to a family that had been in the coffee business for three or four generations. My parents died when I was only seven, and after that I lived in various places—mainly with my sisters and my grandmother. I went to public school and have very good memories of those years.

I played sports at school and worked in a pickle factory. I started working there peeling vegetables, then I was able to cook, and finally I was allowed to do all the other procedures.

I went to university, and during that time I also worked and was a runner for the university, competing in the 1,800 meter. I had only about two trimesters to go when I found a job in a big hydroelectric project in the north of the country.

I came to Oregon in 1979. I traveled on a tourist visa, but after talking with some people I was able to register for classes at the university.

Later, I found a job cooking in a restaurant. I worked in restaurants for some time while I studied. At one of those restaurants I met my wife, Rosemary, who is a teacher. The day we were married, I was roasting coffee for my coffee company. I stopped work, got married, and came back to finish the roasting. I had told Rosemary that if I finished, we would go to the coast for our honeymoon for a couple of days, but I didn't finish the roasting that day. My coffee roaster was too small, and the orders had started to increase. That was the first limitation I had because of the business, but she understood. Later, when I finished roasting the coffee, we went on our honeymoon.

The coffee business has been good and has produced good income. Of course you have good days and bad days—that is part of the risk. We experienced growth for the first eight years. One time we had a bad day that turned into a bad month and then into a bad year, but that time is past. Now we have ten employees and a small diversified company.

We import coffee from producers and also trade it through brokers in various ports—San Francisco, New Orleans, New York. We can sell coffee in its different stages. Sometimes we distribute it to other roasters as well. And our business is not just coffee; we have a restaurant, milk products, olive oil, and different teas.

Alberto Miranda at his coffee roasting business in Eugene.

What I achieved, I achieved on my own. There are certain levels of indifference to foreign vendors here. Just as there once was indifference toward the Japanese and the Germans, Hispanic vendors also face barriers. This is a sole proprietorship, but I have a group of people who have worked for me for several years. We are in a very competitive market, but we are not afraid of competitors.

CATALINA TRUJILLO
Mexican, Salem

My father and a friend came up from Mexico looking for work and ended up in Corvallis, Oregon. My mother stayed in Mexico, because she had a young baby. The baby died on the way up from Mexico. I was born in Oregon and my brothers and sisters were born here, too. My folks spoke Spanish, and most of us learned some of it, but at the time we were with other kids and wanted to speak more English than Spanish. We were speaking English to our parents, but they would answer us in Spanish—it got kind of complicated sometimes. My mother used to bawl us out in Spanish, but none of us really understood Spanish very well, so none of us really understood everything she was talking about.

I had problems academically because my parents didn't read or write English. I had a hard time because in the beginning I couldn't read myself. Later, I had a girlfriend who helped me with some of my classes and explained things to me. When I got to high school, things were different. I was able to read and write. Then I could write letters for my folks.

It was kind of hard in grade school because of the fact that we were the only Mexicans there. I don't remember ever not having friends but at times you do feel as if they didn't like you or something like that. But other than that, I don't remember ever having a big problem of not having friends. They were always asking me why I was a different color. But there were some who were really nice, and of course there were some who would tease me but I'd tease back so there was never any hardship. Of course when I got into high school, well, then I never had any trouble because by that time the kids already knew about our background and being Mexican and stuff like that. One time when I was younger, they would tease us and they thought that we were Negroes because they had never seen Mexicans. One little kid used to joke around and call me "Cadillac," so I says, "Okay, Chevrolet, how are you?" I didn't feel like I was out of place, just once in a while I would think something but I didn't let it get me down.

When my father worked for the railroad, we were crammed into a "railroad house." They would take railroad cars and set them down and they would be our homes. Of course we didn't have any electricity or anything like that. We had kerosene stoves, and we had to heat water on the wood stove. My mother would give us baths in a big old laundry tub. We used to have to take turns, and it was a hassle because there were seven of us. We had a garden near the river, and I can remember my parents growing vegetables using water from the river. My father was a great one for doing a lot of chores. He was great at gardening, and we raised chickens. My father was also the midwife for my mother. He delivered us all—no problems there.

My father was a musician and used to love to play the mandolin and violin. He made most of his instruments. He made a really beautiful violin and a mandolin, and he could play anything. He always had friends over who had guitars, and the house was always cheerful. Of course we had no t. v. and radios were very rare, so it was mostly people coming over and just sitting and visiting and singing in Spanish.

We were kept well fed. Of course my mother would make tortillas every day, and we'd eat beans. That was our main staple. We had a lot of chicken, because we raised them, and a friend who had a cow supplied us with milk. There was no store nearby, so when we needed groceries we would send an order to Albany and they would bring them to us by railroad. They would stop the boxcars and unload our groceries, and of course the engineers would always throw us candy and stuff like that. We enjoyed being out in the country, where we could go swimming anytime.

When my father left the railroad, we moved back to Toledo and bought a house. He worked for a lumber mill there.

CARLOS E. CAMUS
Chilean
Carlos Shoe Service, Portland

Life in Chile is so different from the one you live in the United States. Here I have everything I want. You only need to be a hard worker and that's all you need and then you can treat yourself to anything you want. This is what I still do, even now that I am 68 years old.

I arrived in the winter. For about three weeks I was without a job and desperate because I didn't speak very good English. The English I spoke was what I learned in the Chilean Air Force. I didn't really know what kind of job I could get so I went to the air base. I got to the airport at 5:00 in the morning and asked for the "chief," who happened to be a colonel. I was told he arrived at 9:00 a.m. and I decided to wait for him. When the colonel arrived, he was told that I had been waiting since 5:00 a.m. I spoke with him about my problem and here is when the American heart comes into play. I let them know about my desire to work in this country to be able to bring my family. This is what I told him and he was interested in helping me. He introduced me to a person who gave me employment and this is when my life started.

This man was the manager of the shoe repair shop in Meier & Frank. He had someone in the shop who spoke Spanish. This person happened to be from Chile as well, and through him we could communicate. He told me that the manager wanted to know if I was willing to do any kind of work that was needed in the shoe shop. Of course I said yes, I would do anything necessary. I also worked as a dance teacher in a studio. I wanted to make more money so through one of my dance students (who worked at a machine shop) I met her manager and he offered me a job in the machine shop. I also went to the Fred Astair Studio to look for a job, so by this time I had four jobs: Meier & Frank, Fred Astair, Arthur Murray, and the machine shop.

I haven't had any financial difficulty since then. I am amazed at how the people here in Portland have helped me in so many ways. I think you have to be honest and show them that you are a hard worker. These are the things that count here and I am sure that if they see this in you, they will do their best to help you. I say this because I have experienced it. I consider that I have been very lucky.

I have been married for forty-one years. I have three children, two boys—forty-three and thirty-nine—and my daughter who is thirty-one years old. The eldest is an inspector for Boeing and works in Seattle; the second is a territorial manager for Pacific Steel. He travels a lot but works here in Portland. My daughter is an actress and now wants to go to New York because she has just been offered a contract there.

FRANCISCA GARCIA
Mexican, Woodburn

I only went to the fifth grade in Texas, but once I got to the fifth grade—since I'm the oldest one in my family—my parents told me that I had to quit school and start helping out. So I got jobs doing housekeeping for different families and I was no longer allowed to go to school. You know, I really loved school. I wish I could have gone on, but my parents said no. I used to make $1.50 for a whole week of house cleaning. My father thought that was a lot of money, because he was only paid a dollar a day, which was about $7 a week. So of course my father was very happy because that was like a day and a half worth of work for him and we were a large family so it really helped us—even the $1.50 helped.

When we lived in a labor camp, we all saw ourselves as a large family, an extended family. We all looked out for one another. At that time you knew who your neighbors were. You could leave your children alone and the other people in the camp would look out for them, and you trusted them. When you went your separate ways, you missed one another. One family would miss another family they had gotten to know. Today you can't leave an 11-year-old as a baby sitter. My daughter was 11 and I would leave her with the little ones. I didn't have to mistrust anyone, because everyone looked out for the other families. Oh, we used to have celebrations of birthdays for the other people that lived there. The children used to have

Carlos Camus mans the counter at his shoe repair shop in west Portland. A photograph of his daughter hangs on the wall (right).

religious celebrations, like their first communion, confirmation, things like that. The first Quinceañera that I remember that was celebrated was my daughter Lupe's. We celebrated that at the camp. I made a huge dinner and all our neighbors who lived in the camps came by and congratulated her. We all had a good time, but the best one that I remember was my daughter Concha's. Because that was celebrated here at the church in Woodburn. Now that was very, very nice.

In about the 1960s we were the first family to buy our home here in Woodburn. After that they started closing the camps, and then people had to start buying or renting. We had a friend who was working for a real estate agency who helped us a lot. He was the one who told us that this house was for sale and helped us do the paperwork so we could get it. We paid $5,000 and I used to make monthly payments of $35. At the time I thought it was a lot of money, but still we finished paying for it.

I think that my children saw themselves as being Anglo. I remember that during the time when the Hispanics would start migrating back to their home towns or to other states, they would come home and say, "Mom, the Mexicans are leaving," and pretty soon when the migration would start returning they'd say, "Oh, it's about time that the Mexicans would start coming." I would sometimes ask them, "What do you think you are? Are you Mexican or are you Anglo?" And they would say, "Well, we're Anglo," and I would have to remind them that no you are not, you are Mexican. They would say, well, "Yeah, we're Mexicans, but we're the other kind." I guess at that time they thought that they were better than the Mexican population. But later on, as they became more educated, they realized that they weren't. They just had had better opportunities, and maybe more experiences. When my children were in school their Anglo teachers shortened their names, or spoke their names in English, like Francisco became Frank, Concepción became Connie, María Guadalupe became Mary. So after my children graduated they wanted to know why they didn't go by their given Spanish names, so they started using their names in Spanish. Like Francisco was no longer Frank, and Concepción was no longer Connie, María was no longer Mary.

When my daughter Lupe started working, she helped us a lot financially. She was one of the first Hispanic employees here in Woodburn. She worked part time at Ben Franklin, a five and dime store, and at the bank. Many times when she was working at Ben Franklin, they would call her from the bank when they had somebody who didn't speak English. She was always going from one business to another to interpret.

When my daughter was working for Ben Franklin, the Chamber of Commerce approached her and asked her for ideas on how they could thank the Hispanic community for helping with all the harvests. She suggested that they have a *fiesta*—that was one way that they could show their appreciation to the Hispanic community. This took place around 1964. They formed committees, they got together, they would have meetings, and she started telling them what they could do, what the *fiesta* meant, activities that could take place, so the *fiestas* got started. The *fiesta* consisted of a parade, booths, and Mexican music. Some of the Hispanic community that was involved on the committees had their children come out in the parade, ride the floats. The Anglo community wanted our booths to be food booths so that's what we had. We set them up behind the pharmacy, the Rexall Pharmacy. We had about twelve booths; I even had a booth. I had a taco booth and that's all I sold was just tacos. Every booth was going to donate a certain percentage to our church—the Catholic church here in Woodburn.

Next to my booth was a tamale booth, and there was an Anglo gentleman who had always wanted to taste the real authentic tamale. He had always bought the canned tamale, which comes wrapped in paper. Well, this man bought himself a tamale and he started to eat it and he couldn't figure it out, he didn't like the taste. He couldn't really chew through it. Finally I looked at him. He was trying to eat the tamale with the corn husk still on! So, I had to show him that you have to peel off the corn husk and eat the center. Oh, he loved them. He said, "I'll never go back to eating canned tamales again; the canned tamales have no taste—now, these taste good."

In 1965 the Saldaña family got involved and they took over, making the *fiesta*. It was over very early because all we had was the parade and the food booths. The Anglo community really liked it, and since then we went on having a *fiesta* every year. To this day, twenty-eight years later, we still only have thirteen committee members. We are always looking for good committee members. The *fiestas* today are much nicer, and much larger. We have so many people come; we have so many booths. The money that we make from the *fiesta*—any profit that we have—we put back into the committee for the next year's celebration. In 1964 when the *fiestas* began, they were started by the Chamber of Commerce because they were so appreciative. Now the Chamber of Commerce has little to do with it. They do send out flyers and put up flyers announcing it, but we have people

Francisca García and her granddaughter.

from as far away as California coming to set up booths. We do have a fee for a booth set up, but that's where our profit comes in—after expenses, of course.

After my children were raised, I was able to return to school. I went to Chemeketa. That was in 1974. It was very difficult. I kept dropping out of school, but I did finish. My daughter Margarita really encouraged me and supported me. I'd say, "This is too hard, I'm going to quit!" but she would say, "No, you can't quit. You are going to go back." She helped me a lot, and because of her I was able to finish. You know, it took me nine years to get my GED. But I did it, because my daughter helped me; she encouraged me. I used to work during the day and go to school at night. Every time I wanted to quit, she would say, "You don't have anything else to do at night, so you are going to school," and I went. And I finished, I got my GED. I always tell my children and my grandchildren that education is very important. Now that they have the opportunity and can get financial aid, they should take advantage of it. You can't get a good job without an education, without a diploma, or a college degree.

I think that my life here has been better than it would have been had I stayed in Texas. Wages there are much lower and life is much more difficult. I like to return to Texas once every couple of years, but my roots are here. I'm glad that I went out and worked in the fields, and I'm glad that I came to Oregon. I feel very peaceful here. My children, grandchildren, and great grandchildren are here. I 'm not saying that we didn't have any sacrifices or that times weren't difficult for us, but for the most part it has been a good life.

REFLECTIONS OF A PERUVIAN IMMIGRANT: THE LETTER THAT WAS NEVER SENT

BY EFRAIN DIAZ-HORNA

The other day you asked me, as you have so many times before,
"How does it feel to be an immigrant in the United States?"

I am glad you have persisted in trying to get an answer from me. It is a question I have been asked by many friends and acquaintances—one that has lingered in my mind during my twenty-six years in this paradoxical and bittersweet land. It is also a difficult question for me to answer because the answer requires reflection, honesty, detachment, courage, love, humor, time, and good manners.

If I were to characterize my experiences as an immigrant in a couple of sentences, it would suffice to say the following: Many years ago I was a FOREIGNER. Then in 1977 I became a citizen of the United States of America (even though I have always felt like an AMERICAN). Later, to my surprise and amusement, I discovered that I had been promoted to MINORITY status and was considered a "PERSON OF COLOR."

I can see you smiling and perhaps enjoying my sense of humor. As you might be aware, many Hispanics believe that humor is the courtesy of despair. But in addition, humor is a tool, an avenue that forces us to reexamine our perceptions under the unforgiving scrutiny of our own reflection. It impels us to go beyond the limits of the discomfort and pain we feel as outsiders, to transcend the burdens that we experience as the OTHER. It redeems us, and tempers us, and gives us the breath (the inspiration) to persist and to accept the challenges which we face *día a día.*(It is important to remember, at this juncture, Ortega y Gasset's dictum: "I'm myself and my circumstance.")

Allow me to dwell a bit on my experiences as a foreigner and as a minority in Oregon.

I came to the United States to go to school. As a foreign student in a strange land, I was suddenly immersed in a world of strange behaviors and perplexing social cues that kept me from acting and behaving as I had done in Peru. During the first several weeks at college, I was overwhelmed by a sense of paralysis and sadness. I felt severed from the group. Nostalgia, the pain of wanting to relive my past, permeated my every thought. I yearned to go back to my roots. Consequence: I developed an annoying and painful gastric ulcer.

Those were the days in which I had to constantly assess (and reassess) my learned social skills: to shake hands or not to shake hands; to embrace or not to embrace. This awareness of not knowing what to do made me feel uncomfortable, and I felt stifled and a bit schizophrenic. The informality of the environment was deceptive, and any affront to the social norms was met with swift disapproval and a subtle and silent admonition against repeating the infraction. Even to this day I find myself reacting occasionally in this manner; but when visiting my native land, I very easily rejoin the flow of the things I learned as a kid. Oh, how strong and persistent are our cultural traits!

I also remember the time when I asked a classmate if I could borrow his class notes. His reaction was one of shock and dismay. How bold of me to make such a request! What gall! Later on, after making several similar requests to other classmates and experiencing similar responses, and being more knowledgeable about the culture, I believe I found the answer to this perplexing behavior: in a society that nurtures competition, the idea of sharing resources that might give someone else the edge to succeed is anathema.

But not all of my experiences were negative. Being a foreigner was also a lot of fun! This in spite of the fact that the word FOREIGNER in any language is a sad word, a cold word,

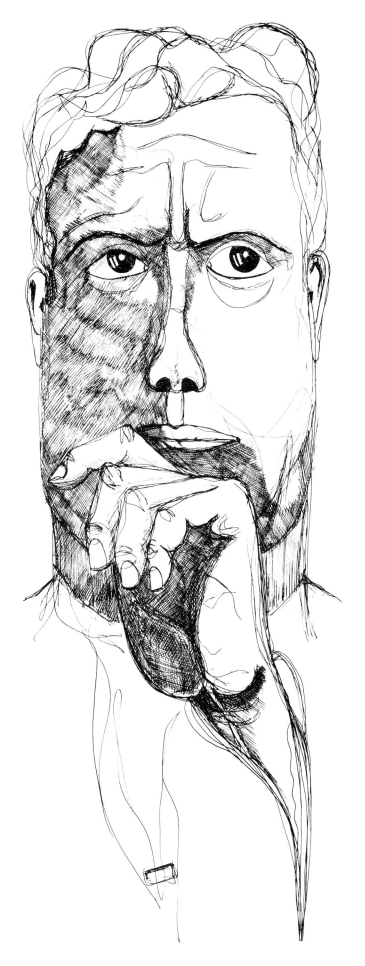

a word that has the smell of oblivion and exile. "Foreigner" evokes feelings and contexts of rootlessness. However, in the midst of these feelings of emptiness I was also able to enjoy the American sense of hospitality in reckless abandon. During this time when I partook of the generosity of those with whom I came in contact, I relished my condition as an outsider. I enjoyed being the other. I enjoyed being different. And I enjoyed the fact that I was treated as a special person. Nevertheless, deep down in my heart I knew all of this was temporary, for I knew that my roots beckoned and I would have to return to Peru.

Those were the days when it was difficult to discern the appropriate social or behavioral response: How to act in a polite and respectful manner when your politeness was seen as a wimpy act? How to behave with the opposite sex when a dutch treat seemed so tacky to me, even though I was broke? What to do about my spontaneity, effusiveness, and expressiveness when they were seen (at least that was my perception) as craziness, displaced eagerness, and mushiness? And how to explain the value of family ties and closeness when those concepts were seen by my classmates as barriers to independence and personal maturity, as the culprits in fostering bonds of dependency? Those were the days of perpetual questioning and turmoil! Oh, and how to deal with my perception of my North American friends—that what many of them said and did in the name of honesty I thought of as rudeness and bad manners?!!

In 1977, when I became a citizen of this country and was "promoted" to minority status, I noticed a dramatic change in the way I was treated and in my behavior as a newly invested American. Perhaps this qualitative change was due to the fact that after so many years, I had decided to make Oregon my home. At this juncture in my life, I was no longer an outsider (at least legally); but because of my accent and the fact that I was "different," the dominant culture kept reminding me that my dreams of inclusiveness (being included 100 percent) were still elusive. On one occasion, my candidacy for an administrative job with the State of Oregon was undermined because several members of the interviewing panel were uncomfortable with my accent. On another occasion, my immediate supervisor wanted me to enroll in a behavior modification program to correct my accent. (I politely refused to do so.) Perhaps my career was slightly affected by these incidents, but certainly I did learn that decisions regarding jobs are many times made on prejudicial assumptions and by persons who think they are not influenced by xenophobia—who sincerely believe they are culturally competent and sensitive to the issues of diversity.

In this regard, I recall the professor who asked me to see him to discuss a paper I had written. I was delighted, felt privileged by his invitation, and had an uplifting conversation with him on the pros and cons of public administration. Several months later I discovered that the purpose of his invitation had been to determine whether I had actually written the paper or had *paid* someone to write it for me. The professor had had a hard time believing that I was so proficient with the English language.

And what about the administrator of a state agency who informed me that he was not a racist because he did not believe that all Hispanics were sexual predators and white-woman chasers? At such times, one experiences the dark side of a culture, the perennial quest to exclude the extraneous and to impose a single way of doing and seeing things. Every culture does this, and we have to be mindful of the fact so as not to fall prey to the culture's alluring and comforting script.

At the same time I was having such experiences, I was also being asked to get involved in the affairs of my community, so I joined several organizations that valued my participation and my contributions as a citizen of Oregon. These organizations included the Oregon Commission on Hispanic Affairs, the Governor's Commission on Senior Services, the Community Housing Resource Board, the Salem Family Services Committee, the Global Tomorrow Coalition, the United Way Allocations Committee, the Oregon United Nations Association, the Salem Catholic Community Services Foundation, the Metropolitan Arts Commission, and several more. My involvement was instrumental in cementing my self-esteem and reassuring me that not everyone was against me. My compulsive need to draw and write poetry and my persistent attempts to transcend the effects of what I perceived as racism also kept me centered and allowed me to face difficult challenges in a positive way.

And let us not forget, my dear son, the support that your mother gave me during these trying times. Know, too, that during such moments I was emotionally sustained by the values and lessons of my parents. (Some of their favorite sayings that helped me were, "Respect breeds respect;" "Never deny your family roots;" "It is not important to arrive first, but to know how to arrive;" "Visit your relatives, even if they are not your favorite ones.") Knowing this, my dear son, you may understand why it is that I do the things I do as I relate to other people.

I would like to share with you a story that has helped me innumerable times in dealing with prejudice and arrogance. The story goes like this: Many North Americans think that Hispanics are lazy, always late, irresponsible, too loud, too macho, too fatalistic, too proud, impossible to work with, too group oriented, and so on. And because North Americans feel

superior to Hispanics, they *like* them. On the other hand, Hispanics think that North Americans are too rigid, too serious, too controlling, too cold—that they lack joy, ignore their elderly, are too interested in working, are obsessed with material things, are rude, lack social skills, and so on. And because Hispanics feel superior to North Americans, they *like* them. The point of the story, I think, is that all of us need to have a good dose of self-esteem to confront our daily challenges as human beings, regardless of

Efrain Diaz-Horna, now a Multnomah County Aging Services administrator, is also an artist and poet. The illustration on page 152 is his.

whether or not we come in contact with other cultures or experience racial indignities.

To be an immigrant is to be in a continual struggle (AGONISTES) to adapt or not to adapt. It is an exercise riddled with paradoxes that cause existential headaches, but also an exercise that provides opportunities to strengthen our capacity to appreciate the diversity of life and to learn new rituals, new things. One of the most difficult dilemmas that we immigrants face, because of our tendency to notice the "wrinkles" of our adopted land, is the question of whether to divulge our perceptions, to keep our thoughts to ourselves, or to be oblique in communicating them so as not to offend. Interestingly enough, I face the same dilemma when I visit the land of my birth. Sometimes I have a strong feeling of being out of place. After having lived in another culture, life is never quite the same, especially when returning home.

Now if you were to ask me, "Who are you? Are you Hispanic? Are you Latino? Are you Peruvian?" I would answer briefly: "I am EFRAIN M. DIAZ-HORNA," and then I would add, "and my circumstance."

Con afecto,
Dad

WRITERS

Herbert K. Beals has authored two books, published by the Oregon Historical Society Press, concerning Spanish explorers in the Pacific Northwest. He was principal researcher and guest curator of the OHS exhibit "Northern Mystery: Spain's Maritime Exploration of the Northwest Coast of America."

Carlos Blanco is the son of a Spanish refugee from the Civil War of 1936 who moved to Puerto Rico in 1950 and married Carlos' mother, a woman who has deep roots in the island. Carlos received his undergraduate education in Puerto Rico and earned an MBA at the University of Texas. He moved to Portland in 1984, where he works in the utility industry.

Steven W. Bender is an assistant professor of law at the University of Oregon School of Law, where he graduated in 1985. His mother is a first-generation Chicana who brought him from East Los Angeles to Eastern Oregon 20 years ago. He teaches a class on Chicanos and the Law in the Ethnic Studies Program at the University of Oregon.

Bob Boyd is a history teacher in the Bend-La Pine School District and Curator of Western Heritage at The High Desert Museum, with responsibility for exhibits that interpret the region's exploration and settlement. In recent years, exhibits have included *Gum San: Land of the Golden Mountain*, which focuses on the Chinese experience, and *Amerikanuak! Basques in the High Desert*. A future exhibit will highlight the contribution of the Hispanic *vaqueros*.

Eliza Buck works as a public sector folklorist for the Oregon Folk Arts Program of the Oregon Historical Society. **Nancy Nusz**, coordinator for the Oregon Folk Arts Program, has directed folklife programming since 1983.

Susan U. Cabello is professor of Spanish at Pacific University. During a sabbatical in the spring of 1992, she worked as a volunteer at the Centro Cultural in Cornelius, where she also conducted research for this chapter.

Efrain Diaz-Horna is an administrator for Multnomah County Aging Services and a member of the Oregon Council for the Humanities board. He has long been active in Hispanic community affairs and is a published poet and an artist.

Erasmo Gamboa first came to Oregon as a child, when his family did seasonal farm work in the Independence area. He is now associate professor of history in the Department of Ethnic Studies at the University of Washington and the author of numerous articles and books about the Hispanic people of the Pacific Northwest.

Cheryl Hartup holds a master's degree in Latin American Studies from New York University. She is currently working towards a graduate degree in art history at the University of Texas at Austin.

Lourdes de León is an anthropological linguist from Mexico who has worked with Mixtecs there and in Oregon. She teaches linguistics at Reed College in Portland.

Kent Patterson, was regional editor for *Oregon Business Magazine* and the author of over 200 magazine articles. Sadly, he died March 14, 1995 at the age of 53.

Mary Romero, until recently an associate professor of sociology at the University of Oregon, is now teaching at Arizona State University. She is the author of *Maid in the U.S.A.* (Routledge, 1992). **Donna Wong** is an instructor in the Academic Learning Center at the University of Oregon.

Antonio Sanchez is a research analyst for the Washington State House of Representatives, adjunct professor at the University of Washington, and founder of AMERICAS: Institute of Art, History, and Culture. He was knighted by King Juan Carlos of Spain in October 1994 for his contributions to the understanding of the history and heritage of Hispanics in the U.S.

Daniel P. Santos, who holds a law degree from Willamette University College of Law, recently served as a special assistant in the office of Oregon Governor Barbara Roberts. Earlier, he was program manager for the Governor's Commission on Agricultural Labor.

Richard W. Slatta, a long-time Oregonian, is professor of history at North Carolina State University and the author of *Cowboys of the Americas* and *The Cowboy Encyclopedia*, both published in 1994.

OTHER CONTRIBUTORS

PHOTOGRAPHERS

Jan Boles has been making photographs in Idaho and the intermountain west for more than 30 years. He has illustrated folk and ethnic projects for the Idaho Commission on the Arts and the Western Folklife Center, Elko, Nevada, as well as for the Oregon Council for the Humanities. His black and white artwork has been exhibited nationally and internationally.

Natalie Brown, the former art director for the Southern Oregon Historical Society in Medford, is a freelance ethnographic and documentary photographer currently based in Pecos, New Mexico. In addition to documenting the lifeways of southern Oregon migrant workers, she has photographed cowboy poets, American Indian ranchers, and Hell's Angels.

Gerry Lewin has worked as a photojournalist in the Pacific Northwest since moving here from Germany in 1960. During the past 35 years, he says, "I covered a magnitude of events. If it was newsworthy enough, I was there. Sports, news, scenery, people features—I loved them all and still do." Lewin's photographs have won many awards.

Barry Peril holds a degree from Harvard Law School and practiced law for 10 years until a battle with cancer brought a career change. Today, Barry works primarily on assignments related to cultural diversity, including a current project on the Vietnamese in Oregon. His work is featured in several exhibitions that are touring various parts of the world and in *Gum San: Land of the Golden Mountain*, a book about Chinese Americans in Oregon.

Francisco J. Rangel is a freelance photographer in Beaverton whose photographs have appeared nationally in numerous magazines and textbooks. He was born in Ixmiquiltan, Hidalgo, Mexico in 1959 and came to the United States in 1977 to study photography. His studies and experiences led to considerable experimentation and ultimately to the distinctive style he uses when photographing his favorite subject—people.

Michal Thompson has been a freelance photographer and photojournalist in Washington County, working with the *Hillsboro Argus* since 1980. His photographs have appeared in *Life* and *Newsweek* and have been used by the Associated Press and United Press International.

ORAL HISTORIANS

Frances Alvarado, an employment training counselor with the Oregon Human Development Corporation, provides migrant workers with emergency assistance and helps them find long-term employment. She interviewed Francisca García.

George and Susan Cabello conducted oral history interviews with Armando Laguardia, Maria Luisa Baragli de Bevington, Roger Iparraguirre, Alberto Miranda, Rosario Salazar-Collett, and Carlos E. Camus. A native of Chile, George came to Oregon in 1975 and is associate professor of Spanish at Portland State University. Susan is professor of Spanish at Pacific University in Forest Grove.

Eva Castellanoz, who interviewed Mary Thiel, Rosario Martinez, and Cristina de la Cruz Vendrell, is a nationally recognized folk artist who has lived in Nyssa for many years. Her work is discussed on pages 97-98.

Maria Cazarez, who interviewed Catalina Trujillo, has been an activist in the Hispanic community and has been involved in migrant labor camp inspections in the Willamette Valley.

Maria Rius, who interviewed Ana Olariz de Morgan, works as coordinator of the Department of Hispanic Affairs for Extended Campus Programs at Southern Oregon State College. In her work, she provides a variety of services to the Hispanic community, including language instruction and translation.

Noël Wiggins, who interviewed Celia Mariscal, has been the director of La Familia Sana clinic in Hood River, a community health promotion agency.

PRODUCTION STAFF

Erasmo Gamboa, a respected authority on the history of Hispanics in the Pacific Northwest, has coordinated oral history projects for the humanities councils in both Idaho and Oregon. As the co-editor of *Nosotros*, he has been the book's principal academic advisor.

Carolyn M. Buan is a Portland writer and editor whose firm, Writing & Editing Services, produces brochures, newsletters, books, and other publications for business and nonprofit clients. She edits *Oregon Humanities* magazine and was co-editor of *The First Oregonians*, both publications of the Oregon Council for the Humanities.

Jeanne E. Galick is a freelance graphic designer in Portland. She designs corporate identity programs and promotional materials for high technology firms and many nonprofit organizations. She designed *The First Oregonians*.

PHOTOGRAPHY CREDITS

(Unless otherwise noted, photo credits are from left to right and top to bottom on each page)

PRELIMINARY AND DIVIDER PAGES. Front Cover, Patricia Casteñeda, photo by Francis J. Rangel. Page i, Oregon State University Archives, P20:518. Page v, Longina Espinoza, photo by Francisco J. Rangel. Page vi, Girl on her First Communion, 1992 and Mass at St. Alexander in Cornelius, photos by Francisco J. Rangel. Page vii, Loyd's Small Camp, Cornelius, 1988, photo by Francisco J. Rangel; photo by Natalie Brown, courtesy of the Southern Oregon Historical Society. Pages viii and ix, Mauricio J. Rodriguez, Portland Policeman; Al Sigala, TV News Producer/Reporter; Enedelia Hernandez-Rodriguez, Principal at Echo Shaw Elementary School, photos by Francisco J. Rangel. Page x, Food stand at Woodburn Annual Fiesta, 1990, photo by Francisco J. Rangel; photo by Nancy Nusz, courtesy of the Oregon Folk Arts Program, Oregon Historical Society. Pages xi and xii, Group Condor; Mexican muralist Jesus Lopez Vega; and Manuel Izquierdo, 1985, photos by Francisco J. Rangel. Page xviii, Legalization Process, Portland, Oregon, 1987, photos by Francisco J. Rangel. Page 45, Photo by Francisco J. Rangel. Page 95, The Guilleu Brothers, 1985, photo by Francisco J. Rangel. Page 117, Photo from the collection of the Oregon Council for the Humanities.

CHAPTER 1. Page 2, Ana Isabel Ramirez, Photo by Francisco J. Rangel; Page 4, Photo by Natalie Brown, courtesy of the Southern Oregon Historical Society.

CHAPTER 2. Page 9, Photo by Natalie Brown, courtesy of the Southern Oregon Historical Society.

CHAPTER 3. Page 11, From the collection of Erasmo Gamboa. Page 12, Map from David Ralston, courtesy of the Southern Oregon Historical Society. Page 13, Photo TR-G-9304-161, courtesy of the Photo Research Group and Tom Robinson. Page 14, Oregon State University Archives P20:1981, Braceros picking hops, Willamette Valley, 1942; OSU Archives 2969, Mexican workers on Horst Ranch taking empty baskets for hop picking, 1943, Polk County; the collection of Erasmo Gamboa. Page 15, Oregon State University Archives P20:1070, Mexican workers playing guitars after work hours, 1942; the collection of Erasmo Gamboa. Page 16, The family of All Gonzalez, courtesy of Maria Rius; the collection of Erasmo Gamboa; photo by Francisco J. Rangel. Page 17, Photo by Francisco J. Rangel. Page 18, Photos by Francisco J. Rangel; photo by Shan Gordon, for *The Oregonian*. Page 19, Photo by Robert Kaiser, for *The Oregonian*. Page 20, Photo by Francisco J. Rangel.

CHAPTER 4. Pages 22-23 and 24, Courtesy of Museo de América, Madrid. Pages 26, 27, and 28, Courtesy of Museo Naval, Madrid. Page 25, Oregon Historical Society Neg.# OrHi45008. Page 29, Courtesy of Commander Antonio Menchca, Spanish Navy. Page 30, Courtesy of Museo Naval, Madrid; Oregon Historical Society Neg.# OrHi87501.

CHAPTER 5. Page 31, Oregon Historical Society Neg. #OrHi91309. Page 32, The High Desert Museum collection; Oregon Historical Society Neg. #OrHi91310. Page 33, The High Desert Museum collection. Page 34, Oregon Historical Society Neg. #OrHi35887; courtesy of Mike Hanley; Bob Boyd collection. Page 35, Bob Boyd.collection, courtesy of Luis Ortega. Page 37, Bob Boyd collection. Page 38, Photo by Francisco J. Rangel. Page 39, The collection of Erasmo Gamboa.

CHAPTER 6. Page 40, Oregon State University Archives, P20:2834, Harvesting potatoes, Klamath Co., 1943. Page 41, The collection of Erasmo Gamboa. Page 42, Oregon State University Archives, P40:304, Braceros picking cucumbers, ca. 1945; P120: Mexican workers getting their noon lunches before heading to orchards, Hood River Co., 1943; P120:2778, "Mail Wall," Hood River, O'Dell Mexican Labor Camp, ca. 1945. Page 43, Oregon State University Archives P20:1066, Braceros working a pea viner, Umatilla Co., ca. 1944; OSU Archives 972, Umatilla County Mexican Labor Camp, loading up to go to fields during cannery pea harvest, 1943. Page 44, Photo TR-A-4025-189 by Simon Hartbauer, courtesy of the Photo Research Group and Tom Robinson.

CHAPTER 7. Page 46, Photo by Gerry Lewin. Page 48, Oregon Historical Society Neg.#OrHi91304. Page 49, Oregon Historical Society, Neg. #OrHi62396. Page

50, Photos by Gerry Lewin; Photo from the collection of Frank Martinez, courtesy of Erasmo Gamboa. Page 51, Photo by Priscilla Carrasco. Page 52, Second photo in the top row from the collection of José Romero; all other photos from the collection of Frank Martinez, courtesy of Erasmo Gamboa. Page 53, Photo by Gerry Lewin. Page 54, Photo from the collection of Francisco J. Rangel. Page 55, Photos by Gerry Lewin. Page 56, Photos from the collection of José Romero. Pages 57 and 58, Photos by Gerry Lewin.

CHAPTER 8. Page 61, Migrant Workers Waiting for Next Employer, June 1988, photo by Francisco J. Rangel. Page 62, Oregon Historical Society Neg.#OrHi91831. Page 63, Photo by Michal Thompson, *Hillsboro Argus*; photo by Francisco J. Rangel. Page 65, Top photos by Michal Thompson, *Hillsboro Argus*; photo by Francisco J. Rangel. Pages 66 and 67, Photos by Natalie Brown, courtesy of the Southern Oregon Historical Society. Pages 68 and 69, Courtesy of Robertson Merryman Barnes Architects.

CHAPTER 9. Page 71-73, Photos by Francisco J. Rangel. Page 74, Photo by Francisco J. Rangel; photo by Michal Thompson, *Hillsboro Argus*. Pages 75 and 76, Photos by Francisco J. Rangel. Page 77, Photo by Francisco J. Rangel; photo by Michal Thompson, *Hillsboro Argus*. Page 78, Photo by Francisco J. Rangel.

CHAPTER 10. All photos by Michal Thompson, *Hillsboro Argus*.

CHAPTER 11. Page 83-85, Photos by Francisco J. Rangel. Page 86, Photo by Jan Boles, Snake Basin Photography. Page 87, Photo by Natalie Brown, courtesy of the Southern Oregon Historical Society; photo by Barry Peril. Page 88, Photos by Francisco J. Rangel.

CHAPTER 12. All photos from the Oregon Council for the Humanities.

CHAPTER 13. Pages 96 and 98. Photos by Jan Boles, Snake Basin Photography. Page 99, Photos by Eliza Buck, courtesy of the Oregon Folk Arts Program, Oregon Historical Society. Page 100, Photo by Michael Wilhelm. Page 101, Courtesy of Cheryl Hartup. Page 102, Courtesy of Lynda Jasso-Thomas. Page 103, Photo by Bastienne Schmidt, courtesy of Luciana Proaño. Page 104, Courtesy of Patricia Villalobos-Echeverría. Page 105, Courtesy of Lynda Jasso-Thomas. Page 106, Photo courtesy of Oscar Flores-Fiol; Photo courtesy of Patricia Villalobos-Echeverría. Page 107, Photo by Gene Faulkner, courtesy of Margarita Leon. Page 108, Photo by Francisco J. Rangel.

CHAPTER 14. Page 109, Photo by Francisco J. Rangel. Page 110, Top photo courtesy of Maria Rius; bottom photos by Michal Thompson, *Hillsboro Argus*. Page 111, Photo by Gerry Lewin; photo by Michal Thompson, *Hillsboro Argus*. Page 112, Photo by Francisco J. Rangel; photo by Natalie Brown, courtesy of the Southern Oregon Historical Society. Page 113, Photo by Barry Peril; Photo by Eliza Buck, courtesy of the Oregon Folk Arts Program, Oregon Historical Society. Pages 114-116, Photos by Francisco J. Rangel.

CHAPTER 15. Page 119, Photo by Francisco J. Rangel. Pages 120 and 121, From *The Codex Nuttall*, Zelia Nuttall, ed. (New York: Dover Publications). Page 122, Top and bottom photos by Santiago Ventura Morales, courtesy of Lourdes de León; middle photos by Bonnie Bade, courtesy of Lourdes de León. Page 123, Photo by Bonnie Bade, courtesy of Lourdes de León. Page 124, Photo by Francisco J. Rangel.

CHAPTER 16. Pages 126 and 129, Photos by Francisco J. Rangel. Page 130, Photo from *The Oregonian*/Randy L. Rasmussen. Page 131, Photo by Michal Thompson, *Hillsboro Argus*.

CHAPTER 17. Page 134, Photo from the collection of Mary Thiel. Page 135, Photo by Jan Boles, Snake Basin Photography. Page 137, Photo by Francisco J. Rangel. Page 138, Photo from the collection of José Romero. Pages 139-141, Photos by Francisco J. Rangel. Pages 142 and 143, Photos by Priscilla Carrasco. Page 145, Photo by Jan Boles, Snake Basin Photography. Pages 147, 149, and 150, Photos by Francisco J. Rangel.

CHAPTER 18. Page 153, Photo by Larry Johnson, from the collection of the Oregon Council for the Humanities.

SELECTED READINGS

When we embarked on the study of Hispanics in Oregon, we quickly discovered the vastness of the experience and the limits of the published material. While Hispanic history spans many decades, there is no authoritative introduction or survey of this community in Oregon and the Pacific Northwest. Creative writers have likewise failed to devote much energy to the wide and locally rooted repertoire of Hispanic life. Judging from the dearth of published material, Hispanics in Oregon are virtually invisible. To a large extent, this is the reason we undertook this book.

Although modern secondary sources on Oregon Hispanics are lacking, there are a small number of publications. For this book we have included a selection of the most significant published books and articles that faithfully reflect the depth and breadth of the Hispanic experience. It is impossible, nor have we tried, to include everything written about Hispanics in Oregon and the Pacific Northwest. In preparation of this list our overriding criterion was to develop a bibliography of materials easily accessible to the public.

The list of publications that follows is intended to serve the general reader. Scholars are aware that there is an expansive social record of the Hispanic community that includes archival materials in various collections, as well as newspapers, church, school, and census records. Government and private agency studies also provide much data on the Hispanic community. Lastly, in the past few years a number of important studies have been undertaken for advanced degrees at colleges and universities in Oregon and other states. These studies, although not included here, also add significantly to our understanding of Oregon Hispanics.

EXPLORATION

Beals, Herbert K., trans. *Juan Perez on the Northwest Coast*. Portland: Oregon Historical Society, 1989.

"Spanish Explorers in the Oregon Country." *Oregon Humanities*, Summer 1992.

Cook, Warren L. *Floodtide of Empire: Spain and the Pacific Northwest, 1543-1819*. New Haven: Yale University Press, 1973.

Cutter, Donald D. *Malaspina and Galiano: Spanish Voyages on the Northwest Coast*. Seattle: University of Washington Press, 1991.

de la Sota, José Rius. *Tras las hellas de Malaspina*. Madrid: R.T.V.E. y Lunwery, 1994.

Engstrand, Iris W. *Spanish Scientists in the New World: The Enlightenment Expeditions*. Seattle: University of Washington Press, 1981.

Gamboa, Erasmo. "Washington's Mexican Heritage: A View Into the Spanish Explorations, 1774-1792." *Columbia* 3 (Fall 1989).

Moziño, Suarez de Figueroa and José Mariano. *Noticias de Nutka: An Account of Nootka Sound in 1792*. Seattle: University of Washington Press, 1974.

Sanchez, Joseph. *Bluecoats: The Catalan Volunteers in the Northwestern New Spain, 1767-1810*. Albuquerque: University of New Mexico Press, 1990.

White, Robert B. *Coastal Explorations of Washington*. Palo Alto: Pacific Books, 1959.

GENERAL HISTORY

Caso, Alfonso, "Mixtec Writing and Calendar." In *Handbook of Middle American Indians*, Vol. 3, Part 2, Austin: University of Texas Press, 1966.

Gamboa, Erasmo. "Mexican Mule Packers and Oregon's Second Regiment Mounted Volunteers, 1855-1856." *Oregon Historical Quarterly* 92 (Spring 1991).

"The Mexican Mule Pack System of Transportation in the Pacific Northwest and British Columbia." *Journal of the West* 29 (January 1990).

"Oregon's Hispanic Heritage." *Varieties of Hope*, ed. by Gordon B. Dodds (Corvallis, Oregon State University Press, 1993), pp 146-151.

"Supply Line to the Frontier." *Columbia* 21 (Winter 1994/1995).

Hanley, Mike and Ellis Lucia. *Owyhee Trails: The Forgotten Corner*. Caldwell: Caxton Printers, 1973.

Oglesby, Richard E. *Manuel Lisa and the Opening of the Missouri Fur Trade*. Norman: University of Oklahoma Press, 1963.

Oliphant, Orin J. "The Cattle Herds and Ranches of the Oregon Country 1860-1890." *Agricultural History* 21 (October 1947).

Rollins, Philip A. *The Cowboy*. New York: Charles Scribner Sons, 1936.

Simpson, Peter K. *The Community of the Cattlemen*. Moscow: Idaho State University Press, 1987.

Slatta, Richard W. *Cowboys of the Americas*. New Haven: Yale University Press, 1994.

Treadwell, Edward F. *The Cattle King*. New York: MacMillan Co., 1931.

Winther, Oscar Osburn. *The Old Oregon Country: A History of Frontier Trade, Transportation, and Travel*. Lincoln: University of Nebraska Press, 1950.

IMMIGRATION AND MIGRATION

Davis, Marilyn P. *Mexican Voices/American Dreams: An Oral History of Mexican Immigration to the United States*. New York: Henry Holt and Company, 1990.

de León, Lourdes, ed. "Invisible Migrants: Mixtecs in Oregon." Videotape, Portland Cable Access, 1990.

Gamboa, Erasmo. "Chicanos in the Northwest: An Historical Perspective." *El Grito* 6 (Summer 1973).

"Braceros in the Pacific Northwest: Laborers on the Domestic Front, 1942-1947." *Pacific Historical Review* 56 (August 1987).

"Mexican Labor and World War II: Braceros in the Pacific Northwest, 1943-1947: A Photographic Essay." *Pacific Northwest Quarterly* 73 (October 1982).

Mexican Labor and World War II: Braceros in the Pacific Northwest, 1942-1947. Austin: University of Texas Press, 1990.

Ourada, Patricia K. *Migrant Workers in Idaho*. Boise: Boise State University Press, 1980.

Saenz, Rogelio. "Interregional Migration Patterns of Chicanos: The Core, Periphery and Frontier." *Social Science Quarterly* 72 (March 1991).

Santos, Daniel. "Agricultural Labor Reform: Implications of the New Labor Law and the 1989 Legislative Farm Worker Package." *Willamette Law Review* 26:2 (Spring 1990).

Slatta, Richard W. "Chicanos in the Pacific Northwest: An Historical Overview of Oregon's Chicanos." *Aztlan* 6 (Fall 1975).

Valle, Isabel. *Fields of Toil: A Migrant Family's Journey*. Pullman: Washington State University Press, 1994.

COMMUNITY AND CULTURE

Baker, Richard. *Los dos mundos: Rural Mexican Americans, Another America*. Logan: Utah State University Press, 1995.

Cook, Annabel K. "Diversity Among Northwest Hispanics." *Social Science Journal* 23 (Spring 1986).

Gamboa, Erasmo. *Voces Hispanas, Hispanic Voices of Idaho: Excerpts from the Idaho Hispanic Oral History Project*. Boise: Idaho Humanities Council, 1992.

"Oregon's Hispanic Heritage." *Oregon Humanities*, Summer 1992.

Gallegos, Joseph S. "Portraits: Four Hispanic Widows of the Portland Area." *Oregon Humanities*, Summer 1992.

Gallardo, Gabriel. "The Composition of Oregon's Hispanic Population." *Oregon Humanities*, Summer 1992.

Gil, Carlos. "Washington's Hispano American Communities." In *Peoples of Washington: Perspectives on Cultural Diversity*. Pullman: University of Washington Press, 1989.

Johansen, Bruce and Roberto Maestas. *El Pueblo: The Gallegos Family's American Journey, 1503-1980*. New York: Monthly Review Press, 1983.

McCarl, Bob, Joanne Mulcahy and Eva Castellanoz. "Hispanic Traditional Arts and Social Change: A View From the Snake River Valley." *Oregon Humanities*, Summer 1992.

Mirandé, Alfredo and Evangelina Enríquez. *Las Chicanas: The Mexican-American Woman*. Chicago: University of Chicago Press, 1979.

Morales, Armando and Mary O'Conner. "Teatro Nuestro and Sandunga: Art Forms with a Proud History." *Oregon Humanities*, Summer 1992.

Perez, Ramón. *"Tianguis," Diary of an Undocumented Immigrant*. Houston: Arte Publico Press, 1991.

Rea, Lori. *Living Treasures: Hispanic Artisans and Traditionalists of the Snake River Valley*. Nampa: Hispanic Folkarts Survey Committee, 1991.

Slatta, Richard W. "Chicanos in the Pacific Northwest: A Demographic and Socioeconomic Portrait." *Pacific Northwest Quarterly* 70 (October 1979).

Slatta, Richard W. and Maxine P. Atkinson. "The Spanish Origin of the Population of Oregon and Washington: A Demographic Profile, 1980." *Pacific Northwest Quarterly* 75 (July 1984).

White, Sid, et al. *Chicano and Latino Artists in the Pacific Northwest*. Olympia: Evergreen State College Press, 1984.

ABOUT THE OREGON COUNCIL FOR THE HUMANITIES

*The Oregon Council for the Humanities, founded in 1971 to promote
community appreciation for the humanities throughout the state,
is governed by a board of 21 Oregonians and is an affiliate of
the National Endowment for the Humanities.
Through competitive grants, publications, and its own projects,
the Council seeks to enrich people's store of ideas and information about their world,
demonstrate the relevance of the humanities to modern life, and help scholars
bring their knowledge into community settings.*

*Of special concern to the Council is the multicultural character of our world
and the role the humanities can play in broadening citizen understanding
of the many different histories, forms of culture, and values
that constitute our human heritage.
Nosotros represents one way in which the Council is trying to focus
public understanding on our state's diverse heritage,
but the book is only one instance of the OCH program at work.*

*From year to year, many exhibits, lectures, publications, films, conferences,
and other programs are supported in all parts of the state,
so that in Oregon there can be a continuing exploration of human experience
and values, a thinking together about shared history and different histories,
shared values and different values, a common future and a multiplicity of futures.*

*Anyone wishing to receive information about the Oregon Council for the Humanities,
to be put on the mailing list, or to contribute to the support of the humanities
in Oregon can write or visit the OCH office at
812 SW Washington Street, Suite 225, Portland, OR 97205
or call us at (503) 241-0543 or 1-800-735-0543.*

ORDER FORM

Please send *NOSOTROS* to:

Name _____

Organization _____

Street Address _____

Mailing Address _____

City _____

State/Zip _____

Telephone _____

Price	Quantity	Total
$16.95	_____	$ _____

Shipping and handling
$2.00 per book $ _____

GIFT: I'm grateful for the Council's
decision to produce such a book.
Here's my tax-deductible gift to
support you. I understand that it
may be matched by the National
Endowment for the Humanities. $ _____

Total enclosed $ _____

Please make checks payable to Oregon Council for the Humanities
Please do not send cash. Sorry, no C. O. D.s

NOSOTROS
The Oregon Council for the Humanities
812 SW Washington, Suite 225
Portland, Oregon 97205
(503) 241-0543 or 1-800-735-0543

*Proceeds from the sales of this book are used to support other
humanities projects throughout Oregon.
Thanks for your support.*

HOJA DE PEDIDO

Por favor envíe NOSOTROS a:

Nombre _____

Organización _____

Domicilio _____

Dirección Postal _____

Ciudad _____

Estado/Código Postal _____

Teléfono _____

Precio	Cantidad	Total
$16.95	_____	$ _____

Gastos de Envio
$2.00 por libro $ _____

DONACION: Agradezco a la
organización por haber hecho posible la
publicación de este libro. Esta es mi
contribución de apoyo. Tengo entendido
que esta contribución puede ser igualada
por la organización llamada "National
Endowment for the Humanities." $ _____

Total adjunto $ _____

Por favor haga los cheques a nombre de "Oregon Council for the Humanities"
No envie efectivo. No hay pago contra entrega.

NOSOTROS
The Oregon Council for the Humanities
812 SW Washington, Suite 225
Portland, Oregon 97205
(503) 241-0543 or 1-800-735-0543

*La ganancia de las ventas de este libro se utilizan para financiar
otros projectos de humanidades en todo el estado de Oregon.
Gracias por su apoyo.*